AF560105

AGRICULTURE UNDER SUSTAINABLE DEVELOPMENT

Edited by

Dr. Ram Krishna Mandal

Head & Associate Professor of Economics

Dera Natung Govt. College

Itanagar - 791 113

Arunachal Pradesh

(India)

e-mail: *rkm_1966@yahoo.co.in*

DISCOVERY PUBLISHING HOUSE PVT. LTD.

NEW DELHI-110 002

Published by:
Tilak Wasan
DISCOVERY PUBLISHING HOUSE PVT. LTD.
4383/4B, Ansari Road, Darya Ganj
New Delhi-110 002 (India)
Phone : +91-11-23279245, 43596064-65
Fax : +91-11-23253475
E-mail : discoverypublishinghouse@gmail.com
sales@discoverypublishinggroup.com
web : www.discoverypublishinggroup.com

***First Edition:* 2015**

ISBN: 978-93-5056-712-8

Agriculture Under Sustainable Development

Printed at:
Infinity Imaging Systems
Delhi

Dedicated

To

Mrs. Archana Mandal

Acknowledgements

The present study is an attempt at a comprehensive and critical analysis for the role of women in socio-economic development with special reference to educational levels, entrepreneurship, attitude of the society towards women, social and religious taboos, women's own awareness and political attainments in society.

The present volume is a collection of fourteen papers contributed by eminent scholars, academicians, policy makers, bureaucrats and thinkers from different parts of India. The publication of this book would not have been possible without their contributions. Their work is based on diverse source materials which consist of official reports, published journals, books and findings of field work. Most of their writings are based either on the social structural aspects or on the social dynamism and rapid regional socio-economic transformation or on the empowerment of women. I have felt the need to put some of their writings together so as to enable the readers to get an overall idea about the same aspect. Some of their writings have been updated, revised and edited for the purpose. I hope that the readers will find it relevant for understanding the features of women in a better way. I hope, this book will benefit immensely the students, teachers, young scholars, planners and administrators in the area of women study in particular and society of our country in general. I am conscious of the bulk of the work which becomes largely inevitable on account of the intrinsic sweep of the subject. I acknowledge my gratitude to all contributors, whose works are consulted in the preparation of this volume.

I would be failing in my duty if I do not extend my gratitude to our Principal, Shri Tomar Ete, Dera Natung Govt. College, Itanagar, Arunachal Pradesh, India for generating in me an interest to edit this book.

I also acknowledge the inspiration received from my beloved teacher and guide, Prof. Chandan Kumar Mukhopadyaya, Department of Economics, University of North Bengal, West Bengal. I express my deep sense of gratitude to him.

I have received supports and cooperation from my colleagues Dr. Madhuparna Bhattacharjee Dr. A.I. Singh, Dr. Suparna Bhattacharya and Miss Anjali Biswas, my Research Assistant, I express a deep sense of gratitude to them.

I am also taking the opportunity to thank profusely to Shri Tilak Wasan, Managing Director, Discovery Publishing House Pvt. Ltd., New Delhi, for publication this book.

Lastly, I am grateful to the members of my family: Mrs. Archana Mandal (wife) and Miss Anusree Krishna Mandal, KVPY Fellow (Daughter) and Master Avinandan Krishna Mandal (son) for their untiring support and patience during the work of this volume.

Dr. Ram Krishna Mandal

Contents

List of Contributors

1. **Dr. Rajashri S. Gudaganavar**, Associate Professor & H.O.D. Economics, C.S. Bembalagi Arts, Sha. M.R. Palaresha Science & G.L. Rathi Commerce College, Ramdurg - 591 123, Belgaum, Karnataka, India.
2. **Dr. Nagaraj V. Gudaganavar**, Associate Professor in Statistics, Anjuman Arts and Commerce Degree College, Dharwad - 580001, Karnataka, India.
3. **Dr. Komol Singha,** Assistant Professor, ADRTC, Institute for Social and Economic Change, Dr. V K R V Rao Road, Nagarabhavi P.O., Bangalore - 560 072, India.
4. **Dr. A.I. Singh**, Associate Professor of Economics, Dera Natung Govt. College, Itanagar, Arunachal Pradesh.
5. **Sanjay Rode,** Assistant Professor, Department of Economics, S.K. Somaiya College, University of Mumbai, Maharashtra, India.
   Correspondent Address: 404 Sukhashanti Apt, Plot No. - 39, Sector - 06, Nerul (W), Navi Mumbai - 400 706, Maharashtra, India.
6. **V. Ramya,** M.phil Scholar, Dept. of Commerce, Bharathiar University, Coimbatore - 641 046, Tamil Nadu, India.
7. **Dr. M. Dhanabhakyam,** Assistant Professor, Dept. of Commerce, Bharathiar University, Coimbatore - 641 046, Tamil Nadu, India.

8. **R. Krishnamoorthy,** Ph.D., Research Scholar, Dept of Economics, The New College (Autonomous), Chennai - 14, Tamil Nadu, India.
9. **Dr. A. Abdulraheem**, Assistant Professor, Dept. of Economics, The New College (Autonomous), Chennai - 14, Tamil Nadu, India.
10. **Devajeet Goswami,** Department of Commerce, Maniram Dewan School of Management, Krishna Kanta Handiqui State Open University, Guwahati - 781 006, Assam, India.
11. **Niteesh Kumar Upadhyay,** Lecturer of Law, CNLU, Patna - 800 001, Nyaya Nagar, Mithapur, Patna - 800 001, Bihar, India.
12. **Kedar Vishnu,** Ph.D., Fellow, ADRTC, Institute for Social and Economic Change, Bangalore - 560 072, Karnataka, India.
13. **Rohi Choudhary,** Research Assistant, ADRTC, Institute for Social and Economic Change, Bangalore - 560 072, Karnataka, India.
14. **Saswathan. M,** Sr. Marketing Manager, 20/17 Sriramapuram 1st Street, Choolaimedu, Chennai - 94, Tamil Nadu, India.
15. **Miss Anusree Krishna Mandal**, KVPY Fellow and Student of MBBS-1st Year, Lady Elliott Hostel, NRS Medical College & Hospital, Sealdah, Kolkata - 700 014, West Bengal, India.
16. **Sanjoy Das**, Department of Agricultural Economics, SASRD, Nagaland University, Medziphema Campus, Medziphema, Nagaland, Pin - 797 106, India.
17. **N.K. Patra,** Department of Agricultural Extension, SASRD, Nagaland University, Medziphema Campus, Medziphema, Nagaland, Pin - 797 106, India
18. **Mrs. Archana Mandal**, PGT, Balupara Colony Nibedita Balika Vidyalaya, P.O.: Gopalganj, Dist. Dakshin Dinajpur, West Bengal, India.
19. **Mr. Toku Chokio,** Asstt. Professor of Economics, Dera Natung Govt. College Itanagar, Arunachal Pradesh - 791 113, India.

Introduction

❖ Ram Krishna Mandal

The changing scenario has recorded that the agriculture becomes more as a business proposition than merely tradition at least in the agriculturally progressive states. The traditional agriculture, which was a way of life of the majority of Indian farmers, has gradually shrunken to fewer pockets. It is rightly believed that the traditional farming was consistent for cropping patterns, mixed crop composition, cultivation practices, etc., and it was based on the hereditary and the community level experiences. In terms of subsistence, the traditional agriculture ensured the farming families more or less self-sufficiency because of an array of harvests even though individual commodities harvested were little in quantities. The farmer did not have to pay for these commodities in the local market. Rather they sometimes earned a little profit by selling their marginal surplus in the weekly haats (Singh, 2004).

Indian Agriculture since 1947

Over 50 years since its independence, India has made immense progress towards food security. Indian population has tripled, but food-grain production more than quadrupled: there has thus been substantial increase in available food-grain per capita.

Prior to the mid-1960s India relied on imports and food aid to meet domestic requirements. However, two years of severe drought in 1965 and 1966 convinced India to reform its agricultural policy, and that India could not rely on foreign aid and foreign imports for food security. India adopted significant policy reforms focused on the goal of foodgrain self-sufficiency. This ushered in India's Green Revolution. It began with the decision to adopt superior yielding, disease resistant wheat varieties in combination with better farming knowledge to improve productivity. The Indian state of Punjab led India's green revolution and earned itself the distinction of being the country's bread basket.

The initial increase in production was centred on the irrigated areas of the Indian states of Punjab, Haryana and western Uttar Pradesh. With both the farmers and the government officials focusing on farm productivity and knowledge transfer, India's total foodgrain production soared. A hectare of Indian wheat farms that produced an average of 0.8 tonnes in 1948, produced 4.7 tonnes of wheat in 1975 from the same land. Such rapid growths in farm productivity enabled India to become self-sufficient by the 1970s. It also empowered the smallholder farmers to seek further means to increase food staples produced per hectare. By 2000, Indian farms were adopting wheat varieties capable of yielding 6 tonnes of wheat per hectare.

The Indian Agricultural Research Institute (IARI), established in 1905, was responsible for the search leading to the "Indian Green Revolution" of the 1970s. The Indian Council of Agricultural Research (ICAR) is the apex body in agriculture and related allied fields, including research and education. The Union Minister of Agriculture is the President of the ICAR. The Indian Agricultural Statistics Research Institute develops new techniques for the design of agricultural experiments, analyses data in agriculture, and specialises in statistical techniques for animal and plant breeding. Recently Government of India has set up Farmers Commission to completely evaluate the agriculture programme. However the recommendations have had a mixed reception.

In November 2011, India announced major reforms in organised retail. These reforms would include logistics and retail of agricultural produce. The reform announcement led to major political controversy. The reforms were placed on hold by the Indian government in December 2011. More than three-fifths of India's population draws their livelihood from agriculture that adds less than one-fifth to its GDP. There are serious concerns about efficient functioning of this sector both in terms of its output and productivity.

Efficient agricultural markets can be potent tools for poverty reduction. "Improved agricultural market systems are important for poverty reduction first because agricultural growth can play a critical and unique role in pro-poor growth; second because improved coordination and exchange are critical for agricultural growth; and third because improved coordination and exchange are also critical for the processes by which pro-poor agricultural growth contributes to wider growth" (Dorward and Kydd 2005).

Indian agriculture is the largest private sector enterprise in the country of over 110 million farmers. It engages two-third of total workforce, contributes to 26 per cent of the GDP and nearly one-sixth of the total export earnings. India inherited a stagnant agriculture at the time of independence growing at an annual rate of growth of 0.3 per cent in the first half of the last century. Due to the planned Government policies, technological support provided by agricultural scientists and hard work put in by the farmers, Indian agriculture has achieved an annual growth rate of 2.7 per cent in the post independence era. During the decade of 1980's the growth in food grain production was most impressive at about 3.7 per cent compared to population growth of 2.2 per cent. Unfortunately, it slowed down in nineties to 1.8 per cent, lower than the population growth of 2 per cent. Further, within the agriculture sector too, the development has been uneven in production and productivity across regions and crops.

Contribution of agriculture and allied sector during 2008-2009 was about 17.1 percent in terms of Gross Domestic

Product (GDP) of India. Agriculture generates employment opportunities for majority of the population. Currently, the agriculture contribution in the gross domestic product (GDP) is 14.8 per cent compared to 30 per cent in 1990-91. Currently, agriculture sector provides employment to about 52 per cent of the workforce that used to be about 61 per cent in 1990-91. Industrial and service sectors have outpaced agriculture sector during the past two decades as evident from the average annual growth of agriculture sector (around 3%) of the overall average growth of the economy (6-7%). However, the proportion of workforce engaged in agriculture did not commensurate with the decline of its share in the gross domestic product. Growth in Indian economy always gets affected by the monsoon as 55.7 percent of area sown in India is dependent on rainfall. If rainfall is normal, it results in good output of agriculture. In case of deficit rainfall, agriculture output is adversely affected that has its impact on growth of Indian economy. Despite shrinkage of cultivated area, extensive research and development has helped to increase farm production in India.

India lives mainly in its 600,000 villages. The village remains the basic unit of the Indian society and roughly 65 per cent of the population is rural. They constitute the backbone of what is still, largely, an agricultural economy. Agriculture is the mainstay of the majority of the population in India. Extremes in climate and a variety of soil conditions have made possible the cultivation of almost every item from cash crops to foodgrains. India's growth in per capita food production during 1979-92 was about 1.6 per cent per annum, which is the highest growth rate in the world during this period. Agriculture provides livelihood to about 65 per cent of the labour force, contributes nearly 29 per cent to the Gross Domestic Product (GDP) and accounts for 8.56 per cent of India's exports. In terms of gross fertilizer consumption, India ranks 4th in the world, after the USA, the erstwhile USSR and China. India has the largest area in the world under pulse crops and is also the first in the world to evolve a cotton hybrid. About 43 per cent of India's geographical area is used for agricultural activity. With the spread of irrigation facilities, the introduction of high yielding variety of seeds and farm mechanization, the vulnerability of the Indian agricultural sector to the vagaries of the monsoons has declined, compared to earlier.

Agriculture production increased during the eighties when the weighted index of agricultural production increased at the rate of 3.6 per cent per annum compared to 2.2 per cent per annum in the seventies and 3 per cent per annum in the fifties and early sixties. The increase in agricultural production during the eighties was due to a significant rise in the yield and a marginal rise in the area. As of 2011, India had a large and diverse agricultural sector, accounting, on average, for about 16 per cent of GDP and 10 per cent of export earnings. India's arable land area of 159.7 million hectares (394.6 million acres) is the second largest in the world, after the United States. Its gross irrigated crop area of 82.6 million hectares (215.6 million acres) is the largest in the world. India has grown to become among the top three global producers of a broad range of crops, including wheat, rice, pulses, cotton, peanuts, fruits, and vegetables. Worldwide, as of 2011, India had the largest herds of buffalo and cattle, is the largest producer of milk, and has one of the largest and fastest growing poultry industries.

A 2003 analysis of India's agricultural growth from 1970 to 2001, by Food and Agriculture Organisation of the United Nations, identified systemic problems in Indian agriculture. For food staples, the annual growth rate in production during the six-year segments 1970-76, 1976-82, 1982-88, 1988-1994, 1994-2000 were found to be respectively 2.5, 2.5, 3.0, 2.6, and 1.8 per cent per annum. Corresponding analyses for the index of total agricultural production show a similar pattern, with the growth rate for 1994-2000 attaining only 1.5 per cent per annum. The low growth rates may constitute in part a response to inadequate returns to Indian farmers. India has very poor rural roads affecting timely supply of inputs and timely transfer of outputs from Indian farms, inadequate irrigation systems, crop failures in some parts of the country because of lack of water while in other parts because of regional floods, poor seed quality and inefficient farming practices in certain parts of India, lack of cold storage and harvest spoilage causing over 30 per cent of farmer's produce going to waste, lack of organised retail and competing buyers thereby limiting Indian farmer's ability to sell the surplus and commercial crops. The Indian farmer receives just 10 to 23 per cent of the price the Indian consumer pays for exactly the same produce, the difference going to losses, inefficiencies and middlemen traders. Farmers in developed economies of Europe and the United States, in contrast, receive 64 to 81 per cent of the price the local consumer pays for exactly the same produce in their supermarkets.

The country recorded impressive achievements in agriculture during three decades since the onset of green revolution in late sixties. This enabled the country to overcome widespread hunger and starvation; achieve self-sufficiency in food; reduce poverty and bring economic transformation in millions of rural families. The situation, however, started turning adverse for the sector around mid-nineties, with slowdown in growth rate of output, which then resulted in stagnation or even decline in farmers' income leading to agrarian distress, which is spreading and turning more and more serious.

India's economic security continues to be predicated upon the agriculture sector, and the situation is not likely to change in the foreseeable future. Even now, agriculture supports 58 per cent of the population, as against about 75 per cent at the time of independence. In the same period, the contribution of agriculture and allied sector to the Gross Domestic Product (GDP) has fallen from 61 to 19 per cent. As of today, India supports 16.8 per cent of world's population on 4.2 per cent of world's water resources and 2.3 per cent of global land. And per caput availability of resources is about 4 to 6 times less as compared to world average. This will decrease further due to increasing demographic pressure and consequent diversion of the land for non-agricultural uses.

Scenario of Indian Agriculture

India is the seventh largest country in geographical level and second largest country in context of quantum of population and twelfth largest country in economic poin of view.The economy of India is as diverse as it is large, with a number of major sectors including manufacturing industries, agriculture, textiles and handicrafts, and services. Agriculture is a major component of the Indian economy, More than 75 per cent of our people have their live hood as agriculture and agriculture oriented works. Mahatma Gandhi said "Indian economy lives in rural villages", and many of the industries getting their raw material from agriculture sector.

Indian agriculture began by 9000 BCE as a result of early cultivation of plants, and domestication of crops and animals. Settled life soon followed with implements and techniques being developed for agriculture. Indian agricultural products are traded around the world via existing trading networks and foreign crops were introduced to India.

The five plans are give importance to the agriculture sector and rural development and rural people's employment. Land and water management systems were developed with an aim of providing uniform growth. Our agriculture sector achived green reveloution during 1970s after that we create white revolution in milk production. Despite some stagnation during the later modern era the policy makers was not concentrate the development of comprehensive agricultural program and rural development compare to urban development and industrial development. Nearly 21.1 per cent of the entire rural population of India exists in difficult physical and financial predicament. But rate of poverty in urban population is 15 per cent. In general, the Government controls the Indian economy, and there remains a great disparity between the rich and the poor.

However, the service sector is greatly expanding and has started to assume an increasingly important role. The fact that the English speaking population in India is growing by the day means that India has become a hub of outsourcing activities for some of the major economies of the world including the United Kingdom and the United States. Outsourcing to India has been primarily in the areas of technical support and customer services. Other areas where India is expected to make progress include manufacturing, construction of ships, pharmaceuticals, aviation, biotechnology, tourism, nanotechnology, retailing and telecommunications. Growth rates in these sectors are expected to increase dramatically. But the other side the slowdown in agricultural growth has become a major cause for concern. India's rice yields are one-third of China's and about half of those in Vietnam and Indonesia.

Due to urbanization and industrialization use of agriculture land is reduced during the last one decade agriculture lands are converted in to residential houses and factories hence the number of agriculture labors lost their work and move to urban areas. This leads to low output in agricultural products, insufficiency and rise in food articles prices. Number of surveys said that the world will go to face food insufficiency in near future.

In India Maximum of landholders are fall under the category of Small farmers, so they are not able to meet out the increasing input cost and not able to introduce any new technological machineries in their farms, due to this reason: *"farmers are born in debt, live in debt and died in debt"*.

Infrastructure is also a significant factor in the process of development but country like our rural India has not possessed the infrastructure such as roads, electricity, fertilizer and pesticides availability which caused the vulnerable damage to the growth of agriculture. While India has a wide network of rural finance institutions, many of the rural poor remain excluded, due to inefficiencies in the formal finance institutions, the weak regulatory framework, high transaction costs, and risks associated with lending to agriculture.

Indian agriculture policy allow some foreign companies to introduce Dangerous genetic engineering technologies in seeds (GMS) and shift towards food grains to cash crops it may helpful to the farmers in one way in initial periods but using this type of GMS and shift our production system from food grains to cash crops in future we will loose our traditional seeds. Now we are seriously talking about fuel and its importance hereafter there is serious arguments and problem will come for *"food or fuel"*. An estimated 100 million tonnes of grain per year are being redirected from food to fuel. (Total worldwide grain production for 2007 was just over 2000 million tonnes. As farmers devoted larger parts of their crops to fuel production than in previous years, land and resources available for food production were reduced correspondingly. This has resulted in less food available for human consumption; Irrigation is key to agricultural production. Irrigation facilities are inadequate, as revealed by the fact that only 52.6 per cent of the land was irrigated in 2003-04, which result in farmers still being dependent on rainfall, specifically the monsoon season. A good monsoon results in a robust growth for the economy as a whole, while a poor monsoon leads to a sluggish growth. The government must allocate funds to start the new irrigation projects to increase the cultivation.

Agricultural reforms and increased private investment is must, especially small farmers. Create a viable model of public-private partnership that allows private investors to invest in agriculture infrastructure in partnership with banks and financial institutions. This will help the farmers to access the high quality technologies and increase the output with international standards to meet the global market requirements.

The policy makers in India have a high responsibility on reducing poverty by raising agricultural productivity and developing the rural population economic status from deprived condition. However, bold action from policymakers will be required to shift away from the existing subsidy-based regime that is no longer sustainable, to build a solid foundation for a highly productive, internationally competitive, and diversified agricultural sector.

The government should instruct to the all universities, colleges, private and Government offices and manufacturing industry canteens to sell agricultural products like tender coconut, cucumber, watermelon, fruits etc, to enhance and promote the agricultural products in these areas it will help the formers to get good demand and price for their products.

We need more number of Agriculture universities and agriculture colleges in India to promote research and development in this area because majority of the population depending this sector for their live hood. So the government should concentrate and give more importance to the research and developments in rural and agricultural sector.

Total population of India as well as total population of the world has rapidly increasing There is no question that improving standards of living for the current poor of the world, plus providing for the billions still to come, will increase global demand for food and levels of per capita consumption are so high. But the rate of food grain growth is substantially slower than the average population growth rate. Worldwide about two billion people are lack food security and 825 million people are chronically malnourished, according to a recent estimate by UN Food and Agriculture Organization (FAO). Hence the very urgent need is the policy makers and government should take responsible steps to improve the agricultural sector and eradicate poverty and food starvation in the world.

Even though, India has shown remarkable progress in recent years and has attained self-sufficiency in food staples, the productivity of Indian farms for the same crop is very low compared to farms in Brazil, the United States, France and other nations. Indian wheat farms, for example, produce about a third of wheat per hectare per year in contrast with wheat farms in France. Similarly, at 44 million hectares, India had the largest farm area under rice production in 2009; yet, the rice farm productivity in India was less than half the rice farm productivity in China. Other food staples productivity in India is similarly low, suggesting a major opportunity for growth and future agricultural prosperity potential in India. Indian total factor productivity growth remains below 2 per cent per annum; in contrast, China has shown total factor productivity growths of about 6 per cent per annum, even though China too has smallholding farmers. If India could adopt technologies and improve its infrastructure, several studies suggest India could eradicate hunger and malnutrition within India, and be a major source of food for the world (Singh, 2004).

Reforms in Indian agricultural markets need to be introduced with caution. A proper regulation and competition regimen needs to be put in place before liberalising agricultural markets in favour of major privatisation. Due diligence needs to be adopted lest undesirable anti-competitive behaviour may offset the likely gains. There has been evidence that a greater number of market participants does not always lead to superior outcomes (Poulton et al 2004). Agricultural markets tend to suffer from vertical market failures, which impair the performance of input markets and output supply chains (Kydd and Dorward 2003). Such market failures result from failures to co-ordinate measures designed to make various market players, within a market system, act interactively to achieve some common goal(s). Consequently, there may be lack of investments by a group of market players, say farmers, due to possible absence of complementary investments by other players at different stages, say input providers, traders and processors, in the supply chain. Such co-ordination failures lead to situations in which everyone is worse off than if there were efficient and successful co-ordination. This would obviously need mutually reinforcing and benefiting investments by farmers or farmer-groups as well as input providers, traders and processors. Such co-ordination will not be achieved by market mechanisms alone. Non-market co-ordination would be equally important. For example, a farmers-group might enter into an interlocking arrangement with relatively powerful trader or processor for making required new investments by all parties (Kydd and Dorwad, 2003).

There had been restrictions on the inter-state sale of agricultural commodities in many states. A number of states (e.g. Uttar Pradesh, West Bengal, Assam, Orissa etc.) have used entry permit, which must accompany the sale invoice without which goods are not allowed to enter the consuming state. Obtaining entry permit is a major source of harassment for the dealers wishing to import goods into the consuming state. There is a practice followed by many states of collecting tax on the entry of commercial vehicle into their jurisdiction. This is an impediment to inter state trade. This causes significant losses to the traders due to delays, payment of entry tax and, possibly bribes (NCAER, 2003).

Price Policy and Agricultural Marketing

The Government of India intervenes in the agricultural markets to achieve certain developmental objectives. The overarching reasons for effective government interventions are stated to be food security and price stability. The government intervenes in domestic market in various forms such as food grain procurement and distribution, price support, input subsidies and marketing legislations. The objectives and forms of intervention have undergone substantial changes over time. The interventions attempted to bring in regulation of various agricultural activities to protect the interests of producers and consumers. But, such regulations did not foster a competitive environment for fair play of market forces.

Procurement and Distribution

The Government of India's food grain policy aims at achieving reasonable price support and procurement system to increase farm income and making available food grains to consumers at reasonable price through distribution of subsidised food grains and price stabilisations/buffer stock operations. The Food Corporation of India (FCI) is entrusted with implementation of food grains policy particularly for rice and wheat. FCI or the designated agency of state government procures paddy and wheat from the farmers at minimum support price (MSP). Additionally, FCI procures rice through a levy system from rice mills. Depending on the state, rice mills are required to deliver to the FCI from 10 to 75 per cent of their milled rice at the prescribed levy price. Wheat and paddy/rice procured thus are used to meet the demand for public distribution system, buffer stocks and other welfare measures. FCI's operations are intended to build buffer stocks to meet any exigency, open market sales to stabilise the domestic price and to meet the food security requirements.

In general, the official procurement operations are carried out through regulated markets set up under APMC Act. A network of regulated markets was created to promote organised marketing of agriculture produce. Except Kerala and Manipur, all the other states had enacted State level APMC Acts. In 2005, there were about 7,557 regulated markets spread across various states in India. The geographical distribution of markets was skewed towards large states: larger the size of area, more the number of markets. States like Andhra Pradesh, Bihar, Maharashtra, Madhya Pradesh, Uttar Pradesh and West Bengal had share of more than 50 per cent of total number of markets. The regulated markets handled about 20 per cent of total marketed surplus (Acharya, 2007).

During initial periods of operations, the regulated markets helped to mitigate the difficulties faced by the agricultural producers in disposing their produce. Despite several drawbacks in the functioning of regulated marketing system, they helped to provide access to the markets and increase income of the farmers. But over a period of time, these regulated markets failed to serve the interests of the farmers in a reasonable manner. Some of the rigidities incorporated in the Act bred inefficiency in the system. There are instances that agricultural produces are marketed bypassing the regulated market yards. Several studies (Acharya, 1998; Jha and Srinivasan, 2004; Gulati et al, 2005; Acharya, 2006; Chand, 2006; NCAER, 2006) and Committees (Government of India, 2001; Government of India, 2002a, Government of India, 2002b) pointed out restrictive provisions of Act and their impact on the efficient functioning of the market.

Food Subsidy

The economic cost of the process of food procurement and distribution includes three components, viz. price paid to the farmers, procurement operations and the cost of distribution. The difference between economic cost of foodgrains and the issue price of FCI is equivalent food subsidy. Food subsidy provided to FCI and decentralised state-level procurement operations increased from Rs. 92 billion in 1999-2000 to Rs. 241.2 billion in 2002-03 and then up to Rs. 436.7 billion in 2008-09.

Definitely, the volume will explore the present scenario as well as the strategy for development of agriculture. It consists of fourteen papers collected from different scholars from different corners of the country.

Changing Scenario of Agriculture Under Sustainable Development

Dr. (Smt). Rajashri S. Gudaganavar &
Dr. Nagaraj V. Gudaganavar

ABSTRACT

Agriculture has changed dramatically especially since the end of World War-II. Food and fiber productivity soared due to new technologies, mechanization, increased chemical use, specialization and government policies that favoured maximizing production. Although these changes have had many positive effects and reduced many risks in farming there have also been significant costs. Prominent among these are topsoil depletion, ground water contamination, the decline of family farms, continued neglect of the living and working conditions for farm labourers, increasing costs of production and the disintegration of economic and social conditions in rural communities. Today a growing movement has emerged during the past two decades towards sustainable agriculture, which is garnering increasing support and acceptance. It not only addresses many environmental and social concerns, but it also offers innovative and economically viable opportunities for growers, labourers, policy makers and many others in the entire food system. Sustainable agriculture integrates three main goals-environmental health, economic profitability, and social and economic equity. Sustainability rests on the principle that we must meet the needs of the present without compromising the ability of future generations to meet their own needs.

Introduction

Sustainable development refers to a mode of human development in which resource use aims to meet human needs while ensuring the sustainability of natural systems and the environment, so that these needs can be met not only in the present, but also for generations to come. The term sustainable development was used by the Brundtland Commission, which coined what has become the most often-quoted definition of sustainable development: "Development that meets the needs of the present without compromising the ability of future generation to meet their own needs".

Sustainable development ties together concern for the carrying capacity of natural systems with the social changes faced by humanity. As early as 1970s, "Sustainability" was employed to describe an economy "in equilibrium with basic ecological support systems". Ecologists have pointed to 'The Limits to Growth', and presented the alternative of a 'steady state economy' in order address environmental concerns.

The concept of sustainable development has in the past most often been broken out into three constituent parts, environmental sustainability, economic sustainability and socio-political sustainability. More recently, it has been suggested that a more consistent analytical breakdown is to distinguish four domains of economic, ecological, political and cultural sustainability.

History of the Concept

The concept of sustainable development was originally synonymous with that of sustainability and is often still used in that way. Both terms derive from the older forestry term "sustained yield", which in turn is a translation of the German term "nachehaltiger Ertrag" dating from 1713. According to different sources, the concept of sustainability in the sense of a balance between resource consumption and reproduction was however applied to forestry already in the 12th to 16th century.

Sustainability is a semantic modification, extension and transfer of the term 'sustained yield'. This had been the doctrine and indeed, the 'holy grail' of forests all over the world for more or less two centuries. The essence of 'sustained yield forestry' was described for example by William A.Duerr, a leading American expert on forestry.

"To fulfil our obligations to our decedents and to stabilize our communities, each generations should sustain its resources at a high level and hand them along undiminished". A fine anticipation of the Brundtland formula.

Not just the concept of sustainable development but also its current interpretations have its roots in forest management. Strong sustainability stipulates living solely off the interest of natural capital, where as adherents of weak sustainability are content to keep constant the sum of natural and human capital.

The history of the concept of sustainability is however much older. Already in 400 BC, Aristotle referred to a similar Greek concept in talking about household economics. This Greek household concept differed from modern ones in that the household had to be self-sustaining at least to a certain extent and could not just be consumption oriented.

The first use of the term "sustainable" in the modern sense was by the Club of Rome in March 1972 in its epoch-making report on the "Limits to Growth", written by a group of scientists led by Dennis and Donella Meadows of the Massachusetts. Institute of Technology. Describing the desirable "state of global equilibrium", the authors used the word "sustainable", "We are searching for a model that represents a world system that is:

- Sustainable without sudden and uncontrolled collapse; and
- Capable of satisfying the basic material requirements of all of its people".

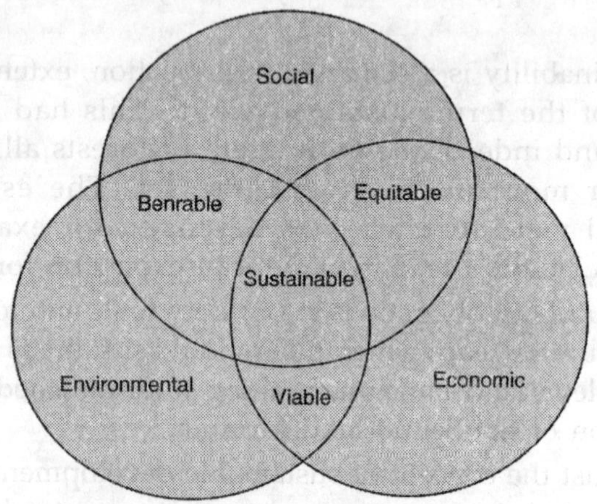

Scheme of Sustainable Development at the Confluence of Three Constituent Parts

Economic Sustainability

The Venn diagram of sustainable development has many versions, but was first used by economist Edward Barbier. However Pearce, Barbier and Markandya [1989] criticised the Venn approach due to the intractability of operationalizing separate indices of economic, environmental, and social sustainability and somehow combining them. They also noted that the Venn approach was inconsistent with the Brundtland Commission Report, which emphasized the interlinkages between economic development, environmental degradation and population pressure instead of three objectives. Economists have since focused on viewing the economy and the environment as a single inter linked system with a unified valuation methodology [Hamilton 1999, Dasqupta 2007]. Intergenerational equity can be incorporated into this approach, as has be common in economic valuations of climate change economics. Thus the three pillars of sustainable development are inter linkages, intergenerational equity and dynamic efficiency.

Economic development has traditionally required a growth in GDP. But this model of growth in GDP may be over. Sustainable development may involve improvements in the quality of life for many, but may necessitate a decrease in resource consumption.

What is Sustainable Agriculture?

Agriculture has changed dramatically especially since the end of world War-II. Food and fiber productivity soared due to new technologies, mechanization, increased chemical use, specialization and government policies that favoured maximizing production.

Although these changes have had many positive effects and reduced many risks in farming there have also been significant costs. Prominent among these are topsoil depletion, ground water contamination, the decline of family farms, continued neglect of the living and working conditions for farm labourers, increasing costs of production and the disintegration of economic and social conditions in rural communities.

Today a growing movement has emerged during the past two decades towards sustainable agriculture, which is garnering increasing support and acceptance. It not only addresses many environmental and social concerns, but it also offers innovative and economically viable opportunities for growers, labourers, policy makers and many others in the entire food system.

Sustainable agriculture integrates three main goals- environmental health, economic profitability, and social and economic equity. Sustainability rests on the principle that we must meet the needs of the present without compromising the ability of future generations to meet their own needs. Therefore stewardship of both natural and human resources is of prime importance. Stewardship of social responsibilities such as working and living conditions of labourers, the needs of rural communities, and consumer health and safety both in the present and the future. Stewardship of land and natural resources involves maintaining or enhancing this vital resource base for the long term.

A systems perspective is essential to understanding sustainability. The system is envisioned in its broadest sense, from the individual farm, to the local ecosystem, and to communities, affected by this farming system both locally and globally. An emphasis on the system allows a larger and more thorough view of the consequences of farming practices on both human communities and the environment. A systems approach gives us the tools to explore the inter connections between farming and other aspects of our environment.

A systems approach also implies interdisciplinary efforts in research and education. This requires not only the input of researchers from various disciplines, but also farmers, farm workers, consumers, policy makers and others.

Making the transition to sustainable agriculture is a process. For farmers, the transition to sustainable agriculture normally requires a series of small, realistic steps. Family economics and personal goals influence how fast or how far participates can go in the transition. It is important to realise that each small decision can make a difference and contribute to advancing the entire system further on the "sustainable agricultural continuum". The key to moving forward is the will to take the next step.

Finally, it is important to point out that reaching toward the goal of sustainable agriculture is the responsibility of all participants in the system, including farmers, labourers, policy makers, researchers, retailers and consumers. Each group has its own part to play, its own unique contribution to make to strengthen the sustainable agriculture community.

National Agricultural Scenario

India's economic security continues to be predicted upon the agriculture sector, and the situation is not likely to change in the foreseeable future. Even now, agriculture supports 58 per cent of the population, as against about 75 per cent at the time of independence. In the same period, the contribution of agriculture and allied sector to the GDP has fallen from 61 to 19 per cent. As of today, India supports 16.8 per cent if world's population on 4.2 per cent of world's water resources and 2.3 per cent global land. And per capita availability of resources is about 4 to 6 times less as compared to world average. This will decrease further due to increasing demographic pressure and consequent diversion of the land for non-agricultural uses.

Around 51 per cent of India's geographical area is already under cultivation as compared to 11 per cent of the world average. The present cropping intensity of 136 per cent has registered on increase of only 25 per cent since independence. Further rain fed dry lands constitute 65 per cent of the total net sown area. There is also an unprecedented degradation of land [107 million ha] and ground water resource, and also fall in the rate of growth of total factor productivity. This deceleration needs to be arrested and agricultural productivity has to be doubled to meet growing demands of the population by 2050. Efficiency mediated improvement in productivity is the most viable option to raise production.

The country recorded impressive achievements in agriculture during three decades since the onset of green revolution in late sixties. This enabled the country to overcome widespread hunger and starvation; achieve self sufficiency in food, reduce poverty and bring economic transformation in millions of rural families. The situation however, started turning adverse for the sector around mid-nineties, with slowdown in growth rate of output, which then resulted in stagnation or even decline in farmers' income leading to agrarian distress, which is spreading and turning more and more serious.

Natural resource base of agriculture, which provides for sustainable production, is shrinking and degrading, and is adversely affecting production capacity of the ecosystem. However, demand for agriculture is rising rapidly with increase in population and per capita income and growing demand from industry sector. There is thus, an urgent need to indentify severity of problem confronting agriculture sector to restore its vitality and put it back on higher growth trajectory. The problems, however, are surmountable when new tools of science and technology have started offering tremendous opportunities for application in agriculture.

The projected production requirements of various agricultural commodities by 2011-12 and growth rates needed to meet those requirements are as follows;

State specific interventions for Higher Agricultural growth

Commodity	Required Production [million tonnes]	Required growth rate [%]
Rice	105.0	2.06
Wheat	79.0	0.95
Total cereals	232.0	2.21
Coarse cereals	48.0	5.15
Pulses	20.0	2.35
Total food grains	252.0	2.21
Milk and Milk products	113.0	3.18
Egg	62.0	6.09
Meat	8.6	5
Fish	8.6	4.39
Edible oilseeds [40% import dependence]	31.8	2.87
Vegetables	109.0	2.51
Fresh fruits	67.0	3.46
Sugar and gur	35.5	3.87

India is required to raise food grains production by more than 2 per cent per year to keep pace with the growth in demand. Growth rate required in milk and milk products towards the end of 11th Five year Plan is 3.18 per cent. Even with 40 per cent dependence on imports, oil seeds production needs to be increased by 2.8 per cent.

Achieving 4 per cent growth in agriculture in 11th plan vis-a vis the present level of about 2 per cent has become critical to avert any crisis in agrarian sector and to fulfil needs of growing economy. The higher growth can very well be realised through adoption of available technologies that minimise yield gaps between experimental farms and farmers' fields. The Government is keen on devising ways and means to facilitate states in adopting these technologies that promise tangible yield gains of 40-100 per cent.

Sustainable Management of Natural Resources

Continued degradation of natural resources under intensive agriculture to attain food sufficiency is one of the reasons for the declining factor productivity and stagnation in food grains production in the country. The health of our soils has been impaired due to emergence of multi nutrient deficiencies and falling of organic carbon levels. The soils are generally not replenished adequately with nutrients removed by crops, particularly micro and secondary nutrients. The wider fertilizer consumption ratios for many states corroborate nutrient imbalance in soils. The soils are, presently, operating on a negative nutrient balance of about 10 million tonnes per annum. Limiting nutrients, not allowing full expression of other nutrients, obviously, lower overall fertilizer-use efficiency and crop productivity. Farmers are resorting to addition of more and more fertilizers to obtain yields similar to previous years and the increased inputs are thus adding to the production cost; marginalizing net returns to farmers.

Site specific integrated nutrient management, envisaging precise use of chemical fertilizers including secondary and micro nutrients, organic manures, composts/vermi-compost, bio fertilizers and green manures, is ideal. This will maintain soil health, enhance nutrient-use efficiency; provide sustained yields, ensuring better economic returns to farmers. The system is also benign environmentally in containing the emissions of green house gases and pollution of surface and ground water resources. The ICAR has generated site-specific nutrient management package that would enable additional yield of 50-60 million tonnes of food grains.

The agricultural sector is going to face grim competition for supplies of fresh water, with its share dropping to 75 per cent from the present 83 per cent in the near future, in the wake of growing industrial and domestic sectors. The judicious management of water resources is, therefore, going to be crucial to sustain agricultural growth in the country. Presently, the ground water is being overdrawn in central Punjab, Haryana, Western Uttar Pradesh, Rajasthan, Tamilnadu, and West Bengal, forcing sharp full in water table in these areas. The excess use of Canal water in South-Western Punjab, Haryana and Rajasthan is leading to water logging and development of secondary salinity. The conjunctive use of water and diversification of rice-wheat is required for solving the emerging problem. Large volumes of waste water need to be utilized for irrigation after their proper treatment, especially in peri-urban areas. The micro irrigation and resource conservation technologies [RCTs], economizing on water and nutrients require to be promoted in a big way.

About 25 million ha of acidic soils in the country have low productivity of less than 1 tonne/ha due to deficiencies as well as toxicities of certain nutrients. Limiting and adequate fertilizer use has the potential to double productivity of these lands. Adoption of cost-effective technology to ameliorate the soils on over 25 million ha could contribute additional 25 million tonnes of food grains to the national food basket per annum.

Nearly 8.5 million ha of soils affected by alkalinity/ salinity in the country have very low productivity and could be reclaimed with gypsum application. Over 1 million ha of such lands have been reclaimed in Haryana and Punjab, raising their productivity by about 6 tonnes/ha. The technology has to be extended to other salt affected areas of Gujarat, Uttar Pradesh, Rajasthan, West Bengal and Andhra Pradesh. The availability of gypsum has to be ensured with fertilizer dealers at a reasonable price. The spread of technology on 5 million ha would provide additional 10 million tonnes of food grains.

Vermi composting is an environment friendly and useful method of conversion of rural and urban organic wastes into good quality manure. It requires less time for decomposition of waste as material passing through gut of earth worms under goes quick enzymatic breakdown. Further, its nutritional quality is better than that of ordinary compost-with higher contents of essential plant nutrients and several growth promoters from secretions of worms and associated microbes. Vermi compost improves physical, chemical and biological environment of soils and also overall crop productivity. Besides economic returns, the avocation provides employment to rural households, especially women and hence, fits well in the Common Minimum Programme of the Government. And it is required to be promoted in a big way in rural India.

Large quantities of biodegradable waste are available from crop residues [350 million tonnes], Vegetable and fruit wastes [5 million tonnes], press mud [5 million tonnes], poultry litter [1 million tonne] and city waste [57 million tonnes]. Besides these 5-6 million tonnes of low grade rock phosphate also available for production of enriched vermi compost.

Farming systems combining crops, horticulture, livestock and fisheries provide ample opportunities of productivity enhancement employment, income generation and nutritional security. The systems are based on recycling of one component for the production of the others.

The rain fed farming practised in over 87 million ha area of the country contributes 40 per cent of food and supports 40 per cent of human and 60 per cent of livestock population. The rain fed areas are characterised by deficient and erratic rainfall, rampant land degradation and small and marginal poor farmers. In the absence of conducive environment, the rain fed areas were by passed by the green revolution in the country. The areas still have low productivity and marketable surpluses. Enabling policy initiatives and absorption of the improved technologies could very well raise the productivity of these areas by half a tonne/ha. The technological interventions required are; water harvesting and ground water recharging for supplemental irrigation [117 million ha-m of rain water going waste as run off], micro-irrigation, adequate and integrated fertilizer use, development and introduction of suitable crops [especially hybrids of maize, pulses and oilseeds], integrated pest management, organic farming, increased credits, low premium crop insurance suiting to rain fed farmers and regular trainings to upscale skills and knowledge of farmers on various aspects of agriculture. All these interventions need to be viewed within the perspective of participatory watershed plus approach for greater transparency, equity, social security and sustainability.

Crop diversification is becoming essential for maintaining soil health, water balance and overall productivity in many parts of the country. This has to be achieved in synchronization with soil, climate, availability of water and market potential, etc, Rice-Whet system and monocultures require to be replaced with legumes, oil seeds, vegetables, fruits and aromatic crops and other cash crops, for which the ICAR has evolved a number of viable and productive options. There is also a need to have assured market outlet for the produce for achieving required diversification in different argo-ecological zones of the country.

Strategy for Sustainable Agricultural Development

Ever increasing human and livestock population particularly in the under developed and the developing world is negating the technology driven progress in agriculture. National resources like soil and water are continuously degrading both in quality and also in quantity. The issues of climate change and global warming caused by the emission of greenhouse gases have emerged as new thrusts. Moreover, the ozone depletion may lead to increase in ultraviolet radiation and will result in adverse impact on earth's environment.

While addressing the issues of productivity, it will be necessary to address growing environmental concerns, especially natural resource conservation. These include the need for better conservation of the land and water base of irrigated agriculture, a reduction of agro-chemical pollution and adverse health effects, protection of fragile eco- systems in mountain, coastal and arid areas, and the containment of deforestation by Traditional shifting cultivation.

The following strategy Clements are suggested for promoting towards sustainable agricultural development and environmental conservation at the farm community level:

- Perception of the environment as fundamental to present and future livelihoods.
- Development of labour souring and time-souring technologies for fuel wood and water collection, food preparation and post-harvest storage.
- Substitution, where possible, of farm-grown inputs which make little demand on household finances, such as integrated pest management, biological nitrogen fixation, organic waste recycling and composting, and biogas production where feasible.
- Creation of non-farm income opportunities to support, not undermine sustainable farming systems.
- Search for other means of supporting household livelihood when common access to resources such as grazing land leads to increase degradation of the resources.
- Improvement of linkages between researchers and their target group formers and rural people to develop sustainable agricultural technologies for marginal lands and small holders, and also develop suitable transfer of these technologies users.
- Adoption of policies that seek to fill those gaps in the food system of critical importance to poor people in low resource areas, such as post harvest technology to avoid food loss, agro forestry, decentralized marketing, better biomass utilization, alternative sources of income generation, which require the development and dissemination of improved agricultural technology.

- Encouragement of the integration of tree growing in farming systems, as well as the integration of fuel, fodder and fuel wood systems.
- Better environmental monitoring (satellite predictions, remote sensing) to improve planning and assessment of land and water resources.

Besides above, following re-orientation suggested for future policies need to be addressed.

- Invest more in research and extension and increase farmer input and feedback into technology generation and the dissemination process.
- Shift crop protection policy from dissemination of chemical pesticides to use of integrated pest management.
- Shift fertilizer policy from an emphasis on increasing the level of use to improving efficiency of nutrient balance and timing and placement of fertilizer.
- Shift emphasis in irrigation policy from investment in new systems to improvement of water-use efficiency and productivity in existing systems.
- Adopt appropriable economic incentives through price policies that keep domestic prices in line with long-term world price trends.
- Reform trade and macroeconomic policy regimes that penalize agriculture to stimulate production by improving short-term input-use efficiency and encourage long-term investment and technological change in the agriculture sector.

The control issue in sustainable agriculture is not achieving maximum yield. It is long term stabilization. Sustaining agricultural productivity will require more than a simple modification of traditional adhoc techniques. The requirements of sustainable agro-eco systems clearly are not only biological or technical, but are also social, economical and political and illustrate the requirements of a sustainable society. Ecological change in agriculture can't be promoted without comparable changes in all other related areas of society. The final requirement for ecological agriculture is an attitude towards nature of existence, not of exploitation. We need to specifically focus on the following:

- Increasing agricultural productivity and production to ensure food and nutritional security and generating surpluses for exports.
- Developing areas of untapped potential, there by correcting uneven development of agriculture across regions.
- Addressing problems of under-employment, unemployment, poverty and malnutrition in the rural areas.
- Diversification of agriculture and accelerating the development of horticulture, sericulture, animal husloandry, poultry and aquaculture with necessary processing and marketing backup.
- Increasing flow of resources and augmenting the rate of capital formation in agriculture.
- Focussing the agricultural research system on the development of economically viable and location-specific low cost technologies and harnessing research in frontier areas of science and technology for the benefit of all sections of the farming community.
- Arresting degradation and depletion of natural resources and maintenance of ecological balance and sustainability of use of resources.
- Increasing the utilization of irrigation potential, promoting water conservation and efficient water management and expansion of irrigation facilities especially in the drought phone areas.
- Revitalizing and democratizing co-operatives for providing credit, inputs extension support and marketing and processing facilities.
- Promoting value addition in agriculture and providing strong market support for disposal of agricultural produce.

- Promotion of exports of agricultural commodities and integration of Indian commodity markets with global markets.
- Pursuing land reforms to channelize the energies of small and marginal and women formers to increase agricultural production.

• Creating quality consciousness among the formers and agro processors and promoting standardization and grading agricultural products for better marketability of the products.

Conclusion

The rapid change in Indian Agriculture particularly since the era of green revolution has been received with mixed response. The development perspective has been definitely encouraging and viewed positively by almost all sectors. However, at the same time, the conservative view has echoed the need for the system sustainability, which many also be arguably right. Both viewpoints have complimentality and also distinct application values, which need to be accepted. Therefore, one should always look forward to addressing both sustainability and development in Indian agriculture in the years to come.

The changing scenario has recorded agriculture more as a business proposition than merely tradition at least in the agriculturally progressive states. The traditional agriculture which was a way of life of majority of Indian formers has gradually shrunken to few pockets. However, developmental pursuits led by the improved technologies have been affecting the traditional agriculture in terms of both content ad extent. This is mainly because of the economic consideration where in traditional forming has gradually become uneconomic and obsolete.

The modern agriculture has become commodity or market oriented where in direct commercial benefit is the main criteria for choice of crop grown by a farmer. The needs of the progressive farmers are to be fulfilled from extrinsic sources. Further in order to organize progressive farming, farmers have to invest in several inputs, such as, tools and farm machinery, improved quality seeds, fertilizers, pesticides, post-harvest processing yards and sheds. As a result their financial needs for primary investment have been on an increase. This required more production and income. Thus the economic and financial considerations became increasingly important, including the costs, returns, markets and profits.

The technological break-through in agriculture has also given way to diversification in several ways, like new varieties of crops, new methods of cultivation, multiple farm enterprises which are important from the perspective of both economics and diversification. With ever increasing population, rapid urbanization, growing external markets more and more demands for farm products competition is also likely to increase. This obviously requires emphasis on fair and efficient regulatory mechanisms and the elaborate legal protection of farmer entrepreneurs and innovations.

The challenge is to develop technologies and packages that may improve productivity and production in a sustainable, environment enriching and energy efficient manner but without competing for human food. An important ray of hope, which one can notice in this complex changing scenario of agriculture, is that at least there is new generation of formers who are more educated, young and energetic. They could be keen on getting more knowledge about the new technology while carrying forward the family traditions more rationally and also logistically.

REFERENCES

Agricultural Productivity Trends in India-Praduman Kumar and Surabhi Mittal.

Indian Economy-Dutt and Sundaram.

Strategies for Sustainable Development in India-Surendra Gupta.

Sutainable agriculture net.

Various issues of Southern Economist, Yojana.

Wikipedia.org

Performance of Centrally Sponsored Scheme in Agriculture
A Case of RKVY in Assam

Dr. Komol Singha

ABSTRACT

The economy of Assam continues to be predominantly an agrarian. At present, agriculture sector provides employment to more than 50 per cent of the rural people in the State. After critical analysis of the sectoral growth of the State economy, it has been observed that the growth of the agriculture and allied sector in the State was not encouraging during the last three consecutive Five-Year Plan (8th to 10th Five-Year Plan) periods. With the apprehension of further slow growth of agriculture and its allied sector in the country, the Rashtriya Krishi Vikas Yojana (RKVY) was implemented by the government of India including Assam.

Background Information

The economy of Assam continues to be predominantly an agrarian. At present, agriculture sector provides employment to more than 50 per cent of the rural people in the State. The net cultivated area or Net Sown Area (NSA) of the State was 28.11 lakh hectares (in 2009-10) which was about

88 per cent of the total land available for agricultural cultivation in the State, and 36 per cent of the State's total geographical area. The Gross Cropped Area (GCA) was 41.6 lakh hectares, estimated at 52.26 per cent of the total geographical area of the State, and the cropping intensity of the State was estimated at around 148 per cent in 2011-12 (Assam Agriculture, 2012; DES, 2012-13). The average annual growth rate of agriculture stood at 1.2 per cent during the 10th Five Year Plan (FYP) and rose to 4.1 per cent in 11th FYP.

Table 2.1 depicts the status of agriculture sector in Assam during the 10th and 11th FYP. It is also clear that the GSDP growth, GCA, NSA, land productivity and cropping intensity have increased during the 11th FYP over the previous plan. Though the contribution of agriculture sector to Gross State Domestic Product (GSDP) was 28.09 per cent during 2002-03 and reduced to 21.74 per cent in 2011-12, overall agricultural growth in the State has increased significantly in the 11th plan. Output of the major crops has increased greatly. Of the crops, the area covered under paddy cultivation was 25.71 lakh hectares and more than 91 per cent of the total area covered under food-grains in the State during 2010-11.

The main reason of achievement of this growth was due to the bumper production of rice, especially the winter rice (DES, 2010-11). Rice is the staple food of the State. As per available estimates, the production of total food-grains in the State was 51.78 lakh tonnes during 2010-11 against 45.57 lakh tonnes during 2009-10, showing an increase of food-grain production at 13 per cent over the previous year. Also, the increase in the production of pulses in 2010-11 was recorded at 9.1 per cent over 2009-10. During the same period, the production of oilseeds has also increased by 8.4 per cent as compared to the previous year (DES, 2011-12).

As of the challenges of agriculture sector in Assam, almost 17 per cent of the State's NSA is identified as chronically flood prone area, and 3.3 per cent of NSA is categorised as chronically drought prone area of the State.

Table 2.1: Status of Agriculture and GSDP in Assam (in 10th and 11th FYP)

Year	Agriculture Growth (in %)	Agriculture GSDP (in%)	GSDP Growth (in%)	NSA (lakh ha)	GCA (lakh ha)	Cropping Intensity (in%)	Land Productivity (Rs/ha)*	Annual Rainfall (in mm)^
2002-03	1.2	28.09	7.1	27.5	39.6	143.8	49532.1	2530.4
2003-04	1.5	26.89	6.0	27.5	39.6	143.7	50282.4	2835.1
2004-05	-1.4	25.57	3.7	27.5	39.0	141.5	49602.8	2890.9
2005-06	2.6	25.37	3.4	27.5	39.5	143.4	50875.1	2314.8
2006-07	1.9	24.70	4.7	27.5	37.6	136.7	51847.8	1777.4
10th FYP	**1.2**	**26.12**	**5.0**	**27.5**	**39.0**	**141.8**	**50428.0**	–
2007-08	2.8	24.23	4.8	27.5	38.4	139.4	53309.2	2414.6
2008-09	1.9	23.36	5.7	28.1	40.0	142.3	53242.0	2271.2
2009-10	6.9	22.91	9.0	28.1	41.0	145.8	56891.5	1851.8
2010-11	5.9	22.49	7.9	28.1	41.6	148.0	60230.5	2475.7
2011-12	2.9	21.74	6.5	28.1	41.6	148.0	62006.4	1717.0
11th FYP	4.1	22.95	6.8	28.0	40.5	144.7	57135.9	–

* Land productivity = Agricultural GSDP/ha of NSA; ^ Annual Average.

Note: GSDP at constant price (2004-05)

Source: DES (2012-13); MoSPI (2013)

Also, 11 per cent of the total geographical area of the State comes under shifting cultivation and 1 per cent of the geographical area of the State is cultivable waste land. Though the State receives good average rainfall, 8 per cent of the cultivable land comes under char area. Besides these natural difficulties, poor technology and weak agriculture infrastructure, especially irrigation facility exacerbate sector's initiatives for better production and productivity of different crops.

After critical analysis of the sectoral growth of the State economy, it has been observed that the growth of the agriculture and allied sector in the State was not encouraging during the last three consecutive Five-Year Plan (8th to 10th Five-Year Plan) periods. With the apprehension of further slow growth of agriculture and its allied sector in the country, the Rashtriya Krishi Vikas Yojana (RKVY) was implemented by the government of India on May 29, 2007, including Assam. The scheme aims at achieving 4 per cent annual growth in agriculture and its allied sector during 11th Five Year plan (2007-12). For further development of agriculture sector, the government of India has spent huge fund under the RKVY scheme. As a result of which, the State economy has witnessed a significant change over the periods and at the same time, the primary sector has witnessed a shift to service sector[1] resulting service sector to flourish very rapidly in the State's economy (DES, 2011-12).

According to DES (2012-13), production and productivity of major agriculture crops in Assam have increased significantly due to RKVY scheme after 3 years (2011-12) over 2007-08 (pre-RKVY scheme). For instances, the growth of production of rice was 52 per cent during the period, 19 per cent of pulses and 7 per cent of oilseeds. As of the productivity of agriculture crops, rice productivity has increased by 39 per cent, 6 per cent of pulses and 8 per cent of oilseeds during the same period (DES, 2012-13). Now, the issue–whether this shift can be credited to RKVY scheme or not. Nevertheless, detail impact of RKVY scheme will be analyzed in the following sections.

Rationale of the Scheme's Evaluation in Assam

Having understood the initiatives made by the government, it is imperative to analyse the impact of the scheme (RKVY) on overall development of agriculture sector in the State in the 11th FYP (post-RKVY period). This will give a direction for the RKVY scheme in the 12th FYP. As of the parameters, there is no definite yardstick to measure impact of centrally sponsored schemes, especially the RKVY. As the RKVY scheme covers not only field crops but also many other agriculture related sectors like, infrastructure, irrigation, marketing, extension services, trainings, etc., mere estimation of area, production and productivity of crops might not give clear picture of the scheme's performance. Also, the agriculture and its allied sector are directly or indirectly supported by multiple agencies and schemes. This made a challenging task for impact evaluation of RKVY scheme in the State. Therefore, estimation of RKVY scheme in isolation is very difficult; some approximations have to be made while evaluating the performance of RKVY scheme. In this study, impact evaluation of RKVY will be carried out as per the following broad parameters:

1. The impact evaluation of RKVY scheme would be made for the period since its inception, covering the 11th Five Year Plan (EFYP).
2. A comparison of the scheme's performance would be made between pre and post-RKVY period, i.e. before 2007-08 and after 2007-08.
3. Impact assessment would be made through increase in area, production and productivity of major crops as well as change in physical infrastructures of the sector in the 11th FYP over the 10th FYP. It includes State budgetary components on agriculture after RKVY.
4. More importantly, expenditure spent by the scheme out of the allocated fund[2] under the scheme in the State would be taken as the main parameter of evaluation.
5. Finally, output and outcome of the scheme would be evaluated. RKVY scheme's claims or achievements would also be cross checked with the State statistics.

Allocated Fund and Expenditure Across the Sectors Under RKVY in Assam

This section focuses on distribution of allocation and expenditure of RKVY projects across the sectors. There are 16 broader sectors of agriculture cover under RKVY scheme in Assam. Based on the expenditure limit across the 16 sectors, 9 major sectors[3] have been taken up for detail evaluation. These sectors utilized 83.36 per cent of the total expenditure of the RKVY scheme and remaining 7 minor sectors utilized only 16.64 per cent of the total expenditure in the State. Accordingly, the sectors have been arranged in descending order in Table 2.2.

Table 2.2: Sector-wise Allocation and Expenditure under 11th FYP

Sl. No.	Sectors	No. of Projects*	Allocation (Rs. in crore)^	Expenditure (Rs. in crore)^	Expenditure/ Project (Rs. in crore)
1		2	3	4	5= (4/2)
1.	Micro/minor Irrigation	4 (4)	173.73 (16.41)	155.19 (22.88)	38.80
2.	Crop Development	13 (14)	91.64 (8.66)	88.48 (13.05)	6.81
3.	Animal Husbandry	25 (38)	104.91 (9.91)	67.63 (9.98)	2.71
4.	Agriculture Mechanisation	4 (7)	121.62 (11.49)	66.02 (9.74)	16.51
5.	Fisheries	19 (24)	75.29 (7.11)	52.54 (7.75)	2.77
6.	Horticulture	11 (27)	72.18 (6.82)	42.31 (6.24)	3.85
7.	Innovative programme/ training/ capacity building	1 (4)	40.86 (3.86)	33.32 (4.92)	33.32

(Contd...)

Sl. No.	Sectors	No. of Projects*	Allocation (Rs. in crore)^	Expenditure (Rs. in crore)^	Expenditure/ Project (Rs. in crore)
	1	2	3	4	5= (4/2)
8.	Research (agri/horti/ animal husbandry)	10 (19)	43.93 (4.15)	30.93 (4.57)	3.09
9.	Marketing and Post-harvest Management	8 (10)	48.44 (4.58)	29.02 (4.28)	3.63
10.	Seed	10 (11)	38.63 (3.65)	28.86 (4.26)	2.89
11.	Extension	6 (8)	145.07 (13.7)	21.18 (3.13)	3.53
12.	Organic farming/ bio-fertiliser	4 (4)	25.07 (2.37)	17.95 (2.65)	4.49
13.	Fertilisers and INM	3 (5)	19.44 (1.84)	15.15 (2.24)	5.05
14.	Natural Resource Management	4 (4)	14.89 (1.41)	14.98 (2.21)	3.75
15.	Dairy Development	13 (17)	28.58 (2.7)	14.71 (2.17)	1.13
16.	Non-farm Activities	0 (1)	15.05 (1.43)	0 (0)	0.00
	Grand Total	**135 (197)**	**1059.34 (100)**	**678.29 (100)**	**5.02**

* Figures in the parentheses in column 2 indicate number of projects based on allocation under RKVY; ^Figures in the parenthesis in column 3 and 4 indicate the percentage to the respective total.

Source: RKVY (2013)

Within the selected sectors, expenditure per project incurred by the Micro/minor irrigation sector was found to be at the highest with Rs. 38.80 crores and lowest expenditure was incurred by the dairy development sector with Rs. 1.13

crore in the State during the 11th FYP. Interestingly, cost per project of a few minor sectors (like, Fertilisers and INM, Organic farming/bio fertiliser, etc.) were found to be higher compared to some other major sectors (like, horticulture, animal husbandry and fisheries). As shown in Table 2.2, RKVY sanctioned Rs. 1059.34 crores to develop 197 projects during 11th FYP in Assam. Out of the sanctioned amount, Rs. 678.29 crore has been spent (64.03%). Out of the total 197 projects sanctioned under RKVY, 135 projects have been initiated during the period and Rs. 5.02 crore was spent per project.

Table 2.3 represents sector-wise allocation of fund, expenditure made by the sectors, expenditure-allocation ratio, status-wise expenditure and fund remaining/left for ongoing projects. As also mentioned in Table 2.3, the micro/minor irrigation sector was allocated the lion's share of the RKVY fund and so as the higher expenditure (e.g. Rs. 173.74 crores was allocated and spent Rs. 155.19 crore). The sectors which allocated fewer funds were– natural resource management, non-farm activities and fertilizer and INM with Rs. 14.89, Rs. 15.05 and Rs. 19.44 crores respectively. Micro/minor irrigation sector spent lion's share of the fund (Rs. 155.19 crore) from the total expenditure (cost) followed by crop development with Rs. 88.48 crore. The sectors which spent less were the dairy development, natural resource management and fertilisers and INM with Rs. 14.71, Rs. 14.98 and Rs. 15.15 crores respectively. Though the allocation of fund under the project of "non-farm activities" under RKVY was made with Rs. 15.05 crore, the project was not initiated and no expenditure was made on this particular project.

With respect to expenditure allocation ratio, it was not appreciable that no sector has made expenditure and allocation ratio at 1:1. Barring natural resource management sector which spent more than allocated amount (expenditure-allocation ratio was 1.01:1), which means, Rs. 14.98 crore was spent against the allocated fund of Rs 14.89 crore, no other sector reached 100 per cent spending of the allocated fund during the period.

Table 2.3: Sector-wise Allocation and Expenditure by Status (2006-07 to 2011-12)

Sectors	Allocation (in Rs. Crore)	Expenditure (in Rs. Crore)	Expenditure Allocation Ratio	Status wise expenditure (Rs. Crore)		Amount to be spent on ongoing Projects
				C&S	A&T	
1	2	3	4=(3/2)	5	6	7= (2-3)
Micro & minor irrigation	173.74	155.19	0.89	150.19	5.00	18.55 (1.76)
Crop development	91.64	88.48	0.97	75.76	12.71	3.17 (0.3)
Animal husbandry	104.92	67.63	0.64	67.63	0.00	37.29 (3.52)
Agriculture mechanization	121.62	66.03	0.54	21.61	44.42	55.60 (5.25)
Fisheries	75.29	52.54	0.70	52.54	0.00	22.75 (2.15)
Horticulture	72.18	42.31	0.59	42.31	0.00	29.87 (2.82)
Innovative programmes, training, capacity building	40.86	33.32	0.82	33.32	0.00	7.54 (0.72)
Research (agri, horti, animal husbandry/etc.)	43.94	30.94	0.70	30.94	0.00	13 (1.23)

(Contd...)

Sectors	Allocation (in Rs. Crore)	Expenditure (in Rs. Crore)	Expenditure Allocation Ratio	Status wise expenditure (Rs. Crore)		Amount to be spent on ongoing projects
				C&S	A&T	
1	2	3	4=(3/2)	5	6	7= (2-3)
Marketing & post harvest management	48.44	29.03	0.60	27.98	1.05	19.42 (1.84)
Seed	38.63	28.86	0.75	27.61	1.25	9.77 (0.93)
Extension Services	145.07	21.18	0.15	1.43	19.75	123.88 (11.7)
Organic farming & bio-fertilizer	25.07	17.95	0.72	10.54	7.41	7.11 (0.68)
Fertilisers and INM	19.44	15.15	0.78	15.15	0.00	4.29 (0.41)
Natural resource management	14.89	14.98	1.01	14.98	0.00	-0.09 (0.00)
Dairy development	28.58	14.71	0.51	11.28	3.43	13.87 (1.31)
Non-farm activities	15.05	0.00	0.00	0.00	0.00	15.05 (1.43)
Total	1059.34	678.29	0.64	583.26	95.03	381.05 (35.98)

Note: C=Completed, S= Substantially Completed project, T= in Progress, A= Approved and ongoing; Figures in the parentheses indicate per cent of the respective sector to total fund allocated; If the ratio is < 1, the approved cost is not fully utilized, if > 1 than the expenditure cost is more than allocation cost and if = 1 then the approved cost is exactly equal to the expenditure.

Source: Same as Table 2.1.

In terms of completed and substantially completed projects, micro/minor irrigation sector has got the highest number of completed and substantially completed projects with an expenditure of Rs. 150.19 crore, followed by crop development, animal husbandry and fisheries sector with the expenditures of Rs. 75.76, Rs. 67.63 and Rs. 52.54 crores respectively. Extension services project has made the least number of completed and substantially completed projects during the period with an expenditure of Rs. 1.43 crores. Some of the sectors completed less projects are – organic farming/ bio fertiliser and dairy development with expenditure of Rs. 10.54, and Rs. 11.28 crores respectively. Though the non-farm sector was allocated Rs. 15.05 crores and supposed to be completed during 11th FYP, the same was not initiated during the plan in the State, has spilled over to 12th FYP.

In terms of approved and on-going project & project in progress (A & T), the agriculture mechanization sector has got the highest number of approved and ongoing projects with Rs. 44.42 crores. It was followed by extension, crop development and organic farming/bio-fertilizer with the expenditures of Rs. 19.75, Rs 12.71 and Rs. 7.41 crores respectively. Marketing & post harvest management, seed and dairy development have got less number of approved and ongoing project & projects in progress with the expenditures of Rs. 1.05, Rs. 1.25 and Rs. 3.43 crore respectively. Fortunately, the sectors like, animal husbandry, fisheries, horticulture, innovative programmes, research, fertilisers & INM sectors found no evidence of A & T. It implies that the work allocated under these projects have been completed or substantially completed during the period. Also, the natural resource management sector has made larger expenditure than that of the approved/allocated fund under the scheme, and no A&T project was found under this sector.

As of the amount left for ongoing projects, extension sector has left the largest amount with Rs. 123.88 crores, estimated around 12 per cent of the allocated fund. It was followed by agriculture mechanization and animal husbandry with Rs. 55.60 and Rs. 37.29 crore respectively which will be spent on the remaining ongoing projects. In the case of abundant and not yet started status, the seed sector has abandoned with an allocation of Rs. 4.00 crore and horticulture sector (with an allocation of Rs. 0.42 crore) has not yet implemented (Refer Appendix I). Although the allocation has been made for non-farm activities sector, no initiative has been made on the sector and no expenditure was found in the 11th FYP. Detail picture/information of the scheme can be had from the analysis of individual projects which will be discussed in the following sections.

Nature-wise Status of Expenditure for Sector, Sub-sector and Flagship Projects

Assam is identified as one of the agriculturally backward States in term of physical infrastructure which includes road and communication, flood control, post-harvest mechanism of agriculture, marketing, etc. Therefore, more emphasis should be given in this regard. There are 54 infrastructure projects and 5 State flagship projects covered under RKVY scheme in the State. The infrastructure projects included under RKVY scheme have spread across the 10 broader sectors listed in Table 2.4 and the other 5 State flagship projects fall under the three major sectors-, viz. micro & minor irrigation, agriculture mechanisation and fisheries. Also, 9 separate sub-schemes which was considered as special schemes by the State and their expenditure are listed.

From the Table 2.4 we can see that among projects (both infrastructure and flagship), micro and minor irrigation spent the highest expenditure under RKVY scheme at the tune of Rs. 155.19 crore. It was followed by crop development, animal husbandry, agriculture mechanisation fisheries, etc. As the State gives more emphasis on infrastructure development, out of the total expenditure of Rs. 678.30 crore under RKVY scheme, a total of Rs. 353.97 was spent in infrastructure projects in Assam in 11th FYP. In percentage term, it was around 52.19 per cent of the total RKVY expenditure that have spent on development of infrastructure in agriculture and allied activities in Assam.

Table 2.4: Sector and Sub-sector wise Expenditure by Nature of the Project

Sectors	Subsectors	Expenditure for Infrastructure Assets Projects	Expenditure for State Flagship Project	Total Expenditure	Percentage to the Total Expenditure
Micro/minor irrigation	Pump sets (diesel/electric)	142.5 (96.62)	130.26 (88.32)	147.5 (100)	21.75
	Tube wells	7.69 (100)	0 (0)	7.69 (100)	1.13
Sub total		150.19 (96.78)	130.26 (83.94)	155.19 (100)	22.88
Crop development	Coarse cereals	0 (0)	0 (0)	21.3 (100)	3.14
	Oilseeds and pulses	0 (0)	0 (0)	23.16 (100)	3.41
	Others (crop development)	0 (0)	0 (0)	40.04 (100)	5.90
	Sugarcane	0 (0)	0 (0)	3.99 (100)	0.59
Sub total		0 (0)	0 (0)	88.48 (100)	13.04

(Contd…)

Sectors	Subsectors	Expenditure for Infrastructure Assets Projects	Expenditure for State Flagship Project	Total Expenditure	Percentage to the Total Expenditure
Animal husbandry	Animal health	0 (0)	0 (0)	7.19 (100)	1.06
	Breed improvement	0 (0)	0 (0)	10.93 (100)	1.61
	Extension and training	0	0	0	0.00
	Feed and fodder	8.43 (73.68)	0 (0)	11.45 (100)	1.69
	Infrastructure	19.67 (72.52)	0 (0)	27.13 (100)	4.00
	Others (animal husbandry)	7.8 (71.24)	0 (0)	10.95 (100)	1.61
	Poultry	0	0	0	0.00
Sub total		35.9 (53.09)	0 (0)	67.63 (100)	9.97
Agriculture mechanisation	Machines and equipment assistance	21.61 (32.73)	44.39 (67.23)	66.03 (100)	9.73
Sub total		21.61 (32.73)	44.39 (67.23)	66.03 (100)	9.73

(Contd...)

Sectors	Subsectors	Expenditure for Infrastructure Assets Projects	Expenditure for State Flagship Project	Total Expenditure	Percentage to the Total Expenditure
Fisheries	Farmers fish ponds/ assistance including training	21.36 (68.6)	9.79 (31.41)	31.15 (100)	4.59
	Fish marketing	0 (0)	0 (0)	3.85 (100)	0.57
	Infrastructure/ponds of fishries/dept./agency	13.82 (91.59)	11.73 (77.76)	15.09 (100)	2.22
	Others (fisheries)	2.47 (100)	0 (0)	2.47 (100)	0.36
Sub total		37.64 (71.64)	21.52 (40.95)	52.55 (100)	7.75
Horticulture	Development of horticulture farms/facilities	19.59 (66.79)	0 (0)	29.34 (100)	4.32
	Fruits	0	0	0	0.00
	Mushroom	0	0	0	0.00
	Nurseries and green houses	0	0	0	0.00
	Others (horticulture)	0 (0)	0 (0)	12.98 (100)	1.91
	Post harvest management	0	0	0	0.00
	Vegetable	0	0	0	0.00

(Contd...)

Sectors	Subsectors	Expenditure for Infrastructure Assets Projects	Expenditure for State Flagship Project	Total Expenditure	Percentage to the Total Expenditure
Sub total		19.59 (46.3)	0 (0)	42.32 (100)	6.24
Innovative programmes/ training/capacity building	Innovative programmes	0 (0)	0 (0)	33.32 (100)	4.91
Sub total		0 (0)	0 (0)	33.32 (100)	4.91
Research (agri/horti/ animal husbandry etc.)	Agri facility	5 (90.34)	0 (0)	5.54 (100)	0.82
	Agri research project	23 (90.56)	0 (0)	25.4 (100)	3.74
	Agri research/teaching facility (infrastructure)	0	0	0	0.00
Sub total		28 (90.52)	0 (0)	30.94 (100)	4.56
Marketing and post harvest management	Others (marketing & phm)	6.18 (58.51)	0 (0)	10.56 (100)	1.56
	Setting up/strengthening of market infrastructure	18.47 (100)	0 (0)	18.47 (100)	2.72

(Contd…)

Sectors	Subsectors	Expenditure for Infrastructure Assets Projects	Expenditure for State Flagship Project	Total Expenditure	Percentage to the Total Expenditure
Sub total		24.65 (84.91)	0 (0)	29.03 (100)	4.28
Minor sectors	Seed production	12.84 (52.92)	0 (0)	24.26 (100)	3.58
	Promotion of organic farming	0 (0)	0 (0)	17.96 (100)	2.65
	New approaches to extension	0 (0)	0 (0)	17.04 (100)	2.51
	Water conservation structures and watershed dev	10.11 (100)	0 (0)	10.11 (100)	1.49
	Micro nutrients labs	0 (0)	0 (0)	8.5 (100)	1.25
	Promotion of milk collection centres	3.07 (47.12)	0 (0)	6.51 (100)	0.96
	Land reclamation	4.87 (100)	0 (0)	4.87 (100)	0.72
	Seed distribution	0 (0)	0 (0)	4.06 (100)	0.60

(Contd...)

Sectors	Subsectors	Expenditure for Infrastructure Assets Projects	Expenditure for State Flagship Project	Total Expenditure	Percentage to the Total Expenditure
	Others (minor sectors)	5.52 (28.22)	0 (0)	19.55 (100)	2.88
Sub total		36.4 (32.26)	0 (0)	112.84 (100)	16.64
Grand total		**353.97 (52.19)**	**196.16 (28.92)**	**678.3 (100)**	**100**

Note: Figures in parentheses are the percentages of the sector's total expenditure.

Source: Same as Table 2.1.

Within the infrastructure projects, the micro/minor irrigation accounted for the highest share of Rs. 150.19 crore, followed by fisheries with 38 crores, animal husbandry with 36 crores and so on. Coming to the State flagship projects, hardly 29 per cent of RKVY fund was spent on State flagship projects, estimated around Rs. 196.16 crore during the 11th FYP in Assam. Within the State flagship projects, once again, micro/ minor irrigation registered highest expenditure with Rs. 130.26 crore, followed by agriculture mechanisation and fisheries in the second and third position respectively.

Overall sector-wise expenditure share under RKVY in Assam during the evaluation period is concerned, micro & minor irrigation spent 22.88 per cent, had made the highest expenditure share followed by crop development with 13.04 per cent and animal husbandry with 9.97 per cent and agriculture mechanisation with 9.73 per cent, and so on. If we club all the minor sectors together, the expenditure share made by it was 16.64 per cent. When it comes to the projects irrespective of the broader sectors, pump sets registered the highest expenditure share with 21.75 per cent, followed by machines and equipment assistance with 9.73 per cent and others (crop development) with 5.90 per cent and so on.

Major Sector-wise Stated and Actual Goals

When we see the impact of RKVY, the present section compares the changes made in 2011-12 over 2006-07. Also, output and outcome of the scheme is analysed. Table 2.5 depicts some visible changes that have made by RKVY over the years in Assam. By doing so, impact in terms of output and outcome was captured. The remark column tells us whether there is any divergence from stated goals and actual implementation and shows that most of the sectors have achieved their stated goals under RKVY scheme. The last column represents the cross-checking of RKVY output and outcome with the State statistics and found that barring post-harvest loss of horticulture sector, remaining sectors have achieved stated goals of the scheme. In term of post-harvest loss of horticulture, the loss were found to be increasing, not decreasing as stated by the State statistics.

Table 2.5: Major Sector-wise Expected, Actual Output and Outcome

Sector*	Components	Out put		Outcome		Remarks	Cross checking	
		Expected	Actual	Expected	Actual		2006-07	2011-12
1. **Micro/Minor irrigation** (25% not available)	Irrigation	235018ha	227018ha	35318ha	15498ha	Achieved 96.6% expected output & 43.9% of expected outcome	323297 ha	↑60.69%
	Copping Intensity	NA	NA	200%	-do-		137%	↑7.6%
2. **Extension** (62.5% not available)	Activities	111780 No.	9267 No.			8.29% expected output implemented.	Consumption of fertilizer 52.27 kg/ha	↑20.09
	Infrastructure	↑	↑	↑	↑			
	Use bio-fertilizer	↑	↑	↑	↑			
	Beneficiaries	–	8600 No.	11370 No.	NA			
3. **Agriculture mechanization** (71.43 not available)	Machineries	182321 No.	7916 No.	NA	NA	43.42 % of expected output achieved & fulfilled stated goal.	tractors 338 & power tiller 2552 No.	↑58.98% & 12%
	Cropping Intensity	NA	NA	↑200%	-do-		137%	↑7.6%
	Farm power	NA	NA	↑	0.03hp/ph		.54 hp/ha	↑40%
	Beneficiaries	NA	NA	9200	NA		NA	NA
4. **Animal husbandry** (66.67% not available)	Activities	8377249	NA	NA	NA	Expected goals are mostly achieved; Activity-wise numbers of beneficiaries are not given.	NA	NA
	Milk production	NA	NA	Rs.1513.5 /animal	NA		823 million litre	↑1.08%
	Meat production	↑	-	↑	↑		28800 MT	↑15.29%
	Piglets	13800	NA	NA	NA		Pork production 12000MT	↑25%
	Calf mortality	↓	↓10%	↓	↓		Total no. of veterinary & dispensary 1672 nNo.	↑182.09 %
	Animals treated	NA	NA	NA	NA			
	Green fodder produced	NA	NA	NA	NA		8000 MT	Same
	Training	10395	7500	NA	NA		NA	NA
	Women employment	NA	2500	NA	NA		NA	NA
	Beneficiaries	NA	NA	NA	41892		NA	NA
5. **Crop development** (57.14 % not available)	Paddy Seed	NA	↑	↑	↑	Farmers have made use of crop development activities, and benefited through improved cultivation	157150 quintals	↑73.04%
	Mustard Seed	39700MT	↑	↑	↑		19250 quintals	↑21.36%
	Black gram Seed	NA	↑	↑	↑		590 quintals	↑98.55%
	Maize Seed	NA	↑	↑	↑		150 quintals	↑98.49%

(Contd…)

	Oilseed Seed	NA		97500 farmer		methods as well as through use of supplied critical inputs.	Total food grain production 3.06lakh MT & oilseeds .13lakh MT	↑40.9% & 16.77%
	Cluster demonstration	NA	4000	NA	NA			
	Micro nutrient	NA	141176 ha	176176 ha	136176			
	Beneficiaries	NA	NA	NA	272353			
6. **Fisheries** (25% not available)	Fisheries	2070.4ha	NA	NA	NA	From expected output, 28.18% land and 81.1% beneficiaries implemented; expected outcome is mostly achieved.	In 2011-12 488696ha	
	Fish	↑	583.54	↑4725MT	NA		181479 MT	↑51.62%
	Prawn	↑	56ha	↑11.25MT	↑49MT/Rs. 35 crore		NA	NA
	Kuchia	↑	21 unit	NA	NA		NA	NA
	pork	NA	NA	70MT	Rs. 0.34 crore		NA	NA
	Fish seed production	NA	NA	↑1500MT			2063 million No.	↑ 21.81%
	Paddy productivity	NA	NA	↑350MT	Rs. 1.38 crore		1332.11kg/ha	↑25.17%
	Beneficiaries	1910	9660	NA	NA		NA	NA
7. **Horticulture** (84.62% not available)	Fruit production	↑	↑	↑	↑	Increase production of horticulture crop & reduce PHL.	14.08MT	↑14.4%
	Vegetable production	↑	↑	↑	↑		39.18MT	↑12.35%
	Spices production	↑	↑	↑	↑		2.18MT	↑11.74%
	Post-Harv. loss	↓	↓	↓	↓		PHL of fruit, vegetable & spices 3.5,.9.8 &.45MT	↑18.6%, 15.15% & 11.76%
	Disease control on coconut & arca nut	2000ha	NA	NA	NA			
	Women training	15800	12500	-do-	-do-			
8. **Marketing & PHM** (30% not available)	Market for organic commodity					Expected goals are mostly achieved.	In 2011-12 market for organic commodity is 1 No..	
	Benefited from direct marketing	6500	9000	7800	-do-		In 2011-12 distribution of three wheeler 162 & four wheeler is 470, community threshing floor 55 No..	
	Benefited from auto van	800	1200	-do-	-do-			
	Training	11460	-do-	-do-	-do-			
	Organic commodity producer	27 district	-do-	-do-	-do-			
	Distribution of four wheeler	309	-do-	-do-	-do-			
	Distribution of three wheeler	152	-do-	-do-	-do-			

(Contd...)

	Threshing floor	86	-do-	-do-	-do-		
9. Research-agri, horti, animal husbandry etc (68.42% not available)	Production of organic inputs	↑	↑	↑	↑	Expected goals are mostly achieved.	In 2011-12 market for organic commodity is 1 No..
	Seed of rice	↑	↑	↑	↑		157150 quintals	↑73.04%
	Seed of mustard	↑	↑	↑	↑		19250 quintals	↑21.36%
	Seed of jute	↑	↑	↑	↑		NA	NA
	Seed of Sugar cane	↑	↑	↑	↑		NA	NA
	Fish seed	↑	↑	↑	↑		2063 million No.	↑ 21.81%
	Poultry chick	↑	↑	↑	↑		Poultry meat was 6000MT	↑
	Area for seed production	12500ha	↑	↑	↑		NA	NA
	Demonstration	20	↑	↑	↑		NA	NA
	Rice fish culture	↑	3	↑	↑		Rice Yield 1332.11kg/ha & fish production 181479 MT	↑25.17% & 51.62%

* In the parentheses indicate project information are not available; ←and →indicate increase and decrease; PHL implies Post-harvest Loss

Source: RKVY (2013); DES (2012-13); MoSPI (2013)

Findings and Concluding Remarks

In Assam, RKVY project comprises of 16 sectors which include 39 sub-sectors. Out of the 16 sectors, 9 sectors absorbed 83.36 per cent of the total expenditure of the scheme. Among the major sectors, minor/micro irrigation utilized the major funds. It was followed by crop development, animal husbandry, agriculture mechanization, fisheries, horticulture, innovative programmes/training/capacity building/others, research (agri/horti/animal husbandry/etc.) and marketing and post-harvest management. The major focus of the scheme's evaluation was given to the magnitude of expenditure. In the State, to develop infrastructure and assets in agriculture and its allied sectors, RKVY spent significant share of funds (52.19 % of the total expenditure). It might have played a crucial role for development of agriculture and its allied sector in the State. Besides, 28.92 per cent of the total expenditure was spent on the State flagship projects, especially the micro/minor irrigation, followed by the agricultural mechanization and fisheries. The State managed to utilize these funds effectively under the RKVY compared to other projects, probably due to autonomy and flexibility given to them. As per the RKVY mandate, the funds were being utilized and spent for development of agriculture and its allied activities in an integrated manner. Though there are few cases of divergence from stated goals, most of the stated goals have been met.

To verify the performance of the nine sectors, first we took basic indicators and then cross checked in two time periods (pre and post RKVY), i.e., 2006-07 and 2010-11. As indicated in Table 2.5 cross-check column, in the micro & minor irrigation sector, the area covered by micro irrigation as well as cropping intensity was found to be increased by 60.69 per cent and 8.03 per cent respectively over a period of five years. In the agricultural mechanization, the distribution of tractors and power tillers increased by 58.9 and 12 per cent respectively while farm power increased by 40 per cent. In the animal husbandry sector, production of milk and meat increased by 1.08 and 12.29 per cent respectively during the period of above mentioned five years. During the 11th plan, RKVY has leveraged the State agriculture expenditure. When RKVY spends Rs 1, State's expenditure share on agriculture increases by Rs 3.8 during the 11th FYP and with the introduction of the scheme, share of agriculture expenditure from the State budget has risen from 12 per cent in 10th plan to 16 per cent in 11th plan. Also, the share of agriculture expenditure out of the agriculture GSDP has increased from 6 per cent in 10th FYP to 10 per cent in 11th plan.

In the crop development sector, availability of paddy, maize, mustard and black gram seed have increased by 73.04, 98.49, 21.36 and 98.55 per cent respectively and the production of food grains and oilseeds have also increased by 40.9 and 16.77 per cent respectively. When we compared to pre and post RKVY period (10th and 11th FYP), area, production and productivity of major crops have increased significantly in 11th FYP over the 10th FYP, especially the food grains. It further rose from negative values to 2.9 per cent; 9.1 per cent and 0.6 per cent respectively (refer Appendix II). Similarly, in the fisheries sector, production of fish seed and fish have improved by 51.62 and 21.81 per cent respectively. Unfortunately, in horticulture sector, post harvest losses (PHL) of fruit, spices and vegetables have increased by 18.6, 15.15 and 11.76 per cent respectively.

In totality, the Assam State has achieved the targeted growth rate of 4 per cent in agriculture as planned in 11th FYP, which is clearly reflected in Table 1. The average agricultural growth rate during the 11th Plan period was 4.1 per cent compared 1.2 per cent of the previous plan period. Also, the State budgetary expenditure on agriculture has increased by 163 per cent in 11th plan over the previous plan. Major increase was visible in the sectors like, crop development, minor/micro irrigation, agri. research and fisheries. Nevertheless, this achievement might not be solely due to RKVY intervention in the State, because there are some significant initiatives like, Tribal Sub-plan, Land Reclamation, NAEP-III, etc. have been taken up by the State in the recent past. But no one can deny the contribution of RKVY in the process of agricultural development in Assam.

Appendix I

Expenditure on Abandoned (B) and not yet implemented (N) project in Assam

(*Rs. in Cr.*)

Sectors	Sub-sectors	Project Name	Allocation	Exp.	Project Status			
					Allocation		Expenditure	
					B	N	B	N
Horticulture	Development of horticulture farms/facilities	Empowerment of Farm women (Horticulture)	0.42	0		0.42		0
Seed	Others (seed)	Support to Institution (Agril) 1. Strengthening ASSCA 2. Strengthening Assam Seed Corp Ltd. 3. Infrastructure Dev of Kokilabari Farm	4	0	4		0	
Grand total			**4.42**	**0**	**4**	**0.42**	**0**	**0**

Source: RKVY (2013)

Appendix II

Average Annual growth in area , production and yield of major crops in Assam

(in Per cent)

Particulars	10th Plan			11th Plan		
	Area	Production	Yield	Area	Production	Yield
Rice	-2.8	-5.1	-2.5	3.0	9.5	3.1
Wheat	-2.7	-3.6	-1.0	-1.3	-0.7	6.1
Total Cereals	**-2.8**	**-5.1**	**-2.4**	**2.9**	**9.2**	**-1.2**
Gram	0.0	0.2	0.0	-2.4	-2.2	6.0
Arhar/Tur	0.1	0.2	0.0	-2.9	-2.7	0.4
Other Pulses	-2.1	-2.0	0.0	-16.0	-16.0	0.1
Total Pulses	**-1.9**	**-1.8**	**0.0**	**2.6**	**3.1**	**-20.0**
Total Food-grains	**-2.8**	**-5.0**	**-2.4**	**2.9**	**9.1**	**0.6**
Rapeseed & Mustard	-2.3	-2.1	-0.4	0.3	3.1	-1.5
Linseed	-4.3	-4.2	0.0	-2.0	-1.3	3.0
Castor	-8.2	5.3	34.5	-19.7	-33.5	0.8

Source: DES (2012)

NOTES

1 Reduced agriculture GSDP from 28 per cent in 2002-03 to 21 per cent in 2011-12 in Assam.

2 Released of fund under RKVY information is not available till date.

3 The 9 Sectors are Micro/minor irrigation, Crop development, Animal husbandry, Agriculture mechanization, Fisheries, Horticulture, Innovative programmes/ training/capacity building/ others, Research (agri/horti/animal husbandry/etc.) and Marketing and post harvest management.

REFERENCES

Assam Agriculture (2012). *Assam Agriculture– General Profile*. [Accessed on September 30, 2013: http://www.agriassam.in/agriHorti_profile/Profile_ofAgri-HortiSector_ofAssam-June2012.pdf]

DES (2010-11). *Economic Survey Assam 2010-11*. Directorate of Economics and Statistics, Planning and Development Department, Guwahati: Government of Assam.

DES (2011-12). *Economic Survey Assam 2011-12*. Directorate of Economics and Statistics, Planning and Development Department, Guwahati: Government of Assam [Accessed on September 2013: http://www.ecostatassam.nic.in/ads_economic%20survey_2011-12.pdf]

DES (2012-13). *Economic Survey Assam 2012-13*. Directorate of Economics and Statistics, Planning and Development Department, Guwahati: Government of Assam [accessed on September 2013: http://www.ecostatassam.nic.in/ads_economic%20survey_2011-12.pdf]

MoSPI (2013). *Gross State Domestic Product*. Ministry of Statistics and Programme Implementation [Accessed on September 24, 2013: http://mospi.nic.in/Mospi_New/site/home.aspx]

RBI (2012). *Handbook of Statistics on Indian Economy*. Mumbai: Reserve Bank of India.

RKVY (2013). Rashtriya Krishi Vikas Yojana (RKVY). [accessed April 2013: http://rkvy.nic.in/]

Livelihood Strategies in North East India
An Empirical Analysis of Lohit and Papum Pare Districts in the Rural Arunachal Pradesh

Dr. A.I. Singh

ABSTRACT

The concept of livelihood strategy has become vital to any development practice in recent years as the market-driven strategy becomes a reality. Nonetheless, precise identification of livelihoods in quantitative data has remained methodologically elusive. This paper uses cluster analysis methods to operationalise the concept of livelihood strategies in rural household data and then uses the resulting strategy-specific income (consumption expenditure of household) distributions to test whether the hypothesized outcome differences between livelihoods indeed exist. Using data from Lohit in eastern part and Papum Pare district in western part of Arunachal Pradesh, we identify five distinct livelihood strategies that exhibit statistically significant differences in mean per capita consumption expenditure and stochastic dominance orderings that establish clear welfare ranking among livelihood strategies. Multinomial regression analysis identifies geographic, demographic and financial determinants of livelihood choice. The result should facilitate targeting of interventions designed to improve rural household livelihoods.

Keywords: Livelihood strategy; Lohit; Papum Pare; marginal farmers; Cluster analysis; Multinomial regression analysis

Introduction

The North East States of India accounts for about 8 per cent of the country's geographical area. It accounts for about 4 per cent of the total population of the country in 2011 Census. The region has inadequate and poor infrastructural facilities in compare to the other regions of the country. These states are the eastern part of the Himalayan range which is hilly and inhospitable mountainous terrains bounded by Nepal and Bhutan in west, China in north and north-east, Burma (Myanmar) in east, and Bangladesh in south. These states are special category states of the country since Independence and are still underdeveloped and backward. Rural households of these states earn their livelihoods from diverse allocation of their natural, physical and human capital assets among various income generating activities. The literature offers many reasons why such diversification occurs (see Ellis, 1998 and Barrett et al. 2001). Among these might be diminishing returns on increasing investment in certain activities due to law and order problem and missing markets that compel self-provision of goods or services the household desires for own consumption. Similarly household may wish to diversify as a strategy for coping with an unexpected shock or to minimize risk ex ante by participating in activities that generate negatively correlated returns. The presumption throughout the literature is that households choose such pattern of diversification so as to achieve the best possible standard of living, broadly defined. The chosen combination of assets and activities is referred to as the 'household's livelihood strategy'. A livelihood strategy encompasses not only activities that generate income but many other kinds of choices, including cultural and social choices, that come together to make up the primary occupation of a household (Ellis 1998).

The concept of livelihood strategy has become vital to any development practice in recent years as the market-driven strategy becomes a reality. Nonetheless, precise identification of livelihoods in quantitative data has remained methodologically vague since a precise operational definition of livelihood remains missing. However, the ability to operationalise the concept of a livelihood strategy becomes vital when one speaks of 'improving' livelihoods, to paraphrase much current development discourse. Implicit in the concept of 'improving' is the suggestion that certain strategies offer households a higher returns on their assets, not least of which is household labour. But if we cannot pin down the boundaries between distinct livelihood strategies, how can we distinguish graduation to an improved livelihood (i.e., better outcome from a different choice) from improvement in the performance of a given livelihood (i.e., higher productivity from the same basic choice, perhaps due to improved technical or allocative efficiency of resources. Hence there exist discernible orderings of distinct livelihood strategies that can be implemented through intervention by facilitating graduation to more desirable livelihood strategies – ones that can be associated with improved well-being of household members.

Objectives

(a) To identify strategies to test whether the hypothesized outcome differences between livelihoods indeed exist.

(b) To examine whether an approach based on statistical cluster analysis methods to identify and order distinct livelihood strategies and to identify the correlates of access to the most desirable of those livelihood strategies.

(c) To analyse the prerequisite to credible targeting of interventions aimed at improving choices and outcomes for rural households data and then uses the resulting strategy-specific income (consumption expenditure of household) distributions to test whether the hypothesized outcome using rural household data from Lohit in eastern part and Papum Pare district in western part of Arunachal Pradesh.

Database and Methodology

The present study is mainly empirical in nature. The data which are used and incorporated in different chapters of the study were collected from primary as well as secondary sources during 2010-11. The State level information has been collected from Arunachal Pradesh Government offices like, Directorate of Economics and Statistics, Directorate of Agriculture, Arunachal Pradesh Remote Sensing and Application Centre, Directorate of Rural Development, Directorate of Environment and Forests and Reports and Publications such as National Sample Survey Organisation, Central Statistical Organisation, Directorate of Census, North Eastern Council, Human Development Report of Arunachal Pradesh, etc. There are several methods of characterizing household livelihood strategies in the literature. Most commonly economists group households by share of income earned in different sectors of the economy. For example, Barrett et al. (2005) analysed the relationship between overall household income and the proportion of income earned in on-farm and off-farm activities, noting how these proportion changed across income quartiles and that different income sources became dominant as one move up the income distribution. Dercon and Krishnan (1996) used income share composition to examine the relationship between income, household characteristics and barriers to entry into higher return activities. Reardon et al. (1992) examined the potential determinants of diversified income portfolios for rural smallholders. The common denominator of this literature is that data on realized incomes underpin most classification. In our case, we take the consumption expenditure of the rural household as denominator since the rural households exaggerate the income data and it is erroneous in the rural dimension since they are mostly illiterate.

We have two concerns with this approach. First, sustainable livelihoods approaches typically focus on asset allocations across distinct activities, i.e. on agents' behavior rather than on income outcomes that are heavily impacted by stochastic, exogenous factors (Ellis 1998; Scoones 1998;

Bebbington 1999). Consequently, categorization based realizations of stochastic incomes involve a subtle but important disconnect from the underlying concept. Second, the categorization used are based on inherently arbitrary decisions by external observers- e.g. why is the sector of employment of primary importance? – and may thereby exaggerate some difference while understanding others.

An alternative method of analyzing livelihood strategies involves direct examination of the individual household's asset endowment. The amount of income earned and even the type of activity undertaken by a households is stochastic function of the assets it controls. Certain activities may be beyond the reach of households without access to the required financial, natural, physical, human or social capital. This asset based approach makes it possible to map a household's asset endowment into its chosen livelihood strategy and then into its (logically subsequent) stochastic income realization (Carter & Barrett 2006). Households with similar bundles of assets might be limited to similar livelihood strategies, but in any given period realize quite different incomes, although they are structurally identical.

The rural households under investigation in the study live in two districts of Arunachal Pradesh- Lohit district in eastern part of the State and Papum Pare district in the western part of the State that exhibit several crucial similarities in terms of food habit and cultural and traditional practices. However population densities are high in Papum Pare district while it is comparatively low in Lohit district. As a result average firm sizes are slightly smaller in Papum Pare than in Lohit. The data used in this paper come out from detailed household and village survey conducted during 2005-06 in Lohit district and 2010-11 in Papum Pare district. There were 6 villages from Lohit district such as Loiliang, Danglat, Karhe, Solungtoo and Tillang Kyong whereas there were 5 villages from Papum Pare district such as Ganga village, Jote, Poma, Jollang and Midpu I. The geographical sizes and population of villages vary from one district to another district. In Lohit, 113 sampled rural households were canvassed and interviewed while 127 were canvassed and interviewed from Papum Pare district. The structured questionnaire had wide information on agricultural production, firm size, livestock holdings, off-farm income activities, earnings, and household characteristics.

Hence, this paper presents an asset-based approach to identifying livelihood strategies, letting the data direct us as to how best to group household assets, and then testing for prospective welfare ordering among the stochastic income distributions associated with each identified livelihood strategy. We apply this method to data from two similar agro-ecological regions in the Kenyan highlands. We find that there exist five distinct livelihood strategies discernible in these data and that one livelihood strategy second degree stochastically dominates the other four. A multinomial logit regression of household characteristics on three slightly broader classifications of livelihood strategy chose (low, medium an high return) highlights key household attributes – geographic location, family size, farming experience, access to credit and remittances – that statistically differentiate households pursuing low, medium, high return livelihood strategies. Asset endowments indeed appear quite important not only in choosing among empirically distinct livelihood strategies but also in the returns earned from these strategies. Categorization of different strategies by asset allocation offers a meaningful and tractable way to operationalize the livelihood strategies concept and to discern broader patterns in livelihood choices for rural households.

Determinants of Livelihood Choice

Assume that a household seeks to maximize its utility over stochastic income by allocating its given asset endowment across a set of feasible activities, i=1,2,3,4 ....., N. Then, a simple revealed preference argument suggests that, where different asset allocation strategies yield different income distributions that can be ordered in welfare terms (e.g. via stochastic dominance criteria), any households observed to have adopted a lower return livelihood strategy must have faced a constraint that limited its choice set relative to those of its neighbors, as no one would freely choose to draw from a stochastically dominated distribution when they had access to a dominating alternative. Identifying low return livelihood strategies and the households that choose them is thus critical to targeting interventions intended to advance poverty reduction policy objectives.

Hence it is assumed that,

$$Y_i = f(A_i) + e_i \quad \text{(i)}$$

Where f_i is an increasing function relating household assets in activity I, A_i to the stochastic return from an activity Y_i with ε_i an error term that represents unexpected shocks to activity income and any measurement error. Household total consumption expenditure $Y = \Sigma y_i$. If the household maximizes its utility defined over income realizations, then the household's choice simply an optimal allocation of its asset endowment A_0.

$$\max_{A_i} U[\Sigma y_i) = \Sigma f_i (A_i) + \varepsilon_i$$

Subject to $\Sigma A_i < A_0$

The resulting choice – an allocation of the household's assets across various activities – represents its chosen livelihood strategy.

Given this conceptual structure for livelihood strategy choice, at any given point in time, the household compares the marginal utility associated with alternative asset allocation taking into consideration the expected income[1] from a given allocation – described by $f(A_i)$- as well as the full underlying distribution of each ε_i which generates a formulation of the above problem, assuming constant returns to scale for all activities and complete, competitive markets that equalize returns across activities $f(A_i) = R'A_i$ because each asset earns a fixed rate of return, R, no matter the volume of the asset or the activity to which it is allocated. More generally, however, returns on assets might vary across activity observed in there exist barriers that restrict household ability to allocate assets freely across all activities observed in an economy – for example, borrowing constraints that limit households ability to supplement their endowment temporarily, market access differences that cause cross-sectional variation in returns of across households, or asset specificity that matches particular assets (e.g., cows, buffalos) with certain activities (e.g., dairy production). As a result, differences in standards of living may persist across households (Dercon Krishnan 1996; Carter & Barrett 2006).

Given the difficulty of observing risk preference, it is typically easier to observe sample information about the probability distribution associated with each activity *i*. Many scholars therefore, commonly use stochastic dominance analysis to rank alternative risky choices given only weak information on preference. In particular, first and second-order stochastic dominance generates clear welfare ordering among alternative choices under the mild assumptions that utility is increasing and weakly concave in income (Whitmore & Findlay 1978)[2]. By the optimum principle, asset allocation under the problem defined in equation (2) – the observed livelihood strategies describing household allocation of assets across a portfolio of activities – should not be second-order stochastically dominated by any other feasible choice. In any given period, a particular asset allocation may yield a low income relative to some feasible alternative(s), i.e. a poor draw from the relevant distribution. But that should result purely from the inherent stochasticity of the income- generating process, not from errors of household livelihood choice, which one would expect would vanish over time in reasonable stable system as people experiment with different portfolio mixes and observes their neighbours' experiments as well.

Common Livelihood Activities

Household in the sample engage in a variety of farm and non-farm activities. We attempted to identify common livelihood activities by summarizing plot-level crop data, types of animal species held and skilled or unskilled off-farm income. As it typical in household-level data, at this level of detail, subtle variations in each household's portfolio holding made it appear as if each farmer in the sample followed a slightly different livelihood strategy from all the others. Such extreme disaggregation of course prevents necessary simplification for the purposes of policy analysis. We therefore sought a theoretically and statistically defensible means of aggregating the data into distinct livelihood categories.

The categories were chosen with many criteria in mind, including distinct input requirement and different roles within the biophysical system from which rural Arunachalee-farming households generate income. We grouped crop production activities into three distinct groups, with one sub-groups: annual food crops (cereals, roots and tubers and leafy vegetables), perennial fodder crops (i.e. Napier grass) and perennial cash crops – with separate sub-group classification for orange and other fruits, the two primary cash crops at the Lohit and Papum Pare districts. We similarly created four livestock groups: improved dairy cattle based on cross- or pure- bed exotic breeds, local breed daily cattle, non-dairy (i.e., beef, Mithun) cattle, and small ruminants (e.g., goats, sheep, hen duck) and pigs. Each of these livestock groups requires different management strategies and produces different outputs, hence their identification as distinct activities. Finally, off-farm income-generating activities were grouped into two categories according to the required skills and associated average earnings: low return, unskilled and high return, skilled. Unskilled employment and self-employed opportunities are universally available, while the more remunerative (on average) options are only open to those possessing the relevant skills, education or both. We thus have N=11 distinct activities in the empirical analysis that follows: annual food crop production, perennial cash crop production, orange and other fruits seasonal crop production, improved daily cattle, local (unimproved) dairy cattle, non-dairy cattle, small ruminants and pigs, unskilled off-farm employment and skilled employment. Table 3.1 summarize the frequencies and means for each activity type in Lohit and Papum Pare districts sample as a whole which is given in next page.

Table 3.1: Frequencies and means of Different Activities in Lohit and Papum Pare Districts of Arunachal Pradesh

Activities	Percentage of Lohit Households	Percentage of Papum Pare Households	Means			
			Lohit (N=113)	Papum Pare (N=127)	Significance	Total (N=240)
Food crops (in acres)	98.2	100.00	1.61	0.94	**	1.25
Cash crop (in acres)	54.9	8.7	0.31	0.08	***	0.19
Orange (in acres)	6.2	0.0	0.04	000	88	0.02
Ginger (in acres)	45.1	8.7	0.23	0.08	**	0.15
Local dairy cattle (head)	4.4	62.2	0.06	1.17	***	0.65
Small ruminants (head)	37.2	27.6	1.46	0.71	*	1.06
Low return off-farm income (No. of individuals)	8.9	49.6	0.10	0.73	***	0.43
High return off-farm income	3.10	31.5	0.08	0.40	*	0.24

Although most of the activity types are found at both sites, Lohit farmers and primarily engaged in food crop production, with fewer households observed cultivating cash crops . They keep fewer improved dairy and non-dairy cattle, and more household members were engaged in unskilled off-farm employment than it Papum Pare. The observed means of the relevant activities, as well as the proportion of each population engaged in each activity type, differed significantly between Papum Pare and Lohit are significant (t-test) either at 5 per cent or 1 per cent level, as shown in table in Table 1, expect in the case of skilled employment and small ruminant holdings. This serves to further emphasize that the livelihood strategies chosen by households in Papum Pare and Lohit are quite different, with Lohit households clearly more often involved in low return activities. As well, Lohit households appear to possess fewer agricultural assets than their Papum Pare counterparts, with smaller average areas for agricultural crops and smaller herd sizes.

Identifying Livelihood Strategies via Cluster Analysis

In the livelihood literature, strategies are commonly identified by broad but inherently arbitrary rules that partition the sample among exogenously defined groupings of activities, for example by looking at activity choices in different income quartiles (Barrett et al. 2005). In this paper we opt instead to let the data tell us how best to partition the sample into statistically distinct livelihood strategies reflecting how households allocated assets across the 11 different activities identified in the preceding section. We do this via cluster analysis techniques.

Cluster analysis is a statistical data reduction method for summarizing a large number of sample observations by assigning them to a smaller, tractable number of distinct groups – or clusters – of observations. The core idea is that there are groups latent common features that enable one to agglomerate individual observations into a small number of groups based on similarity along particular, pre-determined dimensions. Similarity is measure with reference to a particular statistics (e.g. mean or median) of the cluster and does not require any assumptions about the distributions describing observations within or between clusters. Cluster analysis is therefore a highly flexible and intuitive, albeit computationally intensive, method for letting the data speak for themselves in defining focal asset allocations that might usefully define distinct livelihood strategies.

In this paper, we use asset allocation across the 11 activities we have identified as the relevant dimensions and an algorithm that group observations around central points by minimizing distances of observations in a group from the central point while simultaneously maximizing the distance between the points. More precisely, we performed a k-means cluster analysis (Jansen et.al 2003) to assign each household to a distinct group based on the following variables: land area cultivated in (*i*) food crops, (*ii*) pure stand perennials, (*iii*) Orange and (*iv*) other fruits (*v*) improved dairy cattle, (*vi*) local (unimproved) dairy cattle, (*vii*) non-dairy cattle and (*viii*) small ruminants owned; and number of household members engaged in (*ix*) unskilled and (*x*) skilled off-farm employment and self employment activities.

K-means cluster analysis is a non-hierarchical method of partitioning data into a predetermined number of groups. Observations are initially randomly assigned to each of the k clusters, and then reassigned using an iterative method so as to minimize within-cluster variance and maximize between – cluster variance. In multivariate cluster analysis, the between – cluster variance is measured with respect to the Euclidean norm of the cluster means across the vector of variables used as defining characteristics. Convergence is achieved when any further reassignment of observations across groups would increase within-cluster variance.

Based on statistical results and commons sense checks of the resulting groupings, we identified five distinct livelihood strategy clusters in these data (i.e. k=5). The mean values for each activity in each livelihood strategy are summarized in Table 3.2.

Table 3.2: Livelihood Strategies Estimated via K-means Cluster Analysis (Mean value of livelihood activity by cluster)

Clustering Variables	Cluster 1	Cluster 2	Cluster 3	Cluster 4	Cluster 5	Sample Means
Food crops (acres)	0.50	0.98	1.44	1.03	0.70	1.25
Cash crop (acres)	0.00	0.09	0.15	0.11	3.08	0.19
Orange (acres)	0.00	0.00	0.01	0.01	0.50	0.02
Other Fruits (acres)	0.00	0.05	0.12	0.09	2.35	0.15
Local dairy cattle (head)	1.00	0.84	0.55	0.85	0.00	0.65
Improved dairy cattle (head)	0.00	0.39	0.92	0.88	2.00	0.81
Non-dairy cattle (head)	0.00	0.16	0.20	0.21	0.20	0.19
Small ruminants (head)	1.00	0.76	0.78	2.59	2.20	1.06
Low return off-farm income	3.40	1.22	0.00	0.79	0.00	0.43
(number of individual)						
High return off-farm income (number of individual)	0.00	0.00	0.27	1.50	0.80	0.39
Other variable						
Fraction of households that are in Lohit and Papum Pare (%)	100.0	83.7	38.8	70.6	0.0	52.9
Daily per capita income (standard deviation)	11.78 (10.02)	31.46 (29.36)	50.06 (42.74)	65.48 (92.94)	136.30 (71.64)	49.44 (53.48)

(Contd…)

Clustering Variables	Cluster 1	Cluster 2	Cluster 3	Cluster 4	Cluster 5	Sample Means
No. of Households	5	49	147	34	5	240
Fraction of Households (%)	2.1	20.4	61.3	14.2	2.1	100
Strategy	Unskilled worker	Mixed smallholders	Staples producers	Off-farm high returns	Diversified commercial	Total

Source: Survey data 2005-2011

Daily per capita household income was computed as the sum of the value of annual crop agricultural output, evaluated at average local prices, plus any earning from livestock or livestock product sales, off-farm income and remittances; that sum was then divided by the headcount of individuals in the household and converted to a daily measure.

Cluster I (First strategy) is employed by a small number of farm households. They have the lowest mean income of the five strategies and smallest land holdings (their mean land area is 0.5 acres). On average, they have one local dairy cow and one small goat farm. They allocate all of their land to annual food crops. However, what ever the production they have is not self-sufficient in food crop production, they supplement their income with low-wage, unskilled off-farm work which include community work. No household members obtain skilled employment or self-employment and on average, 3/4th of them are engaged in unskilled off-firm employment. In our sample, cluster 1 households appear only in Loiliang Village of Lohit District of Arunachal Pradesh.

Cluster 2 (Second strategy) represents 20.4 per cent of the total sample. Most of them are from western Kenyan village sub-sample. They farm a little more than twice as much land (1.09 acres) as that in cluster 1 but with nearly all of it in food crops, and just a small fraction in perennial forage and cash crops, mostly tea. Cluster 2 households' total livestock holdings are similar to those of the part-time subsistence unskilled workers, but they are most likely to have an improved dairy cow and some non-dairy cattle. Average employment in unskilled off-farm work is above 1/3 that of cluster 1 households, but still without any skilled employment or self-employment. Cluster 2 households' mean per capita daily income is one and two thirds times greater than that of cluster 1 households.

Cluster 3 (Third strategy) represents just over 60 per cent of the total sample. On average, they farm 1.6 acres of land, i.e. more than three times as much as cluster 1 and half again as much as cluster 2. While about 90 per cent of their land holdings are in annual food crops, as with the cluster 2 households, the staples producers grow more of both annual food and perennial cash crops by virtue of their greater land holdings. Indeed, cluster 3 households have the largest area in food crops of all the five groups, hence the 'staple producers' label. They have more livestock on average than households in the first two clusters, with improved dairy cattle for more common. None of these households engage in unskilled off-farm employment, although they do enjoy off-farm from skilled employment, roughly one quarter of a person per household, on average. The key features which distinguish cluster 3 from cluster 2 households are the greater total stock of land and livestock – especially improved dairy cattle – and access to skilled employment.

The distinguishing feature of cluster (fourth strategy), representing a little more than 4 per cent of the sample households, is their greater reliance on skilled off-farm employment as a source of income. They also keep more small ruminants than any of the other clusters. They keep improved and local breeds of dairy cattle in roughly equal proportions (nearly one head of each, on average, per household), and farm just over one acre on average, again about 90 per cent in annual food crops. Unlike the staples producers, many cluster 4 households supplement their farm and skilled off-farm employment with unskilled off-farm employment. They are thus the most diversified in terms of varied activities, earning returns across semi-subsistence and commercial farming along with unskilled and skilled off-farm employment.

In Cluster 5 (fifth strategy) the average per capita income is over twice that of the next highest strategy (cluster 4). Households in this cluster put far less emphasis on food crop production – devoting as much land area to perennial fodder production as they do to annual food crop production – and putting nearly 70 per cent of their land into perennial cash crops, mainly orange and other fruits. The farming operation integrate relatively large improved dairy herds – more than twice as large a any other cluster's – and sizable small ruminant herds – more than twice as large as any but cluster 4's – to constitute highly diversified commercial farms. They have no local dairy cattle and no household member engaged in unskilled employment, but do supplement their on – farm income with some skilled, off-farm employment. Cluster 5's livelihood strategy is the only that generates an average per capita income greater than Rs. 96 a day.

Are there barriers to adoption of the dominant livelihood strategy?

Very few households in the sample chose the dominant, diversified commercial agriculture livelihood strategy, however. This suggests the possibility of significant barrier to adoption of most remunerative livelihood strategy. In order to test for patterns in the adoption of distinct livelihood strategies, we performed a multinomial logit regression on livelihood observed in the part-time smallholder/unskilled worker and the diversified commercial strategies, the households pursuing these strategies were combined with those in the neighboring strategies to generate a trinomial dependent variable. Key household level covariates are summarized in Table 3.3.

The parameter estimate and marginal effects are presented in table 3.4. The likelihood of choosing the staples producer livelihood strategy over the mixed smallholder strategy (the comparison case) is substantially lower in the more degraded western Kenyan soils. This may be partly due to higher population density, as the probability of being a staples producer modestly, but significantly, decreases between the two lesser performing livelihood strategies was farmer experience, which increases the probability of choosing the staples producer strategy, consistent with the idea that this reflects superior productivity that includes full engagement of all unskilled household labour on-farm. The significance of the village dummy accords with distribution of households in the sample and reinforces the point that the lowest return strategies are most often found in Vihiga, where both high population density, which leads to extremely small farm sizes, and lack of access to a large market such Nairobi must surely play a part in this phenomenon.

Table 3.3: Summary of Household Characteristic

Variable	Mean	S.D.	Min.	Max.	Missing
Smallholders (Strategies 1 and 2)					
Household in Lohit and Papum Pare (y/n)	0.85	0.36	0	1	0
Household size (numbers)	5.06	1.89	1	9	0
Farm Size (acre)	1.20	2.73	0.20	20.06	0
Total livestock)	1.43	1.20	0	5	0
Age of household head (years)	54.81	15.12	29	88	1
Head's year of farming experience (years)	22.53	14.53	1	67	3
Self-reported access to credit (y/n)	0.22	0.42	0	1	5
Receives remittances (y/n)	0.20	0.41	0	1	0
Household head has no education (y/n)	0.32	0.29	0	1	0
Household head has secondary education or above (y/n)	0.26	0.44	0	1	0
Staples producers (strategy 3)					
Household in Lohit and Papum Pare	0.39	0.49	0	1	0
Household size (numbers)	5.01	2.35	1	13	0
Farm size (numbers)	1.82	3.21	0.13	26.00	0
Total livestock	1.75	1.43	0	7	0
Age of household heac (year)	57.70	15.17	23	88	5
Head's year of farming experience (years)	30.16	15.89	0	67	17

(Contd...)

Variable	Mean	S.D.	Min.	Max.	Missing
Self-reported access to credit	0.60	0.49	0	1	3
Receives remittances	0.35	0.48	0	1	0
Household head has no education	0.22	0.41	0	1	0
Household head has secondary education or above	0.21	0.41	0	1	0
Off-farm high return and commercial (strategies 4 & 5)					
Household in Lohit and Papum Pare	0.62	0.49	0	1	0
Household size (numbers)	5.74	1.97	2	10	0
Farm size (numbers)	1.32	1.44	0.00	5.50	0
Total livestock	2.23	1.69	0	8	0
Age of household head (year)	48.74	12.83	28	77	0
Head's year of farming experience (years)	19.77	13.72	1	54	4
Self-reported access to credit	0.69	0.47	0	1	4
Receives remittances	0.51	0.51	0	1	0
Household head has no education	0.03	0.16	0	1	0
Household head has secondary education or above	0.51	0.51	0	1	0

Source: Survey data, 2005-2011

Table 3.4: Multinomial Logit Regression of Livelihood Strategy Choice

Variable	Coefficient	Std. Error	Marginal Effects
Staples producers vs. smallholder			
Household in Lohit and Papum Pare	-1.598	0.608	-0.288
Household size (numbers)	-0.169	0.104	0.035
Farm size (numbers)	0.414	0.272	0.050
Total livestock	-0.078	0.161	-0.037
Age of household head (year)	-0.023	0.022	-0.002
Head's year of farming experience (years)	0.047	0.020	0.009
Self-reported access to credit	0.636	0.517	0.007
Receives remittances	0.731	0.476	0.012
Household head has no education	0.134	0.796	0.082
Household head has secondary education or above	0.437	0.535	0.018
Constant	2.075	1.164	
Off-farm high return and diversified commercial Vs marginal farmers			
Household in Lohit and Papum Pare	-0.303	0.716	0.108
Household size (numbers)	0.011	0.131	0.017
Farm size (numbers)	0.386	0.286	0.005

(Contd...)

Variable	Coefficient	Std. Error	Marginal Effects
Total livestock	0.229	0.197	0.033
Age of household head (year)	-0.035	0.029	0.002
Head's year of farming experience (years)	0.004	0.028	0.004
Self-reported access to credit	1.353	0.626	0.092
Receives remittances	1.349	0.586	0.089
Household head has no education	-0.768	1.329	0.078
Household head has secondary education or above	0.712	0.618	0.041
Constant	0.524	1.433	
Number of observation	203		
Per cent correctly predicted	63.8		
Log-likelihood value	-148.58		
Pseudo R-Squared	0.211		

The year of farm experience variable may represent the ability over time to adopt somewhat higher return strategies, but also the inability of asset accumulation alone to move households into the highest return livelihoods.

Credit access and receipt of remittances are the only statistically significant determinants of household self-selection into the combined off-farm high return / diversified commercial strategy. Recall that households in these two clusters have more land invested in cash crops, own more improved dairy cattle and have more household members engaged in skilled off-farm income than the rest of the sample, on average. The ability to diversity into these higher return activities appears to be a function of their relatively greater financial liquidity, facilitated by access to credit and remittances, in comparison to households pursuing the lower return livelihood strategies, consistent with previous studies on the importance of financial liquidity to livelihood choice and household welfare (Dercon & Krishna 1996, Ellis 1998, Mosley 2001, Barrett et al. 2005).

Findings and Conclusions

This paper introduces a novel approach to identifying distinct livelihood strategies in household survey data using cluster analysis. The resulting data-given partitioning of the data enables us to test the hypothesis that some livelihood strategies demonstrably offer households higher returns on investment of their assets yet are unattainable for some households given their endowments, including their geographic location.

The results from a sample of 240 farming households in eastern and western district of Arunachal Pradesh yield an intuitive partitioning of the complex set of activities – we work with distinct, aggregated activity categories – into five distinct livelihoods. Households with more land and more individuals working off farm in skilled employment are able to achieve higher average per capita incomes than their neighbours. The two most remunerative livelihood strategies, on average, first – or – second order stochastically dominate each of the other strategies income distributions. Yet, despite the difference between the strategies in the sample, only the highest return livelihood generated an average income above Rupees 32 per day benchmark and only the three highest earning strategies yielded mean per capita daily incomes in excess of the Rs. 862 per person per day. So variations in livelihood strategies exist, but the overall picture is still one of considerable and broad-based poverty in the rural Arunachal Pradesh. Further use of the methodology described here among other, more representative, population samples may suggest focal points for targeting interventions to help households adopt higher return livelihood strategies.

NOTES

1 In the Interests of Simplicity of Exposition, we Treat this as a Static Problem and ignore the Investment in Assets.

2 First-order Dominance only Requires Monotonicity; Second-order Dominance Requires Concavity, Reflecting Income Risk.

REFERENCES

Barrett, C B, Reardon, T & P. Webb (2001): Non-farm Income Diversification and Household Livelihood Strategies in Rural Africa: Concepts, Dynamics and Policy Implication, *Food Policy*, 26 (4), 315-31.

Barrett, C B. Bezuneh, M, Clay, D & T. Reardon (2005): Heterogeneous Constraints, Incentives and Income Diversification Strategies in Rural Africa. *Quarterly Journal of International Agriculture* , 44 (1), 37-60.

Barrett, CB et al. (2006) Welfare Dynamics in Rural Kenya and Madagascar, *Journal of Development Studies*, 4 (2), 248-77.

Bebbington, A(1999): Capitals and Capabilities: A Framework for Analyzing Peasant Viability, Rural Livelihood and Poverty. *World Development* , 27 (12), 2021-44.

Dercon, S & P. Krishnan (1966): Income Portfolios in Rural Ethiopia and Tanzania: Choices and Constraints, *Journal of Development Studies* , 32 (6), 850-75.

Ellis, F (1998): Household Strategies and Rural Livelihood Diversification, *Journal of Development Studies*, 35 (1), 1-38.

Jansen, H G P, Damon, A, Pender, J, Wielemaker, W & R.Schipper (2003): *Policies for Sustainable Development in the Hillsides of Honduras:*

A Quantitative Livelihoods Approach, Discuss paper, Environment and Production Technology Division, International Food Policy Research Institute (IFPRI), Washington, DC.

Mitra, A (1998): 'Environment and Sustainable Development in Hilly Regions of North East India - A Study of Arunachal Pradesh', *International Journal of Social Economics*, Vol.25, No.24, pp. 196-206.

——— (1999): 'Planning for Forestry and Environment Development in Arunachal Pradesh', in A Banerjee and B Kar (ed), *Economic Planning and Development of North-Eastern States*, Kanishka Publishers, New Delhi.

Reardon, T, Delgado, C & P. Matlon, (1992): Determinants and Effects of Income Diversification Amongst Farm Households in Burkina Faso, *Journal of Development Studies* , 28(2), 264-96.

Scoones, I, 1998, Sustainable Rural Livelihoods: A Framework for Analysis. University of Sussex. IDS (Institute of Development Studies) Working Paper No. 72.

Singh, A I (2010): *Forest and CPR Management in Eastern Himalayas*, Akansha Publication, Delhi.

Whitmore, GA & M.C. Frindlay (1978): *Stochastic Dominance: An Approach to Decision-making under Risk*, Lexington Books, Toronto.

Employment Patterns Among Informal Sector Workers in Mumbai City

Sanjay Rode

ABSTRACT

The city of Mumbai is the financial capital of India. Most of the manufacturing, services and construction works require labour on a regular basis. Many skilled and unskilled workers migrate to the city from rural and other urban areas of the country for employment purposes. Workers differ in terms of education, skills and health status. They provide various services, and their services are subject to demand in the city. Most of the work and services are seasonal and time bound. Present study shows that female unskilled workers are more engaged in construction related jobs. Educational achievements are lower among construction and self-employed workers. Therefore, income generation is also low. Such data is compared of workers with regular job in city. The multi-nominal logit model result shows that educational achievement and income are negatively co-related to self-employed and construction workers as compare to regular workers. Healthcare expenditure is positively co-related and statistically significant among self-employed and construction workers. The policies of training workers with technical skills, provision of healthcare at workplace, water supply at the doorstep in slums will bring good results. Government must provide subsidized food through a public distribution system to workers. It will improve their standard of living, health and nutrition capacity. Such policies will help to improve income earning capacity, and get rid of poverty.

Introduction

The processes of in formalization of jobs observed during the past decades have affected both high and low income countries (Beneria Lourdes 2001). India is not an exception to such changes as far as employment pattern is concerned. Some cities have either restructured employment or developed new trends in employment pattern. Mumbai is the financial capital of India. Apart from corporate head-quarters of number of Indian companies and multinational companies (MNCs), most of the financial institutions such as stock exchange and central bank are located in the city. The growth of service sector which includes finance, information technology (IT), telecom, tourism, entertainment, advertising, communication is higher than any other sector. Due to its vast potential to provide enormous employment opportunities to people, it lures people to from rural areas to the city. Therefore, it is not surprising that very few skilled and unskilled migrants remain unemployed in the region. They are easily consumed in the vast labour market in the city. Educational qualifications and skills of the workers are the two pre-requisites to get higher income. Highly educated workers play an important role in the production process. A highly trained worker will always work for innovation oriented and skilled jobs. Similarly, more educated workers do better in acquiring skills compared to the less-educated ones (Chakravarty 2004). In the city, the segments of services that have grown faster in recent past and provided employment with relatively higher levels of earning, have high human capital requirements and have, therefore, mainly benefited the skilled workers. At the same time, the employment structure in the service sector is sharply polarized between a few high end jobs in large corporations and a mass of low paid jobs in small and informal units. The industrial sector, on the other hand, has thrown up the demand for a wider spectrum of skills. Thus, it benefits workers with different skill levels and from all sections of society (Topala 2009).

A large proportion of the workforce in Mumbai is still in the informal sector. These workers are engaged in economic activities with lower productivity and production, and it results in minor income. They are also engaged in activities with fewer stable employment contracts (including self-employed) and fewer social security benefits. While the wages and salaries of the formal sector workers are revised periodically to counter inflation, no such benefits accrue to the large proportion of workers in the informal sector (Unni Jeemol 2002).

However, due to lack of formal employment, these workers are doing various economic activities and live in the various slums across the city. Many workers are involved in furniture making and polishing, carpentry etc. The city has also witnessed rapid developments in real estate sector. There is a high demand of furniture in newly established malls, residential flats, shops, hospitals, etc. Some workers are engaged in the textile industry. The City boasts a great history of being the centre of big textile mills. Although the textile industry shifted to other cities, leftover workers still carry out weaving, dyeing, twisting, sari-cutting, spinning jari, gilding, etc. in small textile units. Self-employment, most of the time, is seasonal and sometimes workers do not find work at all. Self-employed male and female are engaged in the variety of jobs in the city. Most of the self-employed workers are less educated and are engaged in driving auto-rickshaw, transportation of goods, etc. to earn their livelihood. These people can be found living in suburbs and small dwellings near railway lines and stations. Some self-employed people work in roadside food stalls and small restaurants while others are hawkers and vendors. There are many who move across several adjacent slums and sell various products or small articles such as cloths, toys, pots or even exchange garlic for pots. Some of self-employed people could be found running *paan-bidi* shops (small shops selling cigarettes, betel leaf etc.), vending milk, selling fruits and vegetables on footpath, etc. Although people regularly purchase goods and services from such self-employed people, having a bad day at hawking or vending can massively impact their daily income generation.

New and old construction activities provide a number of informal sector jobs to different kinds of workers, both male and female. The male workers are involved in different construction activities. The women workers also work as causal labourers. They cart materials to and from building sites. They usually wake up early in the morning and prepare food for the family. If drinking water facilities are not available near the house, then it is a laborious activity to carry water from long distances. In such circumstances, women and children usually carry water from extended distances in the slums. The number of trips to carry enough water depends on the family size, the distance to the source of water, the price of water, the hygiene of family, the availability of time, etc. For each household the water requirement and use is different. Generally, the households engaged in causal labour have fewer skills and work only in nearby areas around their house. Most of the women usually walk to their workplace. Competition is considerably high for the unskilled jobs in the city because of availability of workers through large-scale migration into this region. If workers fall sick and have to visit a health centre, the facilities are usually overcrowded and visiting them consumes a lot of precious time which they otherwise could utilize for their work. Women workers are required to go early and stand in a long queue in order to take their prescriptions from the doctor. The direct and indirect cost of visiting health facility, including travelling and medicines is often to forego their daily wages. Regular check-ups may raise the economic burden caused by medical care even further. In order to avoid getting sacked and in hope of regular income, the workers might opt for private health facilities and medical treatment. However, visiting private health facilities is costly because of high consultancy fees and medicine charges. Most of the time, poor people borrow money for medical treatment from their relatives, friends, contractors, etc. To avoid such debts and save money, many workers also try to find solutions to their health problems with home remedies.

The rising population in the city is putting added pressure on existing civic amenities in Mumbai and its Municipal Corporation. Inadequate civic amenities such as water supply, housing, transportation, health care, solid waste, sanitation affect the quality of life inversely. Most of the slums are neglected in terms of provision of infrastructural facilities. They are either declared as illegal settlements or referred to as new settlements. Most of the basic services such as water supply, electricity, housing and sanitation are beyond the reach of poor living in slums. Poor people living in these slums have no choice but to purchase such services from the private providers who charge exorbitant prices. There are few studies which are conducted on workers of slums in Mumbai city. This study is unique because we have conducted primary survey of the workers living in *kutcha* slums and involved in different sectors' in Mumbai.

In the light of above discussion, this paper looks at the employment patterns of workers in the urban slums of Mumbai. The first part of the paper explains the data and methodology used in the course of the study. Second section describes the employment patterns within the city in the context of income, educational attainment and body mass index of construction workers, self-employed and regular workers. Third section examines the association of type of employment with socio-economic characteristics of respondents using multinomial logit regression. Finally, the concluding section explores the policy implications of the study.

Data and Econometric Model

Data for this study was collected from the *kutcha* slums in Mumbai city. We had chosen stratified random sampling for collecting primary data for this study. The *kutcha* slums houses are of plastic sheet and they are without piped water supply, electricity and sanitation facilities. In Mumbai city, there are different pockets of *Kutcha* slums. After selecting particular household, we have interviewed household head and took weight and heights of each member. The sample was undertaken in May-June 2011. We administered detail questionnaire and collected data of 1050 households in Mumbai city. The details of the survey and households covered in it are explained in the appendix. Workers information is collected in detail about income, education, health and measured weight and height. Such data has been collected from the eastern and western suburbs of 15 slum settlements. We categorized workers as self-employed, construction and domestic workers and regular workers in the city. The primary data has been analyzed in Stata12 software. We used multinomial logit regression to examine the socio-economic characteristics of each type of workers in Mumbai city. Such regression helps to find the co-relation between different kinds of workers. Based on nature of dependent variable, an econometric model gets used for study. There are different types of regressions but it is the best fit regression for this study. We have compared the workers of regular jobs with self employment, construction and domestic workers.

The multi-nominal logit model is defined as follows:

$$\Pr(y_i=j) = \frac{\operatorname{Exp}(X_iB_j)}{1 + \Sigma^J_j \exp(X_iB_j)} \quad (1)$$

and

$$\Pr(y_i=0) = \frac{1}{1 + \Sigma^J_j \exp(X_iB_j)'} \quad (2)$$

Where for the ith worker, y_i is the observed outcome and X_i is a vector of explanatory variable. The parameters B_j are estimated by maximum likelihood. The positive and negative parameters are compared with the reference category workers of regular jobs (Greene, W.H.2003). The results are presented in the following table.

Methodology

In order to calculate the total workforce in the city, we have assumed that there are manufacturing and service sectors. We cannot study the entire population and employment pattern of city. But for model building, we are assuming the total workforce which is fixed for particular time period. We assumed that there is no worker involved in agriculture-related activities since agriculture within the city is a rare possibility. Therefore, in terms of equation it is represented as.

$$\sum_{t=1}^{i} wf = \sum_{t=1}^{i} m + \sum_{t=1}^{i} s \qquad (3)$$

Where, *wf* is work force in the city in time *t* and i^{th} number of workers. We can further write as *t=1...n* and *i=1...n* work force. In above equation, summation *m* represents the work force involved in manufacturing sector. Similarly, summation *s* represents the work force involved in the services sector with time *t* and i^{th} workforce. Both *t* and *i* again noted from *1 to n* in the above equation.

$$\sum_{t=1}^{i} m = \sum_{t=1}^{i} f + \sum_{t=1}^{i} if \qquad (4)$$

The workers in manufacturing sector in city are further classified as the workers in the formal and informal sector at time *t* and i^{th} number of worker. In city, the numbers of worker in the manufacturing formal sector are very less.

Therefore, we assume that $\sum_{t=1}^{i} f = 0$ for analysis.

$$\sum_{t=1}^{i} s = \sum_{t=1}^{i} f + \sum_{t=1}^{i} if \qquad (5)$$

For services sector in city, the workers in the formal and informal sector at time *t* and i^{th} number of worker are explained in above equation. Here we again assumed that workers of formal services sector are $\sum_{t=1}^{i} f = 0$. Therefore, workforce in the informal sector in city comprises as follows:

$$\sum_{t=1}^{i} if = \sum_{t=1}^{i} m + \sum_{t=1}^{i} s \tag{6}$$

The number of worker of the informal sector consists of worker of manufacturing and services sector. They are at time *t* and *i=1to n*. We have further classified the workers of the informal sector as follows:

$$\sum_{t=1}^{i} if = \sum_{t=1}^{i} c + \sum_{t=1}^{i} se + \sum_{t=1}^{i} re \tag{7}$$

We have categorized the informal sector workers as workers of construction and domestic work (c), self-employment (se) and regular workers (re). All three categories of workers are considered for time *t* and *i=1 to n* workers.

The workers of the three informal sectors maximize their income subject to following constrains:

$$\sum_{t=1}^{i} Y = TE + (H_t^i + E_t^i + T_t^i + G^i) \tag{8}$$

Total income in the *t* period for (*i=1 to n*) worker depends on the type of employment (TE), health status (H), educational achievement (E), time spend (T) in informal sector labour market and gender (G). All of the above variables decide the income for the ith worker in time *t*. Construction sector, self-employment and regular job workers have three different functions for income maximization.

Results

Pattern of Employment in the Informal Sector of Mumbai City

The workers in Mumbai city are engaged in a variety of economic activities. Fcr analysis, we have categorized the workers into three categories. The major categories are self-employed workers, construction labourers and other occupations. A large number of the work force of the urban slums is engaged in construction sector and providing domestic help. Workers engaged in the construction sector are working as *kadias, mistrys* (mason), and labourers carting materials at building sites, window fitters, painters, earth workers and layers of gutter lines. Women are also involved in the construction sector, and they work as casual labourers carting materials to and from building sites. Other than this, women hold jobs in the informal sector where they work as domestic helps, petty traders, etc.

The self-employed workers are involved in sales, production, processing, repairs, and services. They mainly work as drivers, including rickshaw drivers, transporters of goods in handcarts, cooks or bearers in wayside hotels and smaller restaurants. People engaged in sales frequently pursue jobs such as hawking and vending, running *paan-bidi* shops, which might also sell small items in retail. These items are generally purchased either outside the slum or in the wholesale market. Self-employed in processing activities comprises of carpenters, tailors and blacksmiths. Some workers are engaged in work of small scale textile industry. They engaged in the activities like weaving, dyeing, twisting, sari cutting, spinning *jari*, gilding etc. These groups of self-employed group comprise those who are trying to respond to the market by adjusting themselves and their trade to changing demand patterns in the city of Mumbai. The workers engaged in sales are generally never able to depend on one area or type of product. There are large variations in earnings by different household groups. It also indicates similar variations in returns from specific occupation, types and jobs. Most of the jobs in the informal and especially in the self-employed sector provide low returns because of the irregularity of employment and a lower profit margin. There is no job security and even contractual jobs are scarce. They are involved in a lower category of less paid and casual jobs.

During the interview, it was repeatedly found that working members tend to report uncertain and lower income.

This is particularly because most of the people are self-employed or casual labour, and their income varies from time to time and there being no income at all at certain times. In Mumbai, informal workers and entrepreneurs are entitled to seven essential securities, which are often denied them: labour market security, employment security (protection against arbitrary dismissal regulation on hiring and firing, employment stability, compatible with economic dynamism), job security (career opportunity to develop a sense of occupation), work security (protection against accidents and illness at work through safety and health regulations, limits on working hours and so on) skills reproduction security (to gain retain skills through innovative means, employment training, income security (provision of adequate income and representative security (protection of collective voice in the labour market through independent trade unions and employers organizations and social dialogue institutions (ILO, 2002).

Type of Labour Force by Slums

We have categorized workers into three categories – construction/domestic work, self-employment, regular job. A little more than 75 per cent of women from Mumbai slums are engaged in construction and domestic work. However, this proportion varies considerably from on slum to another. For instance – 20 per cent of all female workers engaged in this sector come from Mazgaon where only 1 per cent comes from Dahisar. About 20 per cent male workers from Mumbai slums are engaged in construction/domestic work.

About 40 per cent male workers from slums are self-employed in Mumbai. About 6 per cent of them come from Govandi. Govandi area has many small shops preparing and selling different items. Everybody in slums is involved in different informal sector activity. The lowest percentages of self-employed workers are found in Borivali and Malad (0.48% each). The proportion of self-employed female workers is about 5 per cent in Mumbai city. They are 0.97 per cent in Lower Parel and Govandi. Male workers with regular job in the slums of city are 41 per cent.

Table 4.1: Place and Type of Labour Force in City (in per cent)

Place	Construction/ Domestic Work		Self-employment		Regular Job	
	Male	Female	Male	Female	Male	Female
Jogeshwari	0.48	1.46	0.81	0.32	1.94	0.16
Malad	0.48	1.46	0.48	0.00	1.05	0.16
Chembur	1.86	3.08	1.29	0.32	2.67	0.65
Mankhurd	1.86	6.65	2.58	0.49	1.29	0.32
Kurla	1.13	2.59	3.47	0.00	3.63	1.62
Lower Parel	0.97	6.97	4.52	0.97	0.00	0.00
Dadar	2.02	4.38	2.75	0.32	5.41	3.73
Matunga	0.81	4.21	1.86	0.32	3.55	1.62
Bandra	2.26	3.89	2.10	0.49	1.13	1.62
Goregaon	1.78	6.97	1.37	0.16	2.26	0.65
Mazgaon	2.34	19.45	7.84	0.65	0.48	0.16
Govandi	0.89	9.56	5.82	0.97	0.00	0.00
Dahisar	0.16	1.30	0.97	0.00	11.07	5.35
Kandivali	1.78	3.24	3.72	0.00	5.82	1.94
Borivali	0.32	0.97	0.48	0.16	0.16	0.00
Total	19.14	76.18	40.06	5.19	40.47	17.99

Source: Compiled from data.

In Dahisar, workers who have regular jobs are 11 per cent. Such workers are absent in the slums of Lower Parel and Govandi. Approximately, about 18 per cent women from Mumbai slums have regular jobs. They are about 4 per cent in Dadar and 6 per cent in Dahisar. None of the female workers in Borivali, Govandi and Lower Parel was engaged in a regular job. With a lower educational attainment, it is difficult to find regular employment for women in the city. Most of the women are working at their home and the number of women even surpasses men in informal employment. However, the gender bias in the informal economy is probably underestimated. Apparel, leather and sports goods sectors, more number of women workers can be seen as they are deemed to be more skilful in working with different kinds of machines for cutting, sewing, stitching etc. Apart from reasons based on grounds of efficiency, women workers are also preferred over their male counterparts because they are less prone to the formation of trade unions and related activities (Deb et.al. 2009). Similarly, Women labours are reluctant to unionize (Absar S.S 2002). Women are more likely than men to be in those informal activities that are under counted such as production for own consumption, paid domestic activities in private households and home work. The challenge is to determine how interventions can be devised that improves the livelihood of the poor while not removing incentives to formalization (Ruffer, Tim and John Knight 2007).

Age Pattern of Workers

It is important to understand the age pattern of the workers involved in construction, self-employment and regular job. Respondents aged 15 to 35 years of age have more chances of having a regular job in the city. The male workers in the age group of 35-45 years in construction/ domestic work are about 5 per cent. Similarly about 30 per cent of all female workers engaged in construction/domestic work were aged between 25 and 35 years. None of male workers in construction work were above 65 years of age. This is mainly because such tasks require more physical energy. It is also possible that at an older age energy for physical labour declines and they drop out of construction jobs. The female workers engaged in the same activities of 65 and above age group are almost negligible. They sometimes work as domestic helps. About 14 per cent of self-employed males belong to the age group 35-45 years. However, only 3 per cent of all female workers belong to 25-35 age groups and are self-employed. It implies that female workers do not accept more self-employment jobs as compare to male workers. About 13 per cent males who have regular jobs belong to the age group of 15-25 years. The female workers in this age group are about 8 per cent of total female workforce.

Table 4.2: Age Pattern of Workers (in per cent)

Age	Construction/ Domestic Work		Self-employment		Regular Job	
	Male	Female	Male	Female	Male	Female
Below 15	0.2	0.5	0.2	0.8	0.2	0.6
15-25	4.5	16.4	8.1	1.1	12.9	7.8
25-35	5.0	30.7	8.4	3.2	11.1	4.8
35-45	5.3	21.2	14.3	1.1	9.0	4.0
45-55	3.5	4.8	8.1	0.3	5.3	0.6
55-65	1.0	1.3	1.1	0.0	1.3	0.0
65-above	0.0	0.2	0.1	0.0	0.2	0.0
Total	19.4	75.0	40.2	6.5	40.0	17.8

Source: Compiled from data.

Educational Attainment Among Workers

Education is a resource and more educated workers can work with skilled jobs and earn more income. Educated workers can understand the new methods of production and work efficiently with modern machines or techniques. However, illiterate workers end up with less-skilled jobs and lower income.

Table 4.3: Educational Attainment Among Workers (per cent)

Education	Construction/ Domestic Work		Self-employment		Regular job	
	Male	Female	Male	Female	Male	Female
Illiterate	6.7	41.4	5.1	2.9	4.2	3.5
Primary	1.8	6.2	2.2	0.2	1.8	1.4
Secondary	10.4	26.3	31.3	3.3	25.5	9.1
high school	0.5	1.1	1.5	0.2	6.9	2.9
Graduate	0.0	0.0	0.1	0.0	1.5	1.0
Post graduate	0.1	0.0	0.0	0.0	0.1	0.0
Total	19.5	75.0	40.2	6.5	40.0	17.8

Source: Compiled from data.

The above table shows that about 41 per cent of all female workers are illiterate and engaged in construction/domestic works such as domestic work, carry material at construction sites, carting etc which do not require any special skill and education. Nearly 26 per cent women workers have education up to secondary level. As for male workers, 10 per cent of them have studied up till secondary level and work in construction work. Another 31 per cent who have an education up to the secondary level are self-employed. About 26 per cent of all male workers have secondary level education and working with a regular job, while among female workers, it is 9 per cent. Maximum numbers of workers from these slums involved in various jobs have mostly attended up till secondary level. The percentage of workers with graduation and post-graduation degrees are very less in the slums. Most of the less-educated workers are engaged in informal sector jobs.

Distribution of Workers by Income Level

Nearly 12 per cent of male workers are earning monthly income between Rs. 3000-6000 in construction work. About 54 per cent of all female workers earn between Rs. 1000-3000 by working in construction sector. Incomes in the construction sector are low and uncertain. During rainy season when all the construction work stops, construction workers remain unemployed. In such situations, some workers migrate to their native place. Most of the female workers work as domestic help. Since there is no specific law for the minimum wage for domestic work, incomes of such female workers are very low. Moreover, if the women worker is absent for a day even due to some inevitable circumstances, the wage is not paid to her. About 25 per cent of all male workers earn between Rs. 3000-6000 by engaging themselves in self-employment. A few of them also earn wages as low as Rs. 1000-3000. As far as regular job with Rs. 3000-6000 is concerned, about 20 per cent male and 7 per cent female workers fall in this category.

Table 4.4: Income Generation Among Workers (per cent)

Monthly Income (in Rs.)	Construction/ Domestic Work		Self-employment		Regular Job	
	Male	Female	Male	Female	Male	Female
0-1000	0.2	0.5	0.0	0.2	0.2	0.0
1000-3000	2.9	54.3	2.1	3.7	1.9	1.6
3000-6000	12.3	15.5	25.2	1.9	19.4	7.0
6000-8000	3.1	4.6	9.2	0.8	11.2	6.4
8000-10000	0.9	0.3	3.6	0.0	5.5	2.2
10000-Above	0.2	0.0	0.2	0.0	1.8	0.5
Total	19.4	75.2	40.2	6.5	40.0	17.7

Source: Compiled from data.

Body Mass Index and Income

Sometimes earnings are dependent on capacity to work and such work capacity is measured in terms of Body Mass Index (BMI). About 50 per cent of all workers who earn Rs. 0-1000 per months have a BMI of 17-18.5 contrary to other income groups. It clearly indicates that low income is positively correlated with low BMI. However, this may not always be true. About 40 per cent of female workers who earn Rs. 1000 or less have a normal BMI (18.5-25). In the Rs. 1000-2000 income category, nearly 38 per cent women workers have normal BMI. About 61 per cent male workers have a normal BMI in Rs. 2000-3000 income category while about 82 per cent female workers who earn Rs. 3000-4000 income category have normal BMI. It implies that as the income rises, the percentage of workers with normal body mass index increases.

Table 4.5 shows that in Rs. 5000-6000 income category, about 63 per cent male workers and 48 per cent of female workers fall in normal BMI category. Similarly, in Rs.6000-7000 income categories, about 63 per cent male workers and 68 per cent female workers are in normal BMI category. The same is true for income categories of Rs.7000-8000 and Rs.8000-10000. Overall about 63 per cent male workers and 69 per cent female workers fall under normal BMI category.

Table 4.5: Income and BMI Characteristics (in per cent)

BMI/Income	<16		16-17		17-18.5		18.5-25		25-30		30-35		35-40		40>	
	M	F	M	F	M	F	M	F	M	F	M	F	M	F	M	F
<1000	0.0	0.0	0.0	0.0	50.0	40.0	25.0	40.0	25.0	20.0	0.0	0.0	0.0	0.0	0.0	0.0
1000-2000	0.0	0.0	0.0	0.0	0.0	12.5	0.0	37.5	33.3	25.0	33.3	25.0	33.3	0.0	0.0	0.0
2000-3000	5.6	1.1	0.0	1.7	11.1	5.1	61.1	82.3	11.1	6.9	11.1	1.7	0.0	0.0	0.0	1.1
3000-4000	5.7	1.4	2.9	1.8	11.4	4.1	67.1	71.1	10.0	13.3	1.4	4.6	1.4	2.8	0.0	0.9
4000-5000	7.9	2.5	4.8	4.9	9.5	7.4	62.7	48.2	11.1	24.7	2.4	11.1	0.0	0.0	1.6	1.2
5000-6000	3.6	2.2	6.3	0.0	14.4	6.5	61.7	58.7	6.3	26.1	5.4	6.5	1.8	0.0	0.5	0.0
6000-7000	2.6	0.0	2.9	0.0	16.8	1.6	63.3	67.7	8.4	19.4	3.7	8.1	2.1	1.6	0.3	1.6
7000-8000	2.2	8.3	2.2	0.0	13.8	16.7	66.7	50.0	8.7	16.7	4.4	0.0	0.7	0.0	1.5	8.3
8000-10000	2.3	0.0	4.1	0.0	11.6	0.0	67.6	56.3	9.8	37.5	1.2	0.0	3.5	6.3	0.0	0.0
>10000	9.2	0.0	4.2	0.0	17.7	0.0	55.5	66.7	8.4	33.3	3.4	0.0	1.7	0.0	0.0	0.0
Total	4.1	1.4	3.8	1.8	14.4	5.3	63.1	68.5	8.8	15.5	3.6	5.1	1.8	1.3	0.5	1.1

Source: Compiled from data.

Nearly 22 per cent male workers and 8 per cent female workers are mild, moderate and severe malnourished in city. Around 23 per cent female workers and 15 per cent male workers are obese in city. Their BMI is above 25.

Higher level of education is normally associated with better income levels. The figure below shows the relationship between per capita income and educational attainment of workers. The educational attainment and monthly per capita income are positively correlated. As the level of education rises, it translates into more skills and capabilities which ultimately enable workers to get higher income. This is also possible in terms of self-employment. Self-employed educated workers work more efficiently and effectively to earn more income in the city. In *kutcha* slums, workers without education cannot earn income. Sometimes workers learn various skills at work and this leads to upward mobility in terms of job and income in the city. The city provides many vertical movement job opportunities as well. Yet, it depends on a worker's effort, job satisfaction, number of working hours, socio-economic background etc. As for self-employment, such opportunities are unlimited. There are self-employed and uneducated workers who earn a monthly income of up to ten thousand rupees. In some cases, auto-rickshaw drivers, sellers of goods, carpenters work more than normal working hours and earn more income. However, the usual trends in the figure show that as the education level of a worker increases, the per capita income also increases. With a post-graduation degree, a worker can earn around fifteen thousand rupees or sometimes more in the city.

Association of Type of Work and Socio-economic Characteristics of the Respondent

Women workers are engaged more in construction related/ domestic works since such a work does not require any special skills. It is should be noted that an overwhelming majority of women is either uneducated or has low educational attainment. Thus, women in construction work as helpers carry stones, bricks and supply cement, etc. to the construction site.

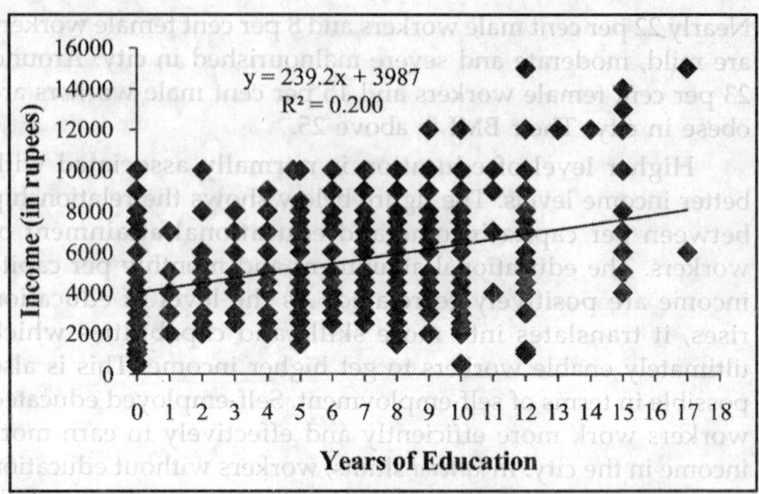

Fig. 4.1: The Relationship Between Monthly Income (in rupees) and Educational Attainment of Workers (in years)

This is reason why women workers have positive correlation with the construction/domestic jobs and it is statistically significant. On the contrary, male workers generally have better skills and better education, and therefore, the number of male workers engaged in construction/domestic work is small. Most of the workers in the construction sector are married. There is no scope for the children to work on the construction sites in the city since child labour is banned by law and it is strictly abided by construction workers now. Moreover, children may have a low work capacity which further reduces the possibility of them getting a job in construction. Therefore, married workers are positively correlated and statistically significant. Age of the workers is negatively associated with construction workers as compared to the workers of the regular jobs. This is because construction work requires more physical strength as compared to regular jobs. Young workers work efficiently on constriction sites and this could be one of the reasons why lower age is positively and significantly associated with construction work. On the other hand, educational attainment of the workers is negatively associated with construction work. It could be due to the fact that workers in construction require less education because it is an unskilled job. Most of the workers have low educational achievement and they work for small wages. The income of the construction workers is less as compared to the regular workers, and it is statistically significant. It is mainly because poor skills and uncertain job fetches lower salary to these workers. Household size among the construction workers is larger as compared to the workers with a regular job. Due to lower educational achievement and small income, most of the workers do not have knowledge of family planning methods. Moreover, high infant mortality and lack of healthcare availability may be other factors behind large family sizes they have. Most of the workers of the construction sector do not receive treatment from public healthcare facility in case of illness. It should be noted that it could be due to the fact that most of the public healthcare facilities in the city are over crowed and visiting such healthcare facilities requires a worker to take a day off from job and stand in a long queue in order to get prescription and treatment. Therefore, repetitive visits to public healthcare facilities are impossible in the city. Most of the workers are removed from informal jobs if they remain absent from their job for a considerable period of time. This perhaps explains as to why healthcare access and medical treatment are negatively correlated with construction workers.

Most of the construction workers spend a sizeable amount of their income on purchasing fuel, necessary for cooking, from market. They either buy wood or kerosene from the private market. Although, government does provide kerosene at subsidized rate, it is often sold in black market at higher rates due to high demand. They have no other option than to buy fuel at higher rates. Therefore, it is positively correlated and statistically significant. The expenditure on clothing is statistically significant and negatively correlated. Construction workers may be spending less on their clothing as they earn less and spend a large part of their salary on their basic needs. The expenditure on the medical services is positively co-related to workers of the construction sector. They work for more hours with maximum physical strength. Due to work pressure, low hygiene and poor food quality in terms of nutritional content affect their day-to-day life and they possibly fall sick more often than others do. Due to overburdened public healthcare facilities, they have to visit the private healthcare facilities where they have to pay more in lieu of services with less/no waiting time. In such a situation, falling ill might lead to unbearable expenditure on the medical services. The expenditure on the *paan* and *bidi* is generally more among construction workers because they generally develop a habit of such items in their peer group, the possibility of usage of such substances is usually less in other kind of works. Hence, the spending on such items is comparatively higher among those who work as construction workers. They also spend significantly more on telephone. It is mainly because they may have to call their relative and friends back home or often make calls in search new jobs. It is also possible that at lower income, the per cent of money spent on telephone shows more weight. Therefore, it is statistically significant and positive.

Self-employment workers are compared with regular workers, and the results are explained as follows. There are few female self-employed workers. This is probably because they do not prefer to take risks and society usually does not support women's engagement in self-employment. In the self-employment category, most of the workers are married therefore it is statistically significant and positive. Perhaps young workers take more risk and start business. In the self-employment category, most of the workers are less educated. It is mainly those individuals with less education who do not find a regular job and decide to start their own businesses or small enterprises. Those who are highly educated usually get regular jobs. Therefore, education is negatively correlated to the workers of the self-employed category but positively correlated in the case of workers who take up regular jobs.

The income earned is negatively associated with self-employed workers. It is mainly because at the initial stages, there is more investment and less returns in self-employment. Secondly, it may also be the case that they might have cited their income less than what they actually earn. They sometimes have to invest again to earn a profit. Therefore, while calculating income, it is not added as a source of income. Self-employed workers may have to carry water from the long distances as most of them are poor. They have no water facility in the premises. Similarly, it is seen that most of self-employed workers do not have a latrine in their house or premises. They have to use the public toilet which is usually at a distance from their houses. The poor people usually live in very small huts where water supply connection and toilet facility are almost impossible to have. They have to use public taps and toilets. The expenditure on fuel is statistically significant and positively associated with the type of employment. The expenditure on clothing is negatively associated possibly because they do not purchase their clothes frequently due to smaller incomes.

In Mumbai, the changes in class relations, increasing inequality and development of new lifestyles and patterns of living among the urban middle class have resulted in the growth of the services. Illiteracy, low caste and migrant status, lack of alternative employment opportunities, dependency on placement agencies and so on make domestic workers vulnerable to various exploitations. Long working hours, low pay, absence of job security and low social status characterize their occupation. Although these are the characteristics of many informal sector occupations, the absence of legal protection makes domestic workers, particularly vulnerable to many labour market exploitations (Neeta, N. 2009). However, there is no any law or regulatory body to monitor the wages, work hours, holidays of informal sector workers. Most of the workers in the city work for a long period of time in the informal sector without any kind of social security.

Table 4.6: Multinomial Logit Regression Results for Different Types of Workers

Variables	Construction/Domestic Work		Self-employment	
	Co-efficient	T-statistics	Co-efficient	T-statistics
Sex of worker	0.68**(0.21)	3.21	-0.3926	-5.9
Married	2.30*(0.32)	7.21	1.84*(0.30)	6.00
Age	-0.02**(0.00)	-2.04	-0.02**(0.00)	-2.42
Body Mass Index	-0.02(0.02)	-1.31	-0.01(0.01)	-1.28
Education	-0.003(0.00)	-7.27	-0.05**(0.20)	-2.52
Income	0.00(0.00)	-9.98	0.00(0.00)	-3.58
Household members	0.24***(0.14)	1.71	0.20(0.14)	1.42
Treatment taken	-0.30***(0.16)	-1.81	0.10(0.15)	0.69
Water carried (minutes)	-0.00(0.01)	-0.62	0.02***(0.01)	1.78
Latrine facility	-0.01(0.36)	-0.04	-1.27**(0.43)	-2.92
Fuel expenditure	0.00**(0.00)	2.05	0.00**(0.00)	2.81
Expenditure on Clothing	0.00(0.00)	-4.06	0.00(0.00)	-4.12
Education	0.00(0.00)	0.75	0.00**(0.00)	2.01
Medical services	0.00*(0.00)	3.83	0.00*(0.00)	4.91
Pulses	0.00(0.00)	0.9	-0.00**(0.00)	-2.11
Eggs	0.00(0.00)	1.09	0.00**(0.00)	2.05
Paan/tobacco	0.00**(0.00)	2.03	0.00(0.00)	1.36
Telephone	0.00**(0.00)	2.56	0.00**(0.00)	2.99
Constant	1.76(0.81)	2.16	-0.38(0.79)	0.48

LR chi^2=1355.09 Prob. >chi^2=0.00, Log likelihood = -1314.49 Pseudo R^2=0.340

*Significant at 1 per cent, **Significant at 5 per cent, ***Significant at 10 per cent

Conclusion

In the city of Mumbai, there is a high demand for skilled and unskilled labour in manufacturing, services and construction sector and that could be one of the basic reasons behind large scale migration to the city from rural areas. The present study finds that the workers engaged in construction and self-employment have lower educational attainment which ultimately later translates into lower income. A female worker with lower education either ends up in construction sector or work as domestic help. Low level of educational attainment and smaller income affect the standards of living among these workers. Most of the workers do not have access to basic infrastructural facilities such as electricity, water supply, sanitation and healthcare. Most of the women and children have to fetch water from long distances. The time spent in carrying water has a high opportunity cost. Healthcare facilities are overcrowded in the city and thus, direct and indirect cost of medical care is very high for causal workers.

In order to overcome of various issues raised in this paper, the Government of Maharashtra should provide technical training to informal sector workers. The female workers should also be given training. Training programmes will enhance skills among women (Anupama, 2008). Empowerment of the poor cannot be a turnkey job. What is even more important to realize is that empowerment of the poor not only needs changes in the poor and their environment but also requires changes in the mainstream institutions in order to make them poor-friendly and supportive of intensive growth (Rao, V.M. 2009).

Microfinance facility could help them start their own small-scale businesses and some technical skills could help them improve the productivity, production and income. Since, most of the workers are causal workers; visiting health care facility in case of even not-very-serious illnesses may forgo their daily wages. Government must provide them either with health check-ups facilities at their workplaces or compensation for foregone wages. Morning and evening camps across the slums in Mumbai city could also be a useful strategy to provide healthcare access to workers and their children. It might help reduce their economic burden by waving off the amount they pay for private healthcare facilities. Government must provide water taps at the doorstep of each household in the slums of Mumbai as it not only helps reducing the physical and economic burden on the slum households but also makes sure that they get good quality potable water. Children can spend such time to study or play. Women can work more in labour market and earn more income. Female workers involved in the informal sector do not get maternity leave. However, female workers should be entitled to maternity benefits, extra leaves in conformity with their biological cycle and crèche facilities for nursing mothers. The equation of equality and equal opportunity needs to be legally resolved (Chandra, Navin 2009). The Non-governmental Organisations and government institutions should work in this direction.

Households in the slums generally purchase food and fuel from the market. They spend a significant portion of their income on such items but their incomes are irregular and seasonal in nature. If government provides fuel and food through a public distribution system, then standard of living could improve to a large extent as it would save a considerable amount of money spent on these items. Although city's growth is fuelled by the cheap labour migrants i.e. slum and pavement dwellers, there is no provision to plan for their housing. However, when the poor build houses in the empty spaces that they can find, a city deems these as an illegal encroachment of land and demolishes such structures. Thus, a constant war of attrition continues while the city demands the poor's economic participation. It refuses to recognize them as legitimate urban citizens who are included in the development plans. This results in the mushrooming of slums (Burra S. and Devika Mahadevan 2005). Overall, government policies towards slums are doubtful. Most of the slums are declared illegal in the city and regularly demolished. Owing to their illegal status there settlements are not provided with the basic infrastructural facilities that other areas of the city get.

Although the slums and migrant workers are an integral parts of the city environment, the workers are expected only to work and not to ask for basic facilities in their community. Government should change its stand about the slum households. More slum redevelopment schemes, affordable and rental housing can help improve the standard of living of the people of the slums. Since this workforce is contributing to the economic growth of city in a big way, denying basic facilities for their settlement is unethical. Government must ensure a decent work environment for worker and secure a better standard of living and respectable life (Choudhury Roy S. 2005). After all, the city of Mumbai also works an engine of economic growth for India. Every worker is contributing to district, state and national domestic product but in return, they also expect the basic amenities be provided to them.

APPENDIX

Table 4.7: The Selected Slums in Urban Area (2011)

Area	Households	Per cent
Jogeshwari	34	3.2
Malad	21	2.0
Chembur	63	6.0
Mankhurd	60	5.7
Kurla	74	7.1
Lower Parel	64	6.1
Dadar	111	10.6
Matunga	61	5.8
Bandra	59	5.6
Goregaon	60	5.7
Mazgaon	126	12.0
Govandi	76	7.2
Dahisar	122	11.6
Kandivali	109	10.4
Borivali	10	1.0
Total	1050	100.0

In our sample, we selected households from the eastern suburbs such as Chembur, Mankhurd, Kurla, Dadar, Govandi. From the western suburb, we selected households of Malad, Jogeshwari, Lower Parel, Matunga, Bandra, Goregaon, Mazgaon, Kandivali and Borivali etc. The survey was undertaken in May-June 2011.

REFERENCES

Absar, S.S (2002) "Women Garment Workers in Bangladesh" Economic and Political Weekly, July 20, 2002, pp. 3012-3016.

Anupama (2008) "Globalization and Employment of Women Workers in the Unorganized Manufacturing Sectors in India" The Indian Journal of Labour Economics, Vol. 51 No. 4. 2008, pp. 687-700.

Beneria, Lourdes (2001) "Changing Employment Patterns and the Informalisation of Jobs: General Trends and Gender Dimensions" Published by International Labour Office, Geneva, Switzerland, August 2001.

Burra, S. and Devika Mahadevan (2005) "Making Markets Work for the Poor: The Small Investors Fund" Economic and PW, July 23, 2005, pp. 3245-3249.

Chakravarty D. (2004) "Expansion of Markets and Women Workers: Case Study of Garment Manufacturing in India" Economic and Political Weekly pp. 4910-4916.

Chandra, Navin (2009) "Labour Rights and the Working Poor" The Journal of Labour Economics, Vol. 52, No. 3, 2009, pp. 471-488.

Greene, William H. (2003) "Econometric Analysis" Fifth Edition, Pearson Education Private Ltd. Indian Branch, Delhi, India.

Choudhury Roy S. (2005) "Labor Activism and Women in the Unorganized Sector: Garment Export Industry in Bangalore" Economic and Political Weekly, May 28-June 4, 2005.

International, Labor Organization (ILO) (2002) "Decent Work and the Informal Economy: Sixth item on the Agenda Report VI: International Labor Conference 90th Session 2002, ILO, Geneva, 22 Switzerland.

Kusum, Deb, Das and Gunajit Kalita (2009) "Are Labour Intensive Industries Generating Employment in India? Evidence from Firm Level Survey" The Journal of Labor Economics, Vol. 52, No. 3, 2009, pp. 411-432.

Neeta, N. (2009) "Counters of Domestic Services-characteristics Work Relations and Regulation" The Journal of Labor Economics, Vol. 52, No. 3, 2009, pp. 489-506.

Ruffer, Tim and John Knight (2007) "Informal Sector Labour Markets in Developing Countries" Oxford Policy Management, 6 S.T. Aldates Counter Yard 38st Aldates, Oxford United Kingdom, February 2007.

Rao, V.M (2009) "Promoting Self-employment Among the Rural Poor: Experiences and Lessons from India" The Indian Journal of Labor Economics, Vol. 52, No. 3, 2009, pp. 387-410.

Topala, T.S. (2009) "India: Growing Fast but also needs to Industrialize" The Journal of Labor Economics, Vol. 52, No. 1, 2009, pp. 57-70.

Unni, Jeemol (2002) " Size, Contribution and Characteristics of Informal Employment in India" The Gujarat Institute of Development Research, Ahmedabad, India, Country Case Study, Commissioned by the ILO, Geneva for Document Relating to ILO conference, June 2002.

A New Paradigm Agriculture for Expansion

Dr. M. Dhanabhakyam and
V.Ramya

ABSTRACT

The agriculture plays essential role that in development of India. Globalization incorporated, value chains, rapid technological and institutional innovations, and environmental constraints have rapidly changed the context for agriculture's role. A new Paradigm is needed that recognizes agriculture's multiple functions for development in that Emerging context, triggering economic growth, reducing poverty, narrowing income disparities, Providing food security, and delivering environmental services. Today's greater willingness to invest in agriculture requires careful prioritization of the functions of agriculture and selection of the corresponding instruments to achieve the functions. The current attention given to agriculture and the new paradigm in using agriculture for development offer unique opportunities to address the extensive remaining development issues. To analyze the growth of agriculture and allied sectors used statistical tools like trend value and annual growth rate.

Keywords: Agriculture, Economic Growth, Globalization, Innovation, Poverty, Paradigm.

Introduction

The structural transformation where the share of agriculture in employment and GDP declines as per capita income rises is a stunning regularity. Agriculture in India has a significant history. A rich literature, both theoretical and empirical, has examined the process of structural transformation of economies, from the least developed in which economic activity is based largely on agriculture, to the high-income in which agriculture typically accounts for less than 5 per cent of GDP. Today, India ranks second worldwide in farm output. Agriculture GDP as one of the world's largest agrarian economies, the agriculture sector contributed approximately14.6 per cent of India's GDP (at 2004-05 prices) during 2009-10. The economic contribution of agriculture to India's GDP is steadily declining with the country's broad-based economic growth. Still, agriculture is demographically the broadest economic sector and plays a significant role in the overall socio-economic fabric of India. Agriculture provides the principal means of livelihood for over 58.4 per cent of India's population. It contributes approximately one-fifth of total gross domestic product (GDP). Agriculture accounts for about 10 per cent of the total export earnings and provides raw material to a large number of industries. Low and volatile growth rates and the recent escalation of agrarian crisis in several parts of the Indian countryside, however, are a threat not only to national food security, but also to the economic well-being of the nation as a whole.

Agriculture as a Trigger of Economic Growth

Agriculture is often the lead export sector and foreign exchange earner since it is the sector with strong comparative advantage in the early stages of development. Most African countries are relatively rich in natural resources, but poor in skilled labor, suggesting comparative advantage for unprocessed primary products. This is re-enforced by a weak business investment climate in terms of infrastructure (roads, electricity, and communications) and institutions (legal, financial, regulatory) that constrain private investment in the formal manufacturing and service industries. In some countries, a combination of natural resources, human capital endowments, and an improving business environment point to comparative advantage in processed primary commodities, as a potential entry point for building a competitive manufacturing sector. Although globalization and new dynamic producers have increased competition in traditional agricultural exports, recent successes such as coffee in Vietnam and cocoa in Ghana suggest that agricultural exports can be major sources of growth.

Agriculture's Power for Poverty Reduction

Three out of four poor people in developing countries—890 million people—lived in rural areas in 2002. Even with rapid urbanization, the developing world is expected to remain predominantly rural in most regions until about 2020, and the majority of the poor are projected to continue to live in rural areas until 2040 (Ravallion, Chen, and Sangraula, 2007). This reflects a large and persistent gap between the share of agriculture in GDP and the share of agriculture in the labor force due to the slow movement of labor out of agriculture.

Objectives

- To study the growth and share of agriculture and allied sectors of the country
- To emphasize the trend of GDP in India
- To analyze the growth rate of GDP
- To find the GDP contribution in Agriculture sector

Table 5.1: The Rates of Growth and Share of Agriculture and Allied Sectors in the GDP of the Country

Figures in Percentage (%)

Sl. No.	Item	2009-10	2010-11	2011-12*
	GDP- Share and Growth (at 2004-05 prices)			
	Growth in GDP in agriculture and allied sectors	1.0	7.0	2.5
1.	Share in GDP-agriculture and allied sectors	14.7	14.5	13.9
	Agriculture	12.4	12.3	–
	Forestry and logging	1.5	1.4	–
	Fishing	0.8	0.7	–
	Share in total gross capital formation in the Country (at 2004-05 prices)			–
2.	Share of agriculture and allied sectors in total gross capital formation	7.1	7.2	–
	Agriculture	6.6	6.6	–
	Forestry and logging	0.1	0.1	–
	Fishing	0.5	0.5	–
3.	Employment in the agriculture sector as share of total workers as per census 2001	58.2		–

* AE=Advance Estimates

Source: Central Statistical Organization (CSO) and Department of Agriculture and Cooperation.

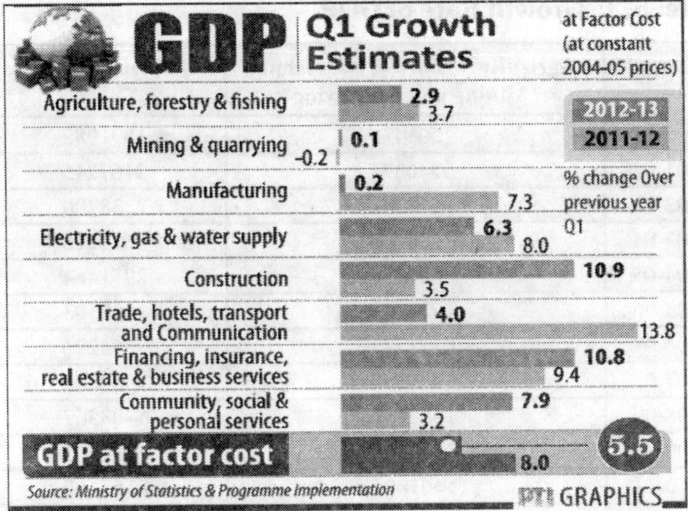

Fig. 5.1: GDP for the Year 2012-2013

Source: CSO & FICCI Research

Table 5.2: Trend of GDP in India

(Values in %)

Sectors	2011-12				2012-13
	Q1	Q2	Q3	Q4	Q1
Agriculture	3.7	3.1	2.8	1.7	2.9
Industry	5.6	3.7	2.5	1.9	3.6
Mining & quarrying	-0.2	-5.4	-2.8	4.3	0.1
Manufacturing	7.3	2.9	0.6	-0.3	0.2
Electricity, gas & water supply	7.9	9.8	9.0	4.9	6.3
Construction	3.5	6.3	6.6	4.8	10.9
Services	10.2	8.8	8.9	7.9	6.9
Trade, hotels, transport & communication	13.8	9.5	10.0	7.0	4.0
Financing, insurance, real estate & business services	9.4	9.9	9.1	10.0	10.8
Community, social & personal services	3.2	6.1	6.4	7.1	7.9
GDP at factor cost	8.0	6.7	6.1	5.3	5.5

Source: CSO & FICCI Research.

Table: 5.3: Growth Rate of GDP

Year	Agriculture, Forestry & Fishing, Mining and Quarrying	GDP at Factor Cost
2000-01	506476	1991982
2001-02	546674	2167745
2002-03	548062	2338200
2003-04	608788	2622216
2004-05	650454	2971464
2005-06	732234	3390503
2006-07	829771	3953276
2007-08	961330	4582086
2008-09	1083032	5303567
2009-10	1236765	6091485
2010-11	1461095	7157412
2011-12	1650396	8279975

Table: 5.3.1: Analyzed Trend Values of GDP

Year	GDP at Factor Cost	Analyzed Trend Values (in %)
2000-01	1991982	100
2001-02	2167745	108.8235235
2002-03	2338200	117.3805787
2003-04	2622216	131.6385389
2004-05	2971464	149.1712275
2005-06	3390503	170.2075119
2006-07	3953276	198.4594238
2007-08	4582086	230.0264761
2008-09	5303567	266.2457291
2009-10	6091485	305.800203
2010-11	7157412	359.3110781
2011-12	8279975	415.6651516

Interpretation

The table 5.3.2 shows that GDP factor trend was analyzed in the year 2000-01 is base year is100.2001-02 are 108.32 per cent. It has increasing simultaneously in following years. Current year 2011-12 it was increased as 415.66 per cent.

Table 5.3.2: Analyzed Trend Values of Agriculture, Forestry Fishing, Mining and Quarrying

Year	Agriculture, Forestry & Fishing, Mining and Quarrying	Analysed Trend Values (in %)
2000-01	506476	100
2001-02	546674	107.9368025
2002-03	548062	108.210853
2003-04	608788	120.2007598
2004-05	650454	128.4274082
2005-06	732234	144.574274
2006-07	829771	163.8322448
2007-08	961330	189.8076118
2008-09	1083032	198.1129521
2009-10	1236765	244.1902479
2010-11	1461095	288.4825737
2011-12	1650396	325.8586784

Interpretation

The table 5.3.2 shows that agriculture, forestry & fishing, mining and quarrying trend was increased simultaneously. Trend analyzed in agriculture sector in the year 2001-2002 is 107.93 per cent and it was highest in the year 2011-12 is 325.85 per cent.

Conclusion

Today's greater willingness to invest in agriculture requires careful prioritization of the functions of agriculture and selection of the corresponding instruments to achieve the functions. The current attention given to agriculture and the new paradigm in using agriculture for development offers unique opportunities to address the extensive remaining development issues. In order to study the trend of GDP in India helps to determine development of agriculture and allies sectors. Agriculture must be given a more prominent part of the development agenda. A GDP growth in actual and projected data it shows the value decline one after year.

Table 5.4: GDP Growth - Actual & Projected

Annual Rates	2005-06	2006-07	2007-08	2008-09	2009-10	2010-11	2011-12	2012-13
1. Agriculture and allied activities	5.1%	4.2%	5.8%	0.1%	1.0%	7.0%	3.0%	2.5%
2. Mining & Quarrying	1.3%	7.5%	3.7%	2.1%	6.3%	5.0%	-2.2%	6.0%
3. Manufacturing	10.1%	14.3%	10.3%	4.3%	9.7%	7.6%	3.9%	7.5%
4. Electricity, Gas & Water Supply	7.1%	9.3%	8.3%	4.6%	6.3%	3.0%	8.3%	6.0%
5. Construction	12.8%	10.3%	10.8%	5.3%	7.0%	8.0%	6.2%	6.5%
6. Trade, Hotels, Transport, Storage & communication	12.0%	11.6%	10.9%	7.5%	10.3%	11.1%	11.2%	10.2%
7. Finance, insurance, real estate & business services	12.6%	14.0%	12.0%	12.0%	9.4%	10.4%	9.1%	9.5%
8. Community and personal services	7.1%	2.8%	6.9%	12.5%	12.0%	4.5%	6.0%	6.0%
9. GDP (factor cost)	9.5%	9.6%	9.3%	6.7%	8.4%	8.4%	7.1%	7.6%
10. Industry (2 + 3 + 4 + 5)	9.7%	12.2%	9.7%	4.4%	8.4%	7.2%	4.3%	7.0%
11. Services (6 + 7 + 8)	10.9%	10.1%	10.3%	10.0%	10.5%	9.3%	9.4%	9.1%
12. Non-agriculture (9 - 1)	10.5%	10.8%	10.1%	8.1%	9.8%	8.6%	7.7%	8.4%
13. GDP (factor cost) per capita	7.8%	8.0%	7.8%	5.2%	6.9%	6.9%	5.6%	6.2%

The functions of agriculture for development include growth, poverty reduction, lesser disparities, food security, and providing environmental services. Priorities vary by country type, with accelerating growth dominant in the agriculture-based countries, reducing disparities in the transforming countries, and enhancing smallholder inclusion in the urbanized countries. In future of agriculture will have to concentrate on maximization production of our daily durables.

Table 5.5: GDP Contribution in Agriculture Sector

Year	1st Quarter Statistics in INR Crores	2nd Quarter Statistics in INR Crores	3rd Quarter Statistics in INR Crores	4th Quarter Statistics in INR Crores
2004-05	135745	108879	172401	148401
2005-06	139404	113023	185750	156309
2006-07	144790	116947	193209	164245
2007-08	151336	122418	211649	169677
2008-09	154307	123389	204748	171675
2009-10	156740	126524	201853	177390
2010-11	161614	132668	224044	190778
2011-12	167548	136806	230359	193955

REFERENCES

BOOKS

Department of Agriculture and Cooperation, Ministry of Agriculture, GOI, New Delhi.

http://agricoop.nic.in/Annual report2010-11/AR.pd

http://india.gov.in/sectors/agriculture/index.php

http://blog.ficci.com/q1-gdp-growth-rate-india/1343/

http://www.dailypioneer.com/business/49900-share-of-agriculture-in-gdp-declines-to-139-in-2011-12.html

http://www.thehindu.com/business/Economy/first-quarter-gdp-growth-at-decade-low-of-55/article3843593.ece

http://www.mindtools.net/GlobCourse/formula.shtml

http://profit.ndtv.com/news/corporates/article-india-gdp-growth-to-slow-to-6-9-for-2011-12-

Agrarian Crisis in India
Reasons and Problems

R. Krishnamoorthy[1]
Dr. A. Abdulraheem[2]

ABSTRACT

The people's protest against Special Economic Zones in various parts of the country, including at Nandigram in West Bengal, stagnation in agriculture, import of foodgrains, widespread suicide of farmers—all these are systems of simmering discontent in the agricultural sector. What is highlighted today in the national scene is the image of "incredible India" and "shining India". We hear often about India as a country with a very high economic growth, a country with the highest numbers of billionaires in Asia, and a country of world renowned information technology. But we do not hear enough about the serious problems in agriculture. Those who govern us do not seem to be concerned about this problem; probably they do not want to. But we cannot easily ignore this problem any longer.

Introduction

Indian is an agricultural country. Even while India's industrial and services sectors are growing by leaps and bounds and where growth rate of agriculture as below 2 per cent the fact remains that India still lives in villages. Over 70 per cent of India's population is supported by agriculture. Even industrial and services sectors are invariably entangled with the fortunes of agriculture due to various intricate forward and backward linkages. There is an ongoing debate in country regarding the state of agriculture. There is a general agreement that the Indian agriculture is in crisis but there is intense debate about the causes which led to such crisis and various way to manage the crisis and put agriculture on healthy footing. According to nutritional emergency (by Samantha) there should be emphasis on pulses. Alagh's approach so ground level with people participation and is realistic in outlook.

The people's protest against Special Economic Zones in various parts of the country, including at Nandigram in West Bengal, stagnation in agriculture, import of foodgrains, widespread suicide of farmers—all these are systems of simmering discontent in the agricultural sector. What is highlighted today in the national scene is the image of "incredible India" and "shining India".

We hear often about India as a country with a very high economic growth, a country with the highest numbers of billionaires in Asia, and a country of world renowned information technology. But we do not hear enough about the serious problems in agriculture. Those who govern us do not seem to be concerned about this problem; probably they do not want to. But we cannot easily ignore this problem any longer.

It was with the Structural Adjustment Programme (SAP) in 1991 that the policy of globalisation was concretely introduced in India. Based on this policy and the directives of the World Bank, International Monetary Fund and World Trade Organisation, the Indian economy was substantially overhauled. The Export-Import policy was liberalised; the import and customs duties of many products were drastically lowered or totally dropped so that they could be imported without any restriction. The government started reducing its investment in agriculture and the industrial sector allowing the private sector to take over. The restructuring of the public distribution system really affected the availability of foodgrains to the poor at subsidised rates. All such measures had implications for the farm sector. This article analyses how the policy of globalisation has affected agriculture in India.

Problems of Agrarian Sector and their Consequences

Fifteen years of economic liberalisation have adversely affected Indian agriculture. The most prominent manifestation of this is in the drastic decline in the growth rate of foodgrains. The rate of growth of agricultural output was gradually increasing in 1950-1990, and it was more than the rate of growth of the population. In the 1980s the agricultural output grew at about four per cent per annum. Thus India became self-sufficient in food and started exporting wheat and rice. But during the 10-year period after the start of liberalisation, the rate of growth declined to two per cent. According to the Mid-term Appraisal of the Tenth Five Year Plan (2002-07), the rate of growth of the GDP in agriculture and allied sectors was just one per cent per annum during the year 2002-05. As a result, per capita availability of foodgrains decreased; the growth rate of population became higher than that of foodgrains, and India started to import foodgrains at a much higher price than that in the domestic market. Secondly, unemployment in the agricultural sector increased during the reform period as agriculture was not profitable due to the fall in the price of farm products. As a result, the number of people who are employed in the primary sector and the area under cultivation decreased, which in turn caused a decline in rural employment. According to the National Sample Survey, the annual rate of growth of the employment in the rural areas was 2.07 per cent in 1987-1984, while it declined to a mere 0.66 per cent in 1993-2000, which corresponds to the period of liberalisation. It is not only the farmers but also the Dalits and tribals, who heavily depend on agriculture, became unemployed.

The suicide of farmers is the third fall-out of stagnation in agriculture. When agriculture was not yielding remunerative income, the life of the farmers became very desperate. Many of them committed suicide as a last resort. As revealed by Sharad Pawar, the Union Agricultural Minister, in the Lok Sabha in 2004, over one lakh farmers committed suicide in India after the economic reform started. According to the National Crime Records Bureau, 17,060 farmers committed suicide in the country in 2006 with Maharashtra having the highest number of (4453) suicide deaths. Punjab is the latest in the list of States having farmers' suicide. This is a record in the agricultural history of India. It points to the acute nature of the problem which has affected the vast majority of the population, and which has created a real crisis. But, unfortunately the government and the people do not consider it a crisis; their lack of seriousness and lukewarm response to the problem points to this reality.

Reasons for the Agrarian Crisis

There is a need for analysing the reasons for the crisis to see whether there is any connection with globalisation and, if so, what measures could be adopted to face this challenge.

Liberal Import of Agricultural Products: The main reason for the crash of prices of agricultural products, especially of cash crops, in India was removal of all restrictions to import these products. As, for example, when the Government of India reduced the import duty on tea and coffee from Sri Lanka and Malaysia, their prices in the domestic market got reduced drastically. Thus cultivation of such products became unprofitable and so their production was fully or partly stopped. Since the removal of quantitative restrictions and lowering of import duties were according to the restrictions of the World Trade Organisations (WTO), the crash in the prices of agricultural products is directly related to the liberalisation policy of the government.

Cutback in Agricultural Subsidies: In the post-reform period the government reduced different types of subsidies to agriculture, and this has increased the production cost of cultivation. According to Ramesh Chand, an economist, cutback in subsidy and control of fertilisers over the last few years has adversely affected the agricultural sector. It has increased the input cost and made agriculture less profitable. Since the decrease in subsidy to agriculture is part of the regulations of the WTO, it is related to the policy of globalisation. Lack of Easy and Low-cost Loan to Agriculture: After 1991 the lending pattern of commercial banks, including nationalised banks, to agriculture drastically changed with the result that loan was not easily available and the interest was not affordable. This has forced the farmers to rely on moneylenders and thus pushed up the expenditure on agriculture. The National Commission for Agriculture, headed by Dr. M.S. Swaminathan, also pointed out that removal of the lending facilities and concessions of banks during the post-reform period have accelerated the crisis in agriculture. When the farmers were not able to pay back loan with high interest, they fell into the debt trap. Studies show that most of the farmers' suicides were due to the debt trap. It is part of the policy of privatisation that banks, even nationalised banks, look for profit over their social responsibilities to the people.

Decline in Government Investment in the Agricultural Sector: Studies show that after the economic reforms started, the government's expenditure and investment in the agricultural sector have been drastically reduced. This is based on the policy of minimum intervention by the government enunciated by the policy of globalisation. The expenditure of the government in rural development, including agriculture, irrigation, flood control, village industry, energy and transport, declined from an average of 14.5 per cent in 1986-1990 to six per cent in 1995-2000. When the economic reforms started, the annual rate of growth of irrigated land was 2.62 per cent; later it got reduced to 0.5 per cent in the post-reform period. The consequences were many. The rate of capital formation in agriculture came down, and the agricultural growth rate was also reduced. This has affected the purchasing power of the rural people and subsequently their standard of living.

Restructuring of the Public Distribution System (PDS): As part of the neo-liberal policy, the government restructured the PDS by creating two groups—Below Poverty Line (BPL) and Above Poverty Line (APL)—and continuously increased the prices of food grains distributed through ration shops. As a result, even the poor people did not buy the subsidized food grains and it got accumulated in godowns to be spoiled or sold in the open market. As the in-take from PDS was less it has affected the food security of the poor, especially in the rural areas, and this has indirectly affected the market and the farmers.

Special Economic Zones: As part of the economic reforms, the system of taking over land by the government for commercial and industrial purposes was introduced in the country. As per the Special Economic Zones Act of 2005, the government has so far notified about 400 such zones in the country. Very often it is fertile land which has been acquired. According to Khasanoki, a writer, the government has acquired five million hectares of land for purposes other than agriculture between 1991 and 2003. This is almost half of what was acquired during the last 40 years. It was in the news that the government decided to acquire 10,120 hectares of land near Mumbai (almost one-third area of Mumbai) for the Reliance Company and reduced it to 5000 hectors due to public pressure. Since the SEZ deprives the farmers of their land and livelihood, it is harmful to agriculture. In order to promote export and industrial growth in line with globalisation the SEZ was introduced in many countries.

Towards a Solution

THE agricultural crisis is affecting a majority of the people in India. The farmers who produce food materials for the country are in deep distress. The marginalised people like the Dalits and tribals, who depend on agriculture, are getting unemployed and struggling for their livelihood. The ordinary people, especially the poor, have lost their food security. The crisis in agriculture is a crisis of the country as a whole and so needs urgent attention. Some of the suggestions are being listed here.

Quantitative restrictions should be imposed on import of agricultural products. Since the import policy was the major reason for the crash in prices of many agricultural products, there should be restrictions on the quantity and customs duty of such products. Necessary import duty and quantitative restrictions should be imposed on imported goods to protect our farmers who should be given priority to the discipline of the WTO.

Subsidy and concessions given to agriculture but removed in the post-reform period should be restored. This is a must to make agriculture remunerative. One of the main disputes in the Doha Round of talks at the WTO is the high subsidy given by the United States and European Union to their farmers in spite of the WTO regulation. India should assert its right to give sufficient subsidy to its farmers to offset the rising cost of cultivation and protect their livelihood.

Bank loans should be easily made available to the farmers, especially since the input cost of agriculture has gone up. The government should seriously think of restoring the low rate of interest to farmers given by banks and other financial institutions as it had done before the reform period. In fact, the M.S. Swaminathan Commission for Agriculture has recommended a low rate of four per cent interest for the farmers.

The government should augment its investment and expenditure in the farm sector. One reason for the agricultural stagnation is low government expenditure. Investment in agriculture and its allied sectors, including irrigation, transport, communication and farm research, should be drastically increased, and the government should aim at integrated development of the rural areas. Effecting Implementation of National Rural Employment Guarantee Scheme can also become a means of revival of the rural economy.

There is a need for periodic revision of the procurement prices for farm produce making those remunerative. This will help the farmers to meet the increasing expenses for farm inputs and ensure at least remunerative income. According to the Swaminathan Commission, unless agriculture is made a profitable enterprise, its present crisis cannot be solved. The Commission has suggested 50 per cent more of the total production cost as supportive price for foodgrains.

The government should revise the policy on Special Economic Zones as it goes against the interest of farmers and the agricultural sector. It should not acquire fertile agricultural land for SEZs. When it does take over land for essential public utilities, it should give just compensation and initiate comprehensive rehabilitation measures. The recommendations of the Swamina-than Commission not to acquire land suitable for agriculture for non-agricultural purposes, to give adequate compensation for the acquired land and to distribute surplus land to the landless farmers should be seriously taken into account when the policy of SEZs is reframed. Over and above the policy of SEZs, there is a need for constitutional structures and mechanisms which will mandate the government, both Central and States, to implement the policy of relief and rehabilitation of people displaced due to SEZs and other developmental projects.

Bold steps should be taken to implement land reforms which were not implemented in most States. Feudal structures and landlordism based on large holdings of land by high caste and class people even now tend to keep a majority of the people, especially Dalits and backward castes, in the rural areas under their control and domination. Neo-liberal policies with privatisation will only reinforce and strengthen these unjust and exploitative structures. Therefore, there is a need for conscious efforts and positive steps from the government side to implement land reforms. Surplus land acquired thus should be distributed to the Dalit and adivasi farmers. According to Amartya Sen, the Nobel Laureate, though the economic growth rate of India is impressive, India cannot play a significant role in the global economic scenario unless it completes land reforms.

Conclusion

The rural economy, particularly agriculture, will be greatly benefit if programmes meant for economically backward sections, including the Integrated Child Development Schemes, mid-day meals for schoolchilden and the National Rural Employment Guarantee Scheme, are effectively implemented. Food security of the poor will be ensured if the public distribution system is efficiently run. All these programmes will increase the purchasing power of the rural people and indirectly help agriculture itself.

REFERENCES

Aerthayil,Mathew (2008): "Agrarian Crisis in India is a Creation of the Policy of Globalisation", Mainstream, Vol. XLVI, No. 13.

Balakrishnan, Pulapre, Ramesh Golait and Pankaj Kumar (2008): Agricultural Growth in India since 1991', : Development Research Group (DRG), Study No. 27, Reserve Bank of India, Mumbai.

Bhat KS and S.Vijaya Kumar (2006): "Undeserved Death: A Study of Suicide of Farmers of Andhra Pradesh (2000-2005)", Allied Publishers Private Ltd, New Delhi.

Economic Survey 2008-09 and previous years.

Kapila, Rak and Uma Kapila (2008): Indian Economy : A Journey in Time and Space, Academic Foundation, New Delhi.

Promoting Organic Farming in the North East Region

An Approach for Sustainable Agricultural Development

Devajeet Goswami

ABSTRACT

NER is an agriculture based region. Its unique bio-diversity and eco- friendly environment make the strongest arguments to develop organic farming in the region. Organic farming is an agriculture method that takes in to account both economy and ecology in providing food to the present and future generations without using chemical fertilizers, pesticide etc. It protects soil health by adopting the system of crop rotation, green manuring etc. The situation after independence called for initiating Green Revolution in India, where high yielding varities and chemical fertilizers were used to face the problem of food crises. However, this system has created certain problems on environment, soil and health fronts. Considering the market potentiality, agro- climatic condition of the NER, organic farming can be developed as an alternative farming system. It needs a systematic approach, cooperation and initiatives from the stakeholders and effective policies to make the entire region as organic region. In this paper an attempt is made to analyze the scope of organic farming and to identify the opportunities and challenges in developing organic farming in this region.

Keywords: Agriculture, Green Revolution, Organic farming, Sustainable Agriculture, Biodiversity.

Introduction

The North East Region (NER) of India is the centre of natural beauty, natural resources and diverse culture. The region comprises of eight states- Assam, Arunachal Pradesh, Meghalaya, Mizoram, Manipur, Nagaland, Sikkim and Tripura. NER is strategically important as it shares international border with Bhutan, China, Myanmar and Bangladesh. The region is the gateway to the South East Asian countries. The region is blessed with highly fertile land, water resources, dense forest, unique bio-diversity and agri-climatic environment. On the economic front, the NER mainly depends on agriculture. Agriculture is the main line of economic activity in all the states of this region. Though the region is agriculture based, agriculture has not been developed to its fullest extent. The traditional farming practices, high dependence on single crop (rice), low agricultural productivity, lack of agricultural marketing facilities, lack of food processing industries etc. resulted in low growth in agriculture sector. Besides that, the region is suffering from various problems like, infrastructural backwardness, low level of per capita income, low level of capital formation, unemployment etc.

In spite of all the problems, the region possesses huge scope for economic development. The potentialities lies in developing the agriculture sector which alone can provide solution to a number of problems the region is currently facing. At the same time, the industry and services sectors should also be developed to bring all round and speedy economic development. So far as agriculture sector in this region is concerned, it provides ample scope for the development of organic farming. The region can be developed as a brand in organic farming in the world map.

Objectives

The objectives of this paper are:

- to analyze the scope of organic farming in the north east region; and
- to analyze the opportunities and the challenges in developing the region as an organic region.

Literature Review

Pugliese (2001) studied the convergence between the notion and implementation of sustainable rural development and some important features of modern organic movement. He studied the linkages and synergies between the sustainable rural development and organic farming.

Charyulu & Biswas (2010) undertaken a study to analyse the status of the organic input units sanctioned under National Project on Organic Farming. The study broadly presented the present status of organic farming in the world and in India. The SWOT analysis had been conducted for organic farming. The study highlighted the economics and efficiency of organic farming besides discussing the various initiatives taken by the government. The study advocated various measures like, the setting up of a single authority at national level for regulating and supervising the organic sector, framing a national policy to tap the opportunities of international organic market, creation of 'Green Market', investment in research and development activities for organic agriculture etc.

Chandrashekar (2010) emphasized the role of organic farming to meet the problem of food security in India. The study addressed the problem of shortage of farmland due to rapid industrialization in rural states of India. The study analysed the importance of organic farming, principle of organic farming, organic farming in rural economy, consumption pattern and export of organically produced products in India.

Yadav *et. a.l.* (2013) reviewed the production of organic crops and products with regard to sustainable agriculture in northern India. He emphasized the importance of organic farming for quality food production without affecting the soil's health and the environment. He advocated the need of identifying suitable crops/products on regional basis for organic production that has international market demand.

Rajalakshmy (n.d.) conducted a study to analyze the scope of the organic farming. He focused on the economic and environmental superiority of organic farming as well as the constraints related to organic farming. He analyzed the problems related to certification, high input cost, lack of awareness, marketing problems, lack of governmental policies etc. He proposed certain measures to promote organic farming in India like, making the certification process simple and affordable to the farmers, development of high- tech market with strict quality control, providing financial support to the farmers during the transition period etc.

Munda et al (n.d.) studied the scope of organic farming in the hills specially the north eastern states of India. They stated that there is huge scope for organic farming in this region because the farmers are not habituated in using inorganic fertilizer. The hill farmers maintain the livestocks which produces sufficient quantity of on-farm manures. These can be efficiently used for organic agriculture. They stated the need of research, development of appropriate technology, human resource development, assistance to farmers in post harvest handling etc. in promoting organic farming in this region.

Research Methodology

This study is based on the secondary data. Various research studies done at the regional, national and international levels as well as the governmental publications were consulted.

Green Revolution in India and its Effects

Immediately after independence, India faced the problems of growing population and severe food crisis. Considering the situation, India adopted the policy of "Green Revolution" in the year 1960. The objective of Green Revolution was to increase the quantity of food production within a short span of time. It required the application of technology in food production in terms of high yielding varieties seeds, use of synthetic fertilizer, pesticide, insecticide, irrigation facilities, use of farm technology etc.

The programme of Green Revolution concentrated mainly on rice and wheat and confined to certain states of the country. The urgent need of increasing food grain production required suitable areas with adequate irrigational facilities and the farmers who could afford the cost of the inputs.

As a result of Green Revolution, India became self- reliant in food production. The other important aspects of green revolution are:

- The agriculture became market oriented as farmers with surplus produce started selling the agricultural produce.
- Build up buffer stock of food grains;
- The demand for industrialized products like fertilizer, pesticide and insecticide, tractors etc. increased leading to industrialization of the economy;
- Creation of employment in the different sectors like, transportation, marketing, storage etc.

However, Green Revolution is not without ill effects. Some of the adverse affect of Green Revolution may be stated a s under:

- Use of chemical fertilizer and pesticide led to serious health and environmental problems;
- Inter- state inequality;
- Economic and social gap increased between the small-scale and large- scale farmers;
- Degrading soil health etc.

All these indicate unsustainability of Indian agriculture. After meeting the urgent need of food shortage, the present situation calls for such a strategy which will lead to sustainable agricultural development. Sustainable agriculture refers to certain measures which arrest the problems of loss of soil health, loss of plant nutrition, water pollution and other environmental hazards by avoiding the use of fertilizer, pesticide etc.

Sustainable development is a multi- dimensional strategy that takes into account ecology, economy, society and human welfare. It has to strike a balance among these dimensions. Sustainable agricultural development must provide enough food with required nutrition to the present generations and at the same time protect the natural resources and environment for future generations as well. The sustainable agricultural development will take care of soil fertility, water resources and the natural environment as a whole. It ensures conservation of natural resources and meeting the need of food of both present and future generations. Sustainable agriculture, on one hand, provides gainful employment and income and on the other hand, meets the nutritional requirements of present and future generations. Sustainable agriculture ensures production and profitability and environmental protection.

As Gracet (1990 as cited in Rao et al) defined "A sustainable agriculture is a system of agriculture that is committed to maintain and preserve the agriculture base of soil, water and atmosphere ensuring future generations the capacity to feed themselves with an adequate supply of safe and wholesome food".

According to Crosson (1992 as cited in Rao et al), "A Sustainable Agriculture system is one that can indefinitely meet demands for food and fiber at socially acceptable, economic and environmental cost."

Various national and international agencies have given great importance to sustainable agricultural development by accepting it as a core area in their agendas.

The UN Food and Agriculture Organization (FAO) defined sustainable agriculture and rural development as follows- "Sustainable development is the management and conservation of the natural resource base and the orientation of technological and institutional change in such a manner as to ensure the attainment and continued satisfaction of human needs for present and future generations. Such sustainable development (in the agriculture, forestry and fisheries sectors) conserves land, water, plant and animal genetic resources, is environmentally non-degrading, technically appropriate, economically viable and socially acceptable" (FAO, 1989).

In 1995, FAO specifically defined sustainable agriculture and rural development as a process that meets the following criteria:

- "Ensure that the basic nutritional requirements of present and future generations, qualitatively and quantitatively, are met while providing a number of other agricultural products.
- Provides durable employment, sufficient income, and decent living and working conditions for all those engaged in agricultural production.
- Maintains and, where possible, enhances the productive capacity of the natural resource base as a whole, and the regenerative capacity of renewable resources, without disrupting the functioning of basic ecological cycles and natural balances, destroying the socio-cultural attributes of rural communities, or causing contamination of the environment; and
- Reduces the vulnerability of the agricultural sector to adverse natural and socio-economic factors and other risks, and strengths and self-reliance."

The National Agricultural Policy (Ministry of Agriculture, 2000) incorporated the element of sustainability. The policy aims at attaining agricultural growth by efficiently using the resources and by conserving soil, water and bio-diversity. It focuses on growth which is technically, environmentally and economically sustainable.

In line with the National Agricultural Policy, the State Agricultural Policy, Assam also emphasized on the sustainable agricultural growth to avoid the adverse effects of green revolution and aims at making available food and nutritional requirement to the masses, both physically and economically.

Organic Farming: An Approach for Sustainable Agricultural Development

Organic farming is one of the approaches for sustainable agricultural development. Organic farming is a widely used method and considered as the best alternative to avoid ill effects of chemical farming (Narayanan, 2005). It is the farming technique which completely avoids the use of chemical inputs and depends on the production capacity of soil and local climatic condition. Organic farming broadens the scope of agriculture. It considers agriculture not only as a system of providing food but a system which takes in to account the well being of each and every living things in the whole planet. It tries to maintain ecological balance so as to protect the present and future generations.

The International Federation of Organic Agriculture Movements (IFOAM) has defined organic farming as, "Organic Agriculture is a production system that sustains the health of soils, ecosystems and people. It relies on ecological processes, biodiversity and cycles adapted to local conditions, rather than the use of inputs with adverse effects. Organic Agriculture combines tradition, innovation and science to benefit the shared environment and promote fair relationships and a good quality of life for all involved." (Infohub.ifoam.org)

The definition is based on the following principles:

- *Principle of Health:* Organic agriculture should sustain and enhance the health of soil, plant, animal, human and planet as one and indivisible.
- *Principle of ecology:* Organic agriculture should be based on living ecological systems and cycles, work with them, emulate and help sustain them.
- *Principle of fairness:* Organic agriculture should build on relationships that ensure fairness with regard to the common environment and life opportunities.
- *Principle of care:* Organic agriculture should be managed in a precautionary and responsible manner to protect the health and well- being of current and future generations and the environment.

The US Department of Agriculture (1980) defined organic agriculture as, "A production system which avoids or largely excludes the use of synthetically compounded fertilizers, pesticides, growth regulators, and livestock feed additives.

To the maximum extent feasible, organic agriculture systems rely upon crop rotation, crop residues, animal manure, legumes, green manure, off- farm organic wastes, mechanical cultivation, mineral bearing rocks, and aspects of biological pest control to maintain soil productivity and tilth to supply plant nutrients, and to control insects, weeds, and other pests." (www.fao.org)

Organic farming is known by different names in various countries like biodynamic, regenerative agriculture, permaculture etc. The common understanding of organic farming is that:

> "Practicing organic agriculture involves managing the agro-eco system as an autonomous system, based on the primary production capacity of the soil under local climatic conditions. Agro- eco system management implies treating the system, on any scale, as a living organism supporting its own vital potential for biomass and animal production, along with biological mechanisms for mineral balancing, soil improvement and pest control. ... farmers, their families and rural communities, are an integral part of this agro - eco system. Both sexes are involved on equal terms" (UNDP, 1992 as cited in Crucefix, 1998)

Technique of Organic Farming

Organic farming uses techniques like, crop rotation, green manuring, recycling of residues, water management. Crop rotation helps in preventing and controlling pests, diseases and weeds. Crop rotation technique provides nutrition for the crops and prevents soil infertility. It uses biological strategy of weed control. Livestock breeding is another important aspect of organic farming where livestock is fed from the food grown in organic farms.

India's Initiatives and Position in Organic Farming

Indian agriculture practiced before the Green Revolution movement was eco-friendly and had some features of organic farming. But organic farming has certain specific guidelines and production standards. Even after Green Revolution, farmers of hilly and tribal areas and areas with heavy rain fall practices organic farming. Herbs, medicinal plants etc. come under organic farming by default. Organic farming is gaining importance from government, entrepreneurs and the farmers. In fact, there is a huge market potential for organic products in the country and in foreign countries as well.

India occupies the 33rd position in terms of total land under organic cultivation and 88th position for agriculture land under organic crops to total farming area. (www.apeda.com). Considering the growing importance of organic farming, the Ministry of Commerce and Industry, Government of India launched the National Programme on Organic Production (NPOP) in the year 2000. This was formally notified in October, 2001 under the Foreign Trade and Development Act. The objective of this programme is to formulate standards for organic production, promoting organic farming in the country, establishing criteria and procedure for accreditation of inspection and certification bodies etc. The standards and procedure are formulated considering the requirements of the country and in connotion with the international standards formulated by Codex and IFOAM. The standards and procedures framed under the NPOP are accepted by European Commission, Switzerland and USDA.

The main organic products produced in India are- Basmati rice, Pulses, Honey, Tea, Spices, Coffee, Fruits, Processed food, Cereals, Herbal medicines, Organic cotton, Fiber, Cosmetics, Body care products etc. India exports organic products mainly to US, EU, Australia, Canada, Japan, Switzerland, South Africa etc.

Feasibility of Organic Farming

Discussions are going on about organic farming in India. The feasibility of organic farming is challenged in India on the ground of ensuring food security to a rising population. The research studies carried out in different parts of the world shows that organic farms are almost as productive as the conventional farms in developed countries whereas in developing countries organic farms may be more productive than conventional farms (Charyulu and Biswas, 2010).

It is not possible to adopt organic farming at one go in India, considering the factors like ensuring food security, population pressure, food inflation, transition period for shifting to organic farming etc. At the same time, the adverse effects of conventional farming cannot be ignored. At the present situation, a combination of organic and inorganic farming can be pursued. The National Academy of Agricultural Sciences (NASS) suggested conjunctive use of organic and inorganic sources of plant nutrients for sustainable productivity (Rajalakshmy) Organic farming is not a short-term but a long- term strategy to be implemented in a phased manner in specific regions in India. Increasing purchasing power capacity, higher standard of living, growing health consciousness, growing knowledge of ill effects of inorganic production system, agricultural sustainability, environment protection, the market potentiality for organic products in foreign countries etc. will compel India to go for organic farming.

Potentialities of Organic Farming in NER

Assam and other north-eastern states remain out of ambit of Green Revolution. Use of chemical fertilizers is very low and the land is almost virgin in this region. It provides a competitive advantage for organic farming. Besides that, certain factors may be put forwarded for promoting organic farming in this region:

- Organic farming ensures long- term soil fertility;
- It yields high quality food;
- It protect the environmental;
- It is labour intensive farming;
- Farmers are not required to depend on costly chemical inputs; and
- Farmers get premium price for organic products.

All these indicate that the strategy of organic farming can be pursued in the entire NER to make it an organic region. In this respect, SWOT analysis of NER so far as the adoption of organic farming is concerned is presented below to identify the various aspects related to it.

Strengths	Weaknesses
• Suitable Agro-climatic condition. • Traditional knowledge of farming. • Availability of labour. • Low capital investment. • Nutritious products. • Prevent environmental degradation. • Achievements in the states of Mizoram and Sikkim in organic farming.	• Lack of access to organic input and technology. • Lack of access to organic market on the part of the farmers. • Lack of processing, packaging, storing, transportation facilities. • Lack of training on the part of farmers. • Less initiative by the government. • Lack of knowledge on the part of consumers about the benefits of organic products.
Opportunities	**Threats**
• Emerging demand in the national market. • Foreign markets for organic products. • Growing health awareness. • Means to solve unemployment problem in rural areas.	• Lack of research studies on probable organic products and local soil. • Lack of fund. • Lack of policy initiatives. • Costly transition period from chemical to organic farming. • National and foreign competitors. • Absence of guidance from successful entrepreneurs. • Organic certification system.

Conclusion and Recommendations

As organic farming is in the primary stage of development, naturally there will be some weaknesses as well as threats. However, on the basis of the strengths and the opportunities, a strong argument can be made in favour of adopting organic farming in this region. It requires adoption of a comprehensive policy on organic farming for the entire north- east region in general and the individual states particularly. In this respect, certain suggestion can be put forwarded:

- Farmers' Group should be formed to take up organic farming;
- Cluster approach can be adopted for the identified organic crops;
- The central and the state governments of the north east region should provide financial support and extension services to the farmers engaged in organic farming;
- Technical, financial as well as marketing support can be sought from the institutions like the Assam State Agricultural Marketing Board, Departments of Agriculture of the respective states, NABARD, APEDA etc.;
- Training to the farmers should be provided regarding standards for organic production, management of organic farms, record keeping for certification etc.
- Contract farming should be welcomed to support the farmers during the transition period, to make available the technical knowhow and the required input to the farmers;
- Information about the benefits of organic farming and organic products should be disseminated to all the stakeholders through Private Public Partnerships; and
- Local organizations and NGOs should be integrated to reach the farmers and to motivate them for organic farming.

REFERENCES

Charyulu K.D. & Biswas S (2010).Organic Input Production and Marketing in India: Efficiency, Issues and Policies. CMA Publication No – 239, IIM, Ahmedabad. (p. 16).

Crucefix D. (1998).Organic Agriculture and Sustainable Rural Livelihoods in Developing Countries. *Department for International Developmental Natural Resources, Advisors Conference, UK.* p. 2. Retrieved fromhttp://projects.nri.org/nret/crucefix.pdf.

G. C. Munda G.C., Das A. & Patel D. P. (n.d.). Organic Farming in Hill Ecosystems: Prospects and Practices.

Ministry of Agriculture (2000). National Agricultural Policy.

Narayanan S. (2005). Organic Farming in India: Relevance, Problems and Constraints. Occasional Paper No. 38. NABARD, Mumbai.

Pugliese P. (2001) Organic Farming and Sustainable Rural Development: A Multifaceted

and Promising Convergence. *Sociologia Ruralis*, 41 (1). Retrieved from cesruc.org/uploads/soft/130221/1-13022115445.pdf.

Rajalakshmy G.(n.d.)Retrieved from www.ecoinsee.org/6bconf/Theme%20F/F.1.3%20Rajalakshmy.pdfý.

Rao V.P, Veeraraghavaiah R. Hemalatha S. & Joseph B (n.d.). Lecture 1: AGRO 303 [Lecture Notes]. Retrieved from www. Angrau.ac.in/media/7392/agro303.pdf

Yadav S.K., Babu S., Yadav M.K., Singh K., Yadav G.S. & Pal S. (2013). A Review of Organic Farming for Sustainable Agriculture in Northern India. *International Journal of Agronomy.2013.*http://dx.doi.org/10.1155/2013/718145

FAO (1989) http://www.fao.org/docrep/w7541e04.htm accessed on 20th August, 2013.

FAO (1995) http://www/fao.org/wssd/sard/index-en.htm accessed on 20th August, 2013.

http://infohub.ifoam.org/en/what-organic/definition-organic-agriculture.

http://www.fao.org/docrep/003/ac116e/ac116e02.htm accessed on 20th August, 2013.

www.apeda.com accessed on 21th August, 2013.

The Farmers (Removal of Indebtedness and Welfare) Bill, 2011 Introduced on 5th August, 2011

Niteesh Kumar Upadhyay

ABSTRACT

Indian economy is an agriculture dominant economy around 66 per cent of its population is involved in agriculture and agricultural plays a major role in the countries total GDP. But the Rate of growth of agriculture sector in the last decade have been poor which become a major cause of rural distress and shows that farming is increasingly becoming an unviable activity now a days . India is also witnessing a serious problem due to increase in life expectancy, the number of old farmers is increasing day by day and sometimes due to bad economical and physical condition these peoples are not supported by their families and children's and they are left on the mercy of god and so they face economic, social, political neglect in the society.

Introduction

The Farmers (Removal of Indebtedness and Welfare) Bill, 2011 Introduced on 5th August, 2011 in Rajya Sabha reasons for introducing this bill are discussed in part 1.

This Review is divided in following parts:

1. Background why there was a need felt of such law?
2. Key features of the Bill?
3. Shortcoming in this Bill?
4. Suggestion
5. Conclusion

Research Methodology

This research is basically a doctrinal research sources are mainly web based government reports, including analysis of different Bills and NGO reports.

What was the need felt to introduce The Farmers (Removal of Indebtedness and Welfare) Bill, 2011?

Indian economy is an agriculture dominant economy around 66 per cent of its population is involved in agriculture and agricultural plays a major role in the countries total GDP. But the Rate of growth of agriculture sector in the last decade have been poor which become a major cause of rural distress and shows that farming is increasingly becoming an unviable activity now a days . In India due to its vastness of the area the natural calamities do occur in one or the other part of India almost round the year. For instance, the whole of Rajasthan, part of Gujarat, West Bengal, Maharashtra, Bihar, Uttar Pradesh, Jharkhand, Madhya Pradesh, Chhattisgarh, etc. are drought prone areas. Every year half of Bihar is flooded and the other half faces drought. Similarly, in Southern States, coastal areas are prone to cyclones or tsunami. Many other parts of the country face earthquake, hailstorm, cloud bursts, extreme cold conditions and other natural calamities so the farmers bear the brunt of such natural calamities. They suffer damage to their crops, livestock, dwelling units, household and other household items including food grains. Despite this, the farmers are hounded by the moneylenders to give back their money taken by the farmers in the form of loan and due to which sometimes these farmers chose suicide as the only way out for this problem. We have also seen that moneylenders charge a huge interest on the money provided to the farmers and due to which farmers are under a constant pressure of paying it back[1] and Moneylender also uses other techniques like advancing the loan so that the farmers submit their agricultural produce to them below the market price[2].

India is also witnessing a serious problem due to increase in life expectancy, the number of old farmers is increasing day by day and sometimes due to bad economical and physical condition these peoples are not supported by their families and children's and they are left on the mercy of god and so they face economic, social, political neglect in the society and we all know that India is a welfare state so taking care of these people is one of the main duty and government is duty bound to provide social security to the farmers by giving them old age pension, remunerative prices and providing them adequate compensation, if they are affected by natural[3] if we see the statics we can trigger out horrible figures reports show that more than 100,000 farmers have taken their lives since 1997 and 86.5 per cent of farmers who took their own lives were financially indebted their average debt was about $835.On average, there has been one farmer's suicide every 32 minutes since 2002. This shows ugly picture of the food providers of the nation (farmers). We don't deny that only the debtness is the cause of the farmer's suicide many of the other issues which are not within the farmer's control like disease, weather, government policy, marriage of daughter etc also add considerable number of farmers doing suicide but no doubt most of the suicide happens due to the harassment of the person and his family by corrupt Money-lenders[4].

Policy makers in India have long recognised the need to provide short and long term institutional credit to agriculture at reasonable rates for meeting farmers' production needs because in India there is no widespread mechanism of crop insurance, bank loans at low rate and hence there is hardly any option left with poor people other than to go to the money lenders for seeking their financial support and in that case moneylenders charge them heavy interest sometimes equal to 25 per cent to 30 per cent and farmers never come out of this vicious cycle

One main reasons for this is failure of co-operative institutions.From 1975-76 to 2005-06 the share of cooperative bank in total credit to agriculture declined from 69.5 per cent to 21.8 per cent whereas the share of scheduled commercial banks increased from 24.2 per cent to 69.5 per cent[5]. which made the large number of farmers to fall back on the moneylender who charges exorbitant interest. The NSSO data further clarified that per cent of indebted farmers taking loans from money lenders is highest (29%), followed by Banks (27%), co-operative society (26%) and finally from Government (3%)[6].

The famers difficulties where added because of the lowpublic investments in agriculture sector[7]. The share of Gross Capital Formation (GCF) in Indian agriculture in total GCF started to decline since the early 1980s. By1995-96, it declined to 6.3 per cent from 16.1 per cent during 1980-81. There was a huge decline in the share of public sector GCF in agriculture to 17.3 per cent in 1999-00 from 43.2 per cent in 1980-81.Contrary to expectations, private investment failed to compensate for the drastic decline in public sector investment. The consequence was that the overall GCF in agriculture as a share of total capital formation in the country declined sharply from 16.1 per cent to 9.2 per cent by 1999-00. Simultaneously, a drastic reduction took place in the share of developmental expenditure on rural development from 11.7 per cent of GDP in 1991-92 to 5.9 per cent in 2000-01

This is not the first instance when government is acknowledging the condition of farmers in India and trying to bring a positive change through a new set of laws we can find various steps taken by government one such steps was introduction was The Payment of Subsistence Allowance to Farmers and Agricultural Labourers Bill, 2007 says that the Central and State Governments are under constitutional obligation to ensure the survival of the farmers and to provide financial resources for agriculture in order to prevent and further loss of lives[8].

This bill proposed that Government shall pay subsistence allowance at the rate ofrupees three thousand per month to the farmers, and rupees one thousand five hundred per month to the agricultural labourers and it also lays down the guidelines for availing the subsistence allowance under the provisions of this Bill from amongst farmers and agricultural labourers who are recorded as owners of land not exceeding four hectares in the official documents or who have been working as farmers or agricultural labourers for the last ten years and have no other source of income.

Main features of The Farmers (Removal of Indebtedness and Welfare) Bill, 2011?

This bill is to provide for the prevention of farmers from exploitation by moneylenders and other unscrupulous elements, removal of indebtedness, extending easy and hassle free loans, compensation to farmers affected by natural calamities by providing them adequate relief and for welfare measures such as old age pension, remunerative prices for their produce to be undertaken by the State and for matters connected therewith or incidental thereto. The motive of this bill is very clear and as the Section 3 of the proposed bill says that appropriate Government shall take such appropriate measures as it may deem necessary and expedient for the removal of indebtedness amongst the farmers and in particular shall endeavour to save them from the local moneylenders who exploit the farmers who charge excess amount of interest on the loan given to the farmers and it also says in the second clause of the Section 3 that the appropriate Government can give remunerative prices and provide compulsory insurance for the produce of the farmers which will be off great help to the farmers because we have discussed above that due to natural calamities and bad agriculture weather lot of people commits suicide so this kind of proposed insurance scheme will keep them far away from the hands of moneylenders and unscrupulous elements.

Section 4 of the proposed Bill is the main provision of the Bill which extends its support to the welfare of the farmers this provision say that it shall be mandatory for all the public, private and co-operative sector Banks and financial Institutions to provide loans on easy terms with nominal or without interest to the farmers affected by natural calamity to restart the agricultural operations and allied activities and fight with the their bad situation due to the natural calamity and it was also mentioned that and other financial institution mentioned in section 4 clause shall also not recover the earlier loan given to the farmers by them who have been affected by natural calamity for at least one year after the calamity and the farmers shall not be denied fresh loans on this ground. This section strengthens the condition of the farmers and gives them reasonable time to start their work normally and get into their normal position and then to think about giving or repaying the loan also according to the first clause the loan to be provided on the easy terms will help farmers to become more prosperous

Section 5 of the proposed bill also put responsibility on the central government to establish the Farmers' Welfare Fund for the purpose of welfare of farmers.

Section 6 expressly deals with the compensation given to the farmers who are hit with the natural calamity and this section of the proposed bill says that these farmers are entitled for the adequate compensation which is decided after keeping in mind the total loss suffered by them in mind. It also provided that a Village Panchayat may apply for compensation for all the affected farmers of the village and it shall be deemed that each farmer has applied for the compensation under this Act and then in the clause 4 of this section it was given that compensation under this Act shall be finalized and the payment should be made within thirty days of filing of the claim and this section also endowed the appropriate government with the responsibility to provide farmers the quality seeds, fertilizers , manure etc. to the farmers who are hit by the natural calamity this section provides the power to the welfare issue of the farmers and shows that this bill is not just related to the providing loan facilities and all but it's also about providing the farmers the necessity needed for their agricultural activity so this Bill is a complete welfare package.

Section 7 of the proposed bill deals with giving pension to the old farmers above the age of 60 years which clearly shows that India is going well with its concept of welfare state and its keeping in consideration for welfare of the of farmers and paying compensation is the way to make them more economically and socially sound.

Section 8 is actually a visionary section of the proposed bill and states that Central Government shall in consultation with the Government of the States, frame a scheme to be known as the "Farmers' Credit Scheme" to be executed by Banks and Financial Institutions and this scheme should provide some relief to the farmers like nominal interest to be charged on farmers credit and also so lay down provision regarding settling the previous loans taken and concessions which can be given to farmers who are hit by natural calamity this section is the best section which can take care of unending problem of farmers about a shortage of funds.

Section 10 speaks that the provisions of this Act, shall be in addition to and not in derogation of any other law for the time being in force in any part of the country dealing with the welfare of farmers and thismeans that this bill will compliment all other laws made for the welfare of farmers.

So above mentioned are the few main features of the proposed Bill but it's time to find out some of the lacuna of this proposed Bill.

Lacuna in the Farmers (Removal of Indebtedness and Welfare) Bill, 2011

Section 2(b) defines "farmer" means a person who owns land or cultivates land for agricultural or horticultural purpose and includes the spouse of such a farmer. And according to my point of view this definition of farmer had narrowed down the approach of this Bill and definition of the word farmer can also be taken from the National Policy For Farmers 2007 , which defines "Farmer" will refer to a person actively engaged in the economic activity of growing crops and producing other primary agricultural commodities and will include all agricultural operational holders , cultivators , agricultural labourers , sharecroppers , tenants , poultry and livestock rearers , fishers , beekeepers , gardeners , pastoralists , non –corporate planters and planting labourers as well as persons engaged in various farming related occupations such as sericulture , vermiculture , and agro-forestry. The term will also include tribal families persons engaged in shifting cultivation and in the collection, use and sale of minor and non-timber forest produce. thedefinition of farmer is very nicely mentioned in the National Policy For Farmers 2007 and which reduce the chances of ambiguity and vagueness so definition of farmers to be relooked .

The Preamble of the instant bill states that it is a bill:

"to provide for the prevention of farmers from exploitation by moneylenders and other unscrupulous elements, removal of indebtedness, extending easy and hassle free loans, compensation to farmers affected by natural calamities by providing them adequate relief and for welfare measures such as old age pension, remunerative prices for their produce to be undertaken by the State and for matters connected therewith or incidental thereto."

The Preamble tries to set forth the intention behind framing this legislation. The instant bill mainly tries to address the issue on the farmers from being exploited by the moneylenders. This can be called a beneficial piece of legislation. But the instant Bill narrows down its ambit when it talks only about 'natural calamities'. 'Natural Calamities' though form a major part of indebtedness of the farmers, but besides there are other factors which have still not been defined in the act.

The Bill only defines 'natural calamity' as:

"natural calamity" includes drought, floods, cyclones, tsunami, earthquakes, hailstorms,extreme cold conditions, and such other conditions as may be notified by the appropriate Government from time to time

The phrase 'natural calamity' though left undefined still has a narrow ambit. The intention shows that it only will define events in regards to natural calamities.

- Taking for instance if a farmers crop is destroyed by insects will he not be covered under the provisions of the bill?
- If a farmers crop is destroyed by some factors for eg riot what cover does he get?

When the intention of the instant Bill is to protect farmers from indebtedness it must take into consideration all relevant factors rather than being narrow in ambit.

Referring to section 4 Clause 1 of the Bill which states that:

1. Notwithstanding anything contained in any other law for the time being in force, it shall be mandatory for all the public, private and co-operative sector Banks and financial Institutions to provide loans on easy terms with nominal or without interest to the farmers affected by natural calamity to restart the agricultural operations and allied activities and to withstand the severity of the calamity and its aftermath.

On one hand the instant bill tries to address the problem of indebtedness but the clause again gives option to public, private and co-operative sector Banks and financial Institutions to provide loans on easy terms with nominal interest. It is true for a fact that no public, private and co-operative sector Banks and financial Institutions will provide loan at no interest basis. Keeping loans on easy terms with nominal interest undefined again raises concerns in relation to the this section of the instant Bill.

Section 3(2) saysthat For the purposes of sub-section (1) the appropriate Government shall, endeavor to give remunerative prices and provide compulsory insurance for the produce of the farmers if we give a harmonious construction than maybe the meaning of this clause is clear otherwise its vague because its talking about the providing compulsory insurance for the produce of the farmers and in some cases we find that after putting seeds there is no crop or sometimes after having a good crop there is no market demand of that crop or no storage facilities so insurance should be given from the day of putting of the seeds to the day of sale of crops in the market.

Section 7(1) speaks about giving the pension of minimum of one thousand rupees to old famers above 60 years of age which is quiet less after looking to today's inflation rate so the minimum limit should also be relooked ones.

Suggestions

1. Involving some part of Farmers' Welfare Fund for farmers knowledge about risk management and sustainable agriculture.
2. Credit counseling centers should be established where severely indebted farmers can be provided a debt rescue package/rescheduling to save them from debt trap.
3. Priority should also be given to the credit cooperative institutions as per the recommendations of Vaidyanathan Committee report[9].
4. We can also take example of the the Karnataka Prohibition of Charging Exorbitant Interest Ordinance, according to which it is illegal to charge an interest rate above 21 per cent in the case of an unsecured loan and 23 per cent in the case of a secured loan even after that we find that rule are violated and also the 21 and 23 per cent is of course a very high rate fixed by the state government of Karnataka[10]. So by taking example of this we can include some provision in the present Bill for fixing up of the maximum amount of interest rate to be charged by anyone (moneylenders , banks etc.)
5. More importance to be given to Regional Rural Banks (RRB)

   Despite their better performance, RRBs have not so far been able to show a worthwhile improvement in financial margins, costs of operation and gross margins. In order to improve their financial performance, the RRBs will have to diversify their investments from low yielding government bonds to more remunerative areas. The government has taken a policy decision to strengthen RRBs by consolidating them. Consequently, the number of RRBs has been brought down from 196 in 2005 to only 96 in June 2007. It has also been decided to expand the rural branch network through the RRBs. In order to improve further the functioning of the RRBs it is important to strengthen their links with microfinance institutions.

6. The successful SHG-Bank Linkage Programme may be extended to farmers by encouraging them to form SHGs. In this context, Sree-KshetraDharmstala Rural Development Programme, which is successful in organizing the farmers, may be emulated. SHGs under Indira Kranti Pathakam in Andhra Pradesh is another successful experiment. These programmes are likely to ensure greater flow of credit to small and marginal farmers.
7. The Minimum Support Price (MSP) mechanism should be implemented effectively across the country.

Conclusion

We have seen that there are significant initiatives in that have already been taken in recent years by the government to reverse the downward trend in agricultural production and to find sustainable solutions for strengthening the farmer's livelihood and income. Some of these important initiatives include:

1 Bharat Nirman
2. National Rural Employment Guarantee Programme
3. National Horticulture Mission
4. Establishment of the National Rainfed Area Authority
5. Reforms in Agricultural Marketing and Development of Market Infrastructure
6. Agri-Business Development through Venture Capital Participation by the Small Farmer Agri-Business Consortium
7. National Rural Health Mission etc.

So this act is furtherance of these initiatives taken by the government for improving the life of farmers in India. But this Bill at this infant stage need some changes to have a wider impact and after that only this bill can succeed in its motive. So after removing the above mentioned lacuna and by using the suggestion given under this project we can find a better law.

NOTES

1 The Farmers (Removal of Indebtedness and Welfare) Bill, 2011 http://164.100.24.219/BillsTexts/RSBillTexts/asintroduced/farmrs.pdf retrieved on 15 Nov 2011 at 11:23 AM IST.

2 Farmers' Suicide in India:Agrarian Crisis, Path of Development and Politics in Karnataka http://viacampesina.net/downloads/PDF/Farmers_suicide_in_india(3).pdf retrieved on 14 Nov 2011 at 12:30 PM IST.

3 Said by Minister R C Singh before Putting The Farmers (Removal of Indebtedness and Welfare) Bill, 2011 forward for the Consideration of Rajya Sabha.

http://164.100.24.219/BillsTexts/RSBillTexts/asintroduced/farmrs.pdf retrieved on 15 Nov 2011 at 4:30 PM IST.

4 International Farmers Suicide Crisis

http://www.un.org/esa/sustdev/csd/csd16/PF/presentations/farmers_relief.pdf retrieved on 15 Nov 2011 at 2:30 PM IST.

see also : National Human Rights Commission Report on following links

http://www.nhrc.nic.in/disparchive.asp?fno=1088

http://www.nhrc.nic.in/disparchive.asp?fno=815

http://www.nhrc.nic.in/disparchive.asp?fno=761

http://www.nhrc.nic.in/disparchive.asp?fno=593

5 Report of the Expert Group on Agricultural Indebtedness, Banking Division, Department of Economic Affairs, Ministry of Finance, Government of India.

July 2007 http://www.igidr.ac.in/pdf/publication/PP-059.pdf retrieved on 15 Nov 2011 at 12:30 AM IST.

6 Farmers' Suicide in India:Agrarian Crisis, Path of Development and Politics in Karnataka http://viacampesina.net/downloads/PDF/Farmers_suicide_in_india(3).pdf retrieved on 14 Nov. 2011 at 12:30 PM IST.

7 Report of the Expert Group on Agricultural Indebtedness,Banking Division Department of Economic Affairs, Ministry of Finance, Government of India.

July 2007 http://www.igidr.ac.in/pdf/publication/PP-059.pdf retrieved on 15 Nov 2011 at 12:30 AM IST.

8 http://164.100.24.219/BillsTexts/LSBillTexts/asintroduced/2738ls-3.pdf retrieved on 15 Nov 2011 at 3:30 PM IST.

9 Report of the High Powered Committee onCooperatives May 2009 Ministry of Agriculture, Government of India.

http://agricoop.nic.in/cooperation/hpcc2009new.pdf retrieved on 15 Nov 2011 at 12:30 AM IST.

10 Farmers' Suicide in India:Agrarian Crisis, Path of Development and Politics in Karnataka http://viacampesina.net/downloads/PDF/Farmers_suicide_in_india(3).pdf retrieved on 14 Nov. 2011 at 12:30 PM IST.

Stages of Indian Agriculture and its Growth Factors

Kedar Vishnu
Rohi Choudhary

ABSTRACT

The present study is the modest attempt to identify the driving forces of Indian agriculture in the post-independence era. Indian agriculture has witnessed a paradigm shift in the post-independence era. In the initial stage of post-reform or liberalization period, Indian agriculture gained a tremendous benefit from the export of agriculture outputs and wiser application of HYV seeds. Horticulture crops have received greater importance during this period. There was a great feeling of strong complementarily between public expenditure and private expenditure in developing Indian agriculture at the national level

Introduction

Indian agriculture has witnessed a paradigm shift in the post-independence era. Expansion of area, institution reform and major irrigation project related expenditure had played important role in shaping Indian agriculture during the pre and early green revolution periods. Higher investment on irrigation during early period of green revolution helped farmers to get relatively better output than those who did not invest on it or benefited from it. However, more dependence on traditional verities of seeds thwarted the sector in enhancing higher productivity in the country. As a result of which, the country faced severe food crisis in the early of green revolution. To overcome this problem, the government of India adopted a few new technologies during the green revolution, in the mid 1960s. Punjab and Haryana were the two major States who started using High Yield Verity (HYV) seed of rice and wheat, and this initiative helped in increasing food-grain production in these States.

In the initial stage of post-reform or liberalization period, Indian agriculture gained a tremendous benefit from the export of agriculture outputs and wiser application of HYV seeds. At the same time, the sector witnessed a substantial shift from food-grain to non-food grain cultivation in the country. Therefore, horticulture crops have received greater importance during this period. A substantial reduction has also been witnessed in the case of subsidy on fertilizers, pesticides and expenditure on irrigation projects. Due to this slight reduction in government attention on the sector, the role of private investment has increasingly been visible during the post-reform period. By virtue of private investment, commercialization and specialization of crops have been widely initiated in Indian agriculture. Unfortunately, greater specialization towards one or fewer crops and higher utilization of fertilizers and pesticide led to negative impact on productivity of different agriculture crops and imbalance in food production in the later stage of reform period.

Fortunately, after a decade of underinvestment, slow growth of agriculture and negligence of the sector, there has been some respite in Indian agriculture sector, especially after 2006-07. Therefore, this period is considered as recovery stage in Indian agriculture. Even majority of the crops has been started registering tremendous growth compared to the later stage of reform period. The recovery phase was characterized by higher growth in the production arising from the both area and yield effects. There are many studies that have captured the impact of green revolution. According to Kathrya (2010), higher application of high yielding variety, fertilizers and pesticides were found to be the most effective drivers for green revolution. Around 50-60 per cent of food-grain production has increased in India since 1990s that have been attributed to increasing use of fertilizers (Birner, et al., 2011). Another study by Chengappa (2013) revealed that institutional credit, subsidized input supply and incentive schemes had played significant role during green revolution period. After the reform period, the debates of the academician and policy makers shifted from green revolution to government and private investment. There was a great feeling of strong complementarily between public expenditure and private expenditure in developing Indian agriculture at the national level (Shetty, 1990; Dhwan and Yedav, 1998). Despite great feeling of private sector involvement in the sector, their role has slowly died down due to declining public support (Misra and Hazell, 1997). It is also revealed that the role of agriculture growth is associated with public expenditure. In the post-reform period, majority of the studies opined that horticulture sector has been the driver of agriculture growth in the country.

The present study is the modest attempt to identify the driving forces of Indian agriculture in the post-independence era. An effort has also been made to see development stages of Indian agriculture. Growth trend of the sector and value of output of the crops were also estimated. The study depends on the secondary data collected from the Directorate of Economics and Statistics, Government of India. Export and import data were collected from Planning Commission of India data base. Crop wise value of output data were collected from Central Statistical Organisation, Govt. of India.

Major Institutional Factors of Agriculture Development in India

In this chapter, four institutional factors have been discussed for development of Indian agriculture. The factors include:

1. Change in the phase of policy making;
2. Subsidy on Indian agriculture/Govt. expenditure;
3. Rising export of agricultural products; and
4. Increasing performance of horticulture crops.

Change in the Phase of Policy making

In this section, we try to trace out the principle government policies for promoting agricultural development. For the overall development of Indian agriculture, many institutional and infrastructural changes have been introduced since Independence. The agricultural policy of the country has impacted the magnitude of agricultural output and direction of its growth. During the last five decades, Indian agricultural policy can be broadly analyzed into three phases. They are– Pre green revolution period (1960s and early 1970s); Green Revolution period (1970s and 1980s); and Reform period (1990s and 2000s)

In the pre-green revolution period, the focus of the policy makers was on area expansion. The period witnessed tremendous agrarian reform, institutional change and the development of major irrigation projects (Chand and Parappurathu, 2011). The serious food-grain crisis in the mid-1960s triggered a significant shift of agricultural policy towards technological development and mechanization, i.e more emphasis was given to technological innovation and started to introduce new agricultural technologies brought from the abroad. During this period, India depended more on the imported food-grain from other country.

In the green revolution period (1970s and 1980s), adoption of technology particularly HYVs and chemical inputs with continued thrust on irrigation and extension boosted agriculture growth to 2.26 per cent. But, this revolutionary was mainly confined to wheat in irrigated areas of north India. Agricultural growth in this period was also mainly supported by institutional credit, subsidized input supply and incentive schemes (minimum support price). However, the same momentum has not been sustained in the later period (Chengappa, 2013). The scope for area expansion diminished considerably.

During the post-reform period (1990s and 2000s), the decade of 1990s saw a sea change in the policy environment of the Indian economy. Agricultural trade liberalization did not cause a major problem during the early year of implementation. India's import policy reform began with the earnest of abolition of quantitative restrictions, and completed in 2001. On the export side, the reform process began in 1994 with the placing of rice and also wheat on the list of freely exportable goods and removing their minimum export prices (Gulati and Mullen, 2013). There was a significant shift in terms of agricultural production from traditional field crops to the horticulture and commercial crops and non-land based activities of livestock and fisheries. Many studies indicate that the high growth in the high value commodity sector has given a push to the growth accomplished by the primary sector at large (Chengappa, 2013). The decade of the 1990s represents a transition period in Indian agriculture from state-led to market-driven growth, and this evolution is still in progress and several roadblocks remain (Gulati and Mullen, 2013).

Subsidy on Indian Agriculture/Govt. Expenditure

In this section an attempt has been made to link the impact of government expenditure on Indian agriculture growth rate. Agriculture is being an important sector of the Indian economy; the impact of its performance (good/bad) is not confined to agriculture alone but also felt in all the sectors of the economy (Kumar, 1992). During the later stage of reform period, Indian agriculture witnessed stagnation and even decline in public investment. As a result, the share of public sector Gross Capital Formation (GCF) in total GCF in agriculture and allied sectors declined from more than 17.1 per cent to 4.5 per cent during 1977-78 and 2010-11 respectively.

Private sector investment also showed stagnation/decline during the 1990s. However, it reverted in 1995-96. We can see from the Figure 1 that there was a perfect complementary between public and private expenditure during 1975-76 to 1981-82. Thereafter, declining public expenditure continued up to 2007-08, but private investment started recovering trend during 1981-82. Thereafter, fluctuating trend was witnessed. Based on above finding, it can be argued that the role of perfect complementary between public and private investment has became very week during the post-reform study. But, one should not forget that even though week complementary between these two sectors, enhancing public investment leverages the private investment into Indian agriculture. Therefore we considered public expenditure as main driver for Indian agriculture performance.

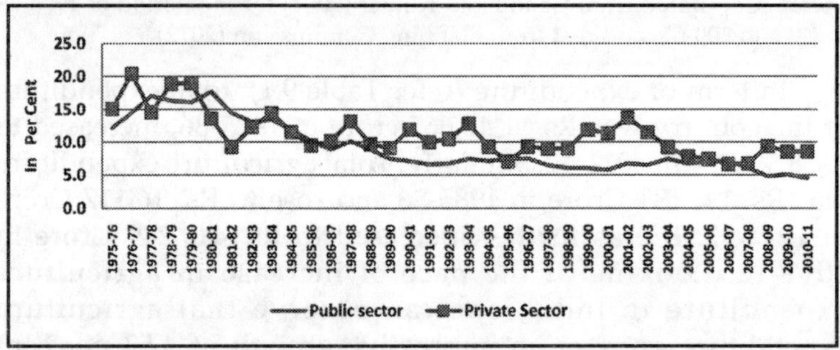

Fig. 9.1: Share of GCF in Agriculture Between Public and Private (at 2004-05 prices)

Source: Planning Commission (2012)

One major reform needed in agriculture sector relates to reduction in subsidies and increase in Investments. It was suggested that the public investment should increase at 16 per cent for achieving 4 per cent growth rate in Indian agriculture (Dev, 2009). It shows that the important of public expenditure on Indian agriculture. There was a trade-off between subsidies and public investment during this period. Public investment declined from 3.4 per cent of agriculture GDP in the early 1980s to 1.9 per cent in 2001-03. On the other hand, subsidies have increased from 2.9 per cent to 7.4 per cent of agriculture GDP (GOI, 2007). It is found from the Figure 9.2 that the subsidy share has increased from 6.2 per cent to 10.8 per cent during 2006-07 and 2007-08 respectively. From the above discussion, it can be clear that the subsidy has played crucial role for improving agricultural growth rate, especially during post-reform period when public expenditure was very meager.

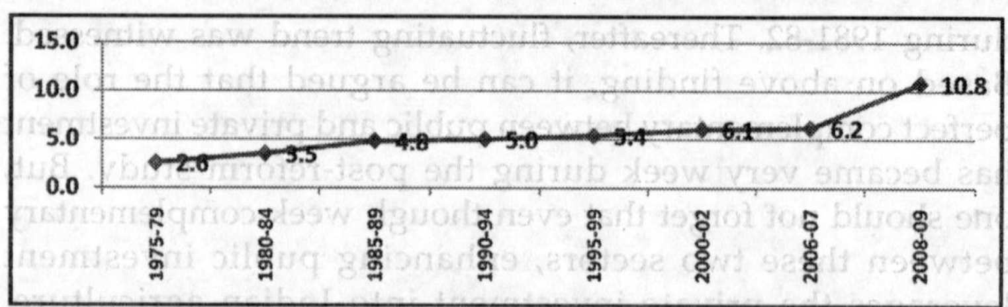

Fig. 9.2: Share (in %) of Input Subsidies in Agricultural GDP (at 1999-00 Prices)

Source: Copulated from Chand and Kumar (2004) for the period of 1975-79 to 200-02, and rest from Planning Commission (2012)

In term of expenditure (refer Table 9.1), total expenditure of the country was Rs. 1, 48,665 crore in 1985-86, increased to Rs. 8, 22,974 in 2011-12. Similarly, Total agriculture expenditure was Rs. 14, 131 Crore in 1985-86 and rose to Rs. 16,117 Crore in 1991-92. It was further increased to Rs. 41, 249 Crore in 2011-12. Looking at the pace of increase in agriculture expenditure in India, one can observe that agriculture expenditure grew at an impressive growth of 4.53 per cent during 1985-86 to 1991-92 but slightly declined at the tune of 1.87 per cent during post reform period. Further, it recovered in the recent past as high as more than 9.81 per cent. from this trend one can observe that post reform period witnessed a visible deceleration of growth in most of the major crops and this can be attributed to a significant diversion of resources away from agriculture to non-agriculture sectors (Chand and Parappurathu, 2011). From the above discussion it is clear that government expenditure has crucial role for influencing agriculture growth rate.

Rising Export of Agricultural Products

Share of agriculture import and export compared to total national import/export in value term is presented in Figure 9.3. It can be seen from the figure that agriculture export has increased from 16.8 per cent during 1992-93 to 20.3 per cent during 1996-97. The initial period of liberalization gives us higher benefit from export to Indian farmers. But, after 1996-97, export trend started declining continuously till 2005-06, and thereafter, marginal recovery situation was initiated.

Table 9.1: Trend of Total Expenditure and Agri. Expenditure in India (at 2004-05 Prices)

	Expenditure in Crore			Growth Rates		
	1985-86	1991-92	2011-12	Pre-reform	Post-reform	Most-recent
Total Exp in India	1,48,665	2,14,553	8,22,974	6.28***	6.40***	8.62***
Agri. Exp. in India	14,131	16,117	41,249	4.53*	1.87***	9.81***

***Significant at 1% level and ** Significant at 5% level

Source: Estimated from RBI (2012)

The share of agriculture export in the India was much higher than that of import. The share of agriculture import has increased significantly in the recent past, from 2.8 per cent during 1990-91 to 8.2 per cent during 1998-99, but, thereafter it started declining and reached as low as 2.7 per cent in 2007-08. The reason for declining agriculture export to total nation export could be due to tremendous increase in share of non-agriculture export, especially after 2000.

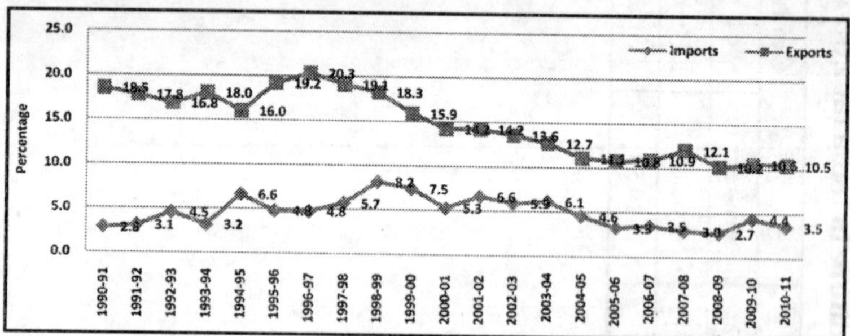

Fig. 9.3: Share (in %) of Agriculture Import/Export in Value term to Total Import/export

Source: Planning Commission (2012)

Within agriculture, the share of each commodity into total agriculture export value has been shown in Figure 9.4. Total food-grains and total horticulture crops are the major contributors into total export. It can be seen from the Figure 4 that the priority of export has shifted from total food-grains to total horticultural crops. Total food-grain export share was found to be around 7.8 per cent to total agriculture export during 1990-91, has reached as high as 25.5 per cent during 1998-99. Afterward, it started showing fluctuating trend up to 2007-08. Rice is the major contributor in total food-grains export. In the recent years, horticulture product has emerged as the second largest contributor into total agriculture export, accounting for over 12.8 per cent during 2010-11. This reflects the important of horticulture commodity in Indian economy. Oil seeds registered the third largest export commodity in the country during the period. But, its share has consistently declining. It is quite interesting to note that import duty has played a dominant role in cotton export from the country. The share of cotton export into total agriculture export was also declining from 14.2 per cent in 1990-91 to 0.3 per cent during 1999-00. Thereafter, its share has started increasing mainly due to BT cotton production in the country.

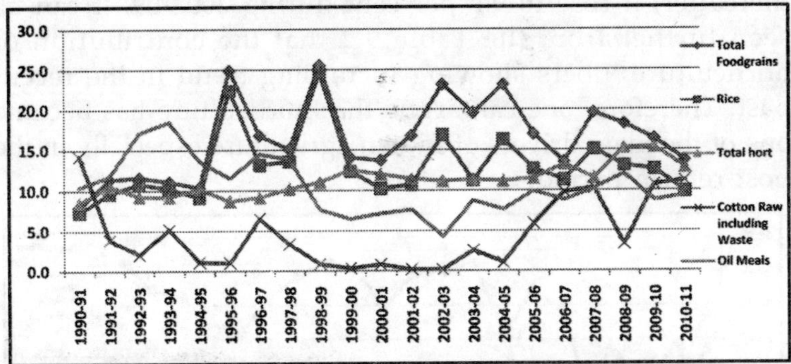

Fig. 9.4: Share of Each Items in Value Term to Total Agriculture Export

The share of each item in value term to total agriculture import is shown in Figure 9.5. Edible oils have emerged as the single largest contributor to total agriculture import to the country, accounting for 52.4 per cent of the total agriculture import. Wood and wooden products have registered the second largest position of agriculture import. It can be seen from the Figure 9.5 that the wood and wooden product's share has been showing a declining trend. Pulses have reported as the third largest import into total agriculture import of the country, probably due to diversification of Indian agriculture from food-grain and pulses toward commercial crops. Cash nut and fruits nut reported less than 10 per cent of total agriculture import to India.

Rising Contribution of Horticulture Crops

It can be seen from the Table 9.2 that the value of output for cereals was 33.7 per cent during 1999-00, and declined to 30.8 per cent during 2008-09. This change was mainly due to the shift of consumption pattern from total food grain to horticulture crops and animal products. The share of fruits and vegetable was 23.2 per cent during 1999-00, and increased to 26.1 per cent during 2008-09. The contribution of total pulses into total agriculture value seems to be stagnant during 1999-00 to 2008-09. Oilseed contributed 8.8 per cent into the total value of agriculture output during 1999-00, and thereafter, it rose to 9.7 per cent during 2008-09. It can be seen further from the Table 9.2 that the contribution of horticulture, fibers showing increasing trend in the recent past. Therefore, one can argue that horticulture has become one of the main drivers of Indian agriculture especially in the post-reform period.

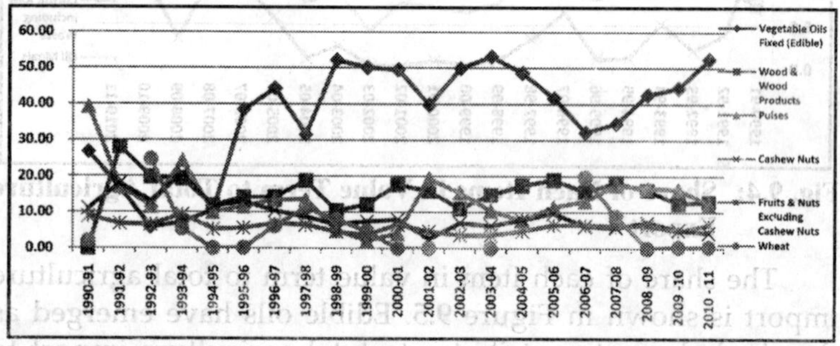

Fig. 9.5: Share of Each Items in Value Terms to Total Agriculture Import

The area under each crop into total Gross Cropped Area (GCA) is shown in Table 9.3. It is found that the area was shifting from food-grain crop to horticulture crops. This is mainly due to higher demand for horticulture crops, especially in the post-reform period. It is also observed that even though the cost of cultivation was higher for horticulture crops, farmers were found to have benefited from this cultivation. Risk evasion (from uncertain climatic condition and poor irrigation) of farmers could have also been another reason for raising the area under horticulture crops. From the above discussion it can be clear that horticulture crops and oilseed crops has become main driving forces for growth of Indian agriculture in the post-reform period.

Table 9.2: Crop wise Value of Output for Indian (at constant prices 2004-05)

Crops	1999-00	2000-01	2001-02	2002-03	2003-04	2004-05	2005-06	2006-07	2007-08	2008-09
Total Cereal	33.7	32.3	32.7	29.9	31.9	30.4	29.8	30.2	30.0	30.8
Total Pulses	4.6	4.1	4.6	4.3	5.1	4.4	4.2	4.2	4.3	4.2
Total Oilseed	8.8	8.4	8.7	7.4	10.2	10.0	10.9	9.8	10.2	9.7
Total Fibers	3.1	2.6	2.6	2.6	3.4	4.1	4.3	4.5	5.1	4.4
Total Drugs & Narcotics	3.1	2.9	2.8	3.1	2.6	3.0	2.8	2.6	2.6	2.7
Total Condiments & Spices	2.9	3.1	3.1	3.3	3.4	3.4	3.4	3.3	3.4	3.4
Total Fruits & Vegetables	23.2	25.4	24.4	27.3	23.4	24.7	25.1	25.3	25.2	26.1
Total By Products	7.2	7.2	6.7	7.0	6.6	6.6	6.3	6.2	5.9	5.9
Kitchen garden	0.5	0.6	0.6	0.7	0.6	0.6	0.6	0.5	0.5	0.5
Total Value of Agri. Output	**100.0**	**100.0**	**100.0**	**100.0**	**100.0**	**100.0**	**100.0**	**100.0**	**100.0**	**100.0**

Source: Computed from CSO, Government of India

Table 9.3: Per cent Change in Area of Major Agricultural Crops in India

Crop Category	TE-1973	TE-1983	TE-1993	TE-2003	TE-2010
Total Cereals	60.73	59.57	54.29	53.26	51.6
Total Pulses	13.37	13.27	9.96	11.91	12.38
Total Food-grains	74.1	72.85	66.32	65	63.98
Total Oilseeds	10.05	10.46	14.09	12.24	13.93
Total Condiments & Spices	1.08	1.24	1.43	1.7	–
Total Horticulture Crops	–	–	**7.00**	**9.46**	**11.56**
Misc. Crops	14.77	15.45	11.16	11.6	10.53
Gross Crop Area	**100**	**100**	**100**	**100**	**100**

Source: DES (2012).

Performance of Indian Agriculture

For better understanding of the performance of Indian agriculture growth rate of the sector has been divided into five periods. They are– Phase I: Pre-green revolution period (1950-51 to 1967-68); Phase II: Early green revolution period (1968-69 to 1985-86); Phase III: Period of wider dissemination (1986-87 to 1996-97); Phase IV: Post-reform period (1997-98 to 2005-06); and Phase V: Period of recovery (2006-07 to 2009-10/2010-11).

Phase I– Pre-green revolution period (1950-51 to 1967-68)

This period was characterized by a sharp decline in growth in GDP agriculture, with the fall in decadal growth rates from 2.78 per cent to 1.06 per cent between the period 1950-51 and 1967-68. Lower allocation of resource during second and third plan was the major reason for reporting lower growth rate in the mid-1960s, as compared to 1950s. Majority of the country's policy makers used to think that the country cannot gain more growth rate in agriculture sector.

Phase II– Early green revolution period (1968-69 to 1985-86)

The green revolution was kick-started from the year 1966 and the effects of adoption of superior technology and institutional reforms were found to have manifested from 1968-69 onwards. Growth trend of Indian agriculture has been slowed, as depicted by Figure 6. At the later stage of this phase, some change in the growth of agriculture GDP was observed. But, the benefit of green revolution was witnessed in the north Indian States, like Punjab, Haryana.

Phase III– Period of wider dissemination (1986-87 to 1996-97)

The major aim of all the government programmes was to transfer the benefit of green revolution from northern States to other parts of the country. We classify this period as wide dissemination of technology for the benefit of the entire country. It was also witnessed that the decade growth of agriculture has reached around 3 per cent by the decade ending with 1985-86.

Phase IV– Post-reform period (1997-98 to 2005-06)

We classified this phase as less productive phase in Indian agriculture. Majority of the Indian policy makers started giving higher importance for services sector. Therefore, tertiary sector found increasing trend and played dominant role in determining the overall growth of Indian economy during this period. This shift towards service sector has been attributed mainly to high marginal propensity to consume and technological advancements in areas such as software development, trade, communications and banking & insurance especially during the most recent period. The deceleration of growth was started from 1997-98 onwards and a clear indication of slumping of the agricultural sector was visible till the year 2005-06. Expenditure on agriculture had experienced a major declining during this period. The declining government expenditure and rising share of revenue expenditure are the major reason for reporting lower growth rate during this period.

Phase V– Period of recovery (2006-07 to 2009-10/2010-11)

A significant recovery of Indian agriculture was observed in the last few years that have pushed the decadal growth rate above the 3 per cent. After decades of underinvestment in the agriculture, especially by the public sector, the declining trends in agricultural spending have recently begun to reverse, particularly after 2006-07. The promotion of Public Private Partnership (PPP) projects to support agriculture could be another reason for reporting higher growth rate during this period. Detail of it can be seen from Figure 9.6.

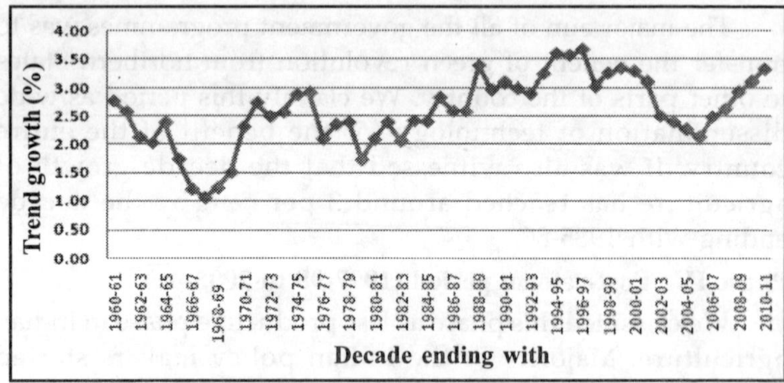

Fig. 9.6: Trend and Growth Rate of Agriculture GDP based on Ten Year Period

Source: Chand and Parappurathu (2011)

Conclusion

From the facts and figures depicted above, it is found that green revolution period has been the golden period for Indian agriculture that witnessed tremendous growth in agricultural output as well as input. The period of wide dissemination of technology can be considers as most successful period in the history of Indian agriculture in which green revolution technologies have shifted from north to south and other remaining part of India. Therefore, we consider shift in policy making as a major driver of Indian agriculture sector mainly during green revolution and wide dissemination period. This paper also revealed that post-reforms period witnessed a visible deceleration of growth in most of the major crops and this can be attributed to a significant diversion of resources away from agriculture to non-agriculture sectors. From the above discussion, it is further clear that government expenditure has crucial role for influencing agriculture growth in the country. But, private investment has played negative role during post-reform period. Moreover, the use of primary inputs in the sector also slowed down, and due to this, the yield of most of the crops went down. During this period, the higher shift of cropping pattern took place from food-grain to horticulture crops. Similarly, the export of horticulture crops was quite higher during this period. Therefore, we can argue that the rising in horticulture sector has become one of the important factors that have been responsible for higher agriculture growth in the country. It is also found that the subsidy has played a crucial role for improving agricultural growth, especially during the post-reform period when public expenditure was very meager. There was a trade-off between subsidies and public investment in Indian agriculture. The public investment rate in Indian agriculture started recovering trend after 2005-06 year. It is revealed that the retardation of growth continued till 2005-06, and thereafter, a sharp recovery in growth was realized. The reason for this can be attributed to a conscious hike in public and private investment and substantial improvement in term of trade in favor of agricultural sector.

REFERENCES

Chand, Ramesh and Parappurathu, Shinoj (2011). Policy Options and Investment Priorities for Accelerating Agricultural Productivity and Development in India. Workshop on Indian Agriculture during November 10-11, 2011. India International Centre, New Delhi.

Chand, Ramesh and Parmod Kumar (2004). Determinants of Capital Formation and Agriculture Growth– Some New Explorations. Economic and Political Weekly, 39(52): 5611-5616.

Chengappa, P.G. (2013). Secondary Agriculture: A Driver for Growth of Primary Agriculture in India. Presidential Address Delivered at the 72nd Annual Conference of the Indian Society of Agricultural Economics held on November 17, 2012 at Banaras Hindu University, Varanasi.

Dev, Mahendra s. (2009). Structural Reforms and Agriculture: Issues and Policies. Key-note Paper Presented at 92nd Annual Conference at Indian Economic Association during December 27- 29, Bhubaneswar, Orissa.

Dhawan, B.D. and S.S. Yadav (1997). Public Investment in Indian Agriculture. Economic and Political Weekly, 32(14): 710-714.

Gulati, Ashok and Kathleen Mullen (2003). Responding to Policy Reform– Indian Agriculture in the 1990s and After. Working paper No. 189, Stanford: Stanford University.

Kathrya, Sebby (2010). The Green Revolution of the 1960s and its Impact on Small Farmers in India. Unpublished Thesis Submitted to University of Nebraska-Lincoln, USA.

Kumar, A. Ganesh (1992). Falling Agricultural Investment and its Consequence. Economic and Political Weekly, 27(42): 2307-2312.

Misra,V.N. and B.R. Peter Hazell (1997). Price and Non-Prices Factors in Agricultural Investment. Economic and Political Weekly, 32(31): 1991-1992.

Planning Commission (2012). Data-book for DCH- 10 April 2012, Page No. 39. New Delhi: Government of India.

Regina, Birner; Gupta, Surpa and Sharma, Neeru (2011). The Political Economy of Agricultural Policy Reform in India– Fertilizers and Electricity for Irrigation. Research Monograph, IFPRI: New Delhi.

RBI (2012). Handbook of Statistics on Indian Economy. Mumbai: Reserve Bank of India.

Shetty, S.L. (1990). Investment in Agriculture– Brief Review of Recent Trends. Economic and political Weekly, 25(7/8): 389-398.

Organic and Inorganic Agriculture System *A Review*

Saswathan, M

ABSTRACT

Agriculture is nothing but the cultivation of land. In India it's believed that agriculture was begun by 9000 BC and rice was believed to be cultivated during Indus Valley Civilization. Now India is the world's largest producer of coconuts, cashew nuts, ginger, turmeric, banana, custard apple, pulses and black pepper. Most of the industries also depend upon the agriculture sector for their raw materials. After the green revolution there is a dramatic change in the cultivation of dry land crops and wet land crops. The advantages of dry land crops are they can be stored for 5 to 6 years where as the rice can be stored for maximum 6 months and the paddy can be stored for maximum of 1.0year.

Introduction

Agriculture is nothing but the cultivation of land. The land can be divided in to two types they are dry land and wet land. Dry Land Farming: It does not use irrigation but depends on precipitation to meet crop requirements. In India the total cultivation land is 141.0 Million Hectare. Out of this 44 per cent of lands are belong to dry land cultivation. Some of the examples of dry land grains are. Pearl Millet, Italian Millet, Finger Millet, Kodo Millet, Proso Millet, Barnyard Millet, Little Millet, Great Millet, Sorghum, etc. Wet Land Farming: A wetland is a land that is saturated with water either permanently or seasonally. Plants that grown in wetland are technically called hydrophytes vegetation. Paddy, sugarcane are the best examples of Wet land Farming. 56 per cent of farming land in India are belongs to Wet land Farming.

After the green revolution there is a dramatic change in the cultivation of dry land crops and wet land crops. The statistical report says the cultivation of paddy are grown more than 400 per cent when compared with the current situation and in the beginning of green revolution (1955). At the same the cultivation of dry land crops are decreased more than 300 per cent. The advantages of dry land crops are they can be stored for 5 to 6 years where as the rice can be stored for maximum 6 months and the paddy can be stored for maximum of 1.0year.

Parts of Trees/Plants/Crops

The trees/plants/crops are divided into the following types. They are: Roots, Stem, Leaves, Flowers and fruits.

Roots: This is further divided in to three types they are Taproot, lateral root, and fibrous root. The Taproot is the main axis of the root that penetrates deeply and is used by certain plants (such as carrot) for food storage. It is in conical in shape form the primary root and produces the secondary root. The lateral roots are extended from the primary roots (Taproot) that helps to anchor the plant into the earth it also contributes to water intake and extraction of nutrition for the growth and development of the plant. Fibrous roots have many secondary roots and help to hold the soil together.

Stem: the stem plays an important role in transferring the water from root to leaves and nutrients from leaves to root. The stem carries the water from root to leaves through the path called Xylem. The food is transferred from leaves to root through the path called Phloem. Cambium plays an important role in distinguish and maintaining both the paths.

Leaves: the food which is required is produced by the leaves through the process of photosynthesis. That is the reason the leaves are exposed to the sunlight.

The following are the important factors which is necessary for the agriculture. They are: Soil, Water, Fertilizer

The agriculture system existing at three different levels:

1. International level
2. National (India) level
3. State (Tamilnadu) level

International Level

The invention of agriculture is one of the great revolutions of human history. In 2011, the International Labour Organization says "one third of world's populations were employed in Agriculture, nevertheless the production level is less than 5 per cent of the gross world products".

In the past century agriculture has been characterized by enhanced productivity, the use of synthetic fertilizers and pesticides, selective breeding mechanization, water contamination, and farm subsidies. Sir Albert Howard argued in the early 20th century that the overuse of pesticides and synthetic fertilizers damages the long term fertility of the soil. The environmental awareness has been increased in the 21st century.

When we see the agriculture in International level, it's mandatory to study the contribution of two eminent persons who did massive changes in agriculture domain. They are:

- Ernest Norman Borlaug
- Mosanobu Fukuoka

Even though their contributions towards agriculture are huge. They travelled in two different paths. Mr. Ernest Norman Borlaug is passionate with Inorganic Agriculture system where as Mr. Mosanobu Fukuoka believes in Organic Agriculture and did tremendous work in that. Their immortal work in Agriculture is discussed below.

Inorganic Farming by Norman Ernest Borlaug

He is also known as the "Father of Green Revolution". He introduces the inorganic agriculture system to many countries during the middle of 20th century. By using his technology the wheat yield was doubled in India during 165 and 1970. He was awarded with Noble prize in 1970 and he also honored with "Padma Vibushan", a second highest civilian honor award in India.

He makes himself involved in research related to genetics and plant breeding. His sixteen years continuous work gave him tremendous success in high yield and diseases resistant wheat. He worked heavily in increasing the diseases resistance through the process called multiline varieties. Normally the plant varieties have pureline diseases resistance it means the plant diseases can overcome this resistance and causes severe damage to the plant. So he discovered multiline varieties which have different genes for diseases resistance without reducing the productivity. Every person in this world has appreciation and criticizes. He too have both the things and the appreciation is most of the people believed that his ideas helped to increase the cultivation without increasing the land size, so he indirectly helped for deforestation because the people would have cut many tree to make the forest as a agriculture land to compensate the food requirement since his technology helped to increase the fold grains without increasing the land size helped for deforestation. So the economist says that his technique saved the ecosystem from the destruction. Most of the people strongly deny this statement because forest is not the source to increase the farm land sources would be many other waste land where the people wouldn't use that for agriculture.

In spite of many appreciations there are many people opposing his ideas and thoughts who consider his techniques are against nature and it leads to affect the environment by using the inorganic fertilizer and pesticides. These people strongly believe that his idea will help to increase the profit of MNC companies like Monsanto and will not useful for the real farmers. In the year 2005 he said 'the world require double the food quantity in 2050". He strongly believes it can possible only by multidisciplinary research. His main aim is to success in "transfer cereals immunity to wheat, maize, sorghum and transfer the wheat based protein to cereals".

The other eminent person who worked totally just the opposite of what Ernest did, it is none other than then Mr. Mosanobu Fukuoka.

Farming (Organic) Agriculture by Mosanobu Fukuoka

The eminent person Mr. Masanobu Fukuoka wrote a book called one-straw revolution in the year 1975 and translated in many languages. In Tamil it is translated in the name of "Ottrai vaikole puratchi". In this book he clearly narrate his philosophy of agriculture is 'Do-Nothing in farming" It means everything will happen by nature and no need to put more efforts other than human labour.

He believes in Natural Farming and follows the below principles.

- No Plowing or tilling the lands
- No weeding
- No fertilizers
- No pesticides
- No Cutting down the branch of trees

No Plowing: Normally after the cultivation, the farmers plow the land to turn over the upper layer of the soil and bringing the nutrients to the surface. Initially the animals were used to plow the soil but now a day's many machines are doing this job. He personally suggests plowing the land is waste of time and most of the times it helps to grow the unwanted weeds. The soil can be plowed naturally with the help of the earthworms, microorganism and also with the help of the roots.

No Weeding: Weeding will ever help to stop them to grow. He suggests spreading the straw which will prevent the growth of weed at the same time it will act as a good fertilizer.

No Fertilizer: He says using fertilizer is waste of money. He suggests using the animals/birds waste especially the duck and chicken dung are the best. The fertilizers also reduces the nutrient content of the soil

No Pesticides: He took some stone salt and poured on earthworms and it died in a few minutes. When the earthworm that is considered as a friend of farmer not able to tolerate the salt how come they can survive when the powerful pesticides used. He strongly suggest not to use the pesticides because it spoil the soil, the water as well as the agriculture products like vegetables, fruits, grains etc.

No cutting down the branch of trees: Normally the branches of orange trees cut down to make them to grow long but he founds that cutting down the branches will help the foreign particles to attack the tree. Sometimes it may leads to death of the tree. So cutting down the branches should be stopped.

So, his principle clearly stated that "Do Nothing in farming" will give more production.

Agriculture in India

Agriculture is the backbone of Indian economy. The sector plays a vital role in the development of India with over 60 per cent of the country's population deriving their subsistence from it. Most of the industries also depend upon the agriculture sector for their raw materials. In India it's believed that agriculture was begun by 9000 BC and rice was believed to be cultivated during Indus Valley Civilization. Now India is the world's largest producer of coconuts, cashew nuts, ginger, turmeric, banana, custard apple, pulses and black pepper.

Even though India occupy top 10 places in cultivation of many products, it faces food crisis in the mid 60's and thus lead to implementation of Green revolution in India which was led by M.S Swaminathan, which makes the way to implement the ideas of the Noble prize winner Ernest Borlaug in India. This is the time where India launched high yielding varieties of wheat along with the other materials like inorganic fertilizers and pesticides. This led to rapid increase of cereal production and transformed India from a food hungry to self sufficient country but in other hand it also brings many negative impact which we are realizing now in terms of contaminated agriculture products and also increasing in the suicide rate of farmers which is estimated around 3.0L farmers have been committed suicide in last 20 years.

In India there is committee called GEAC – Genetic Engineering Approval Committee. The function of this committee is to test the products of new seeds before it is introduced in the market and give approval if it doesn't cause any illness to the people. But it has approved the BT seeds in India without doing any experiment on the same.

In India Ministry of Agriculture is responsible for development of the agriculture sector in India. This ministry is responsible for formulation and implementation of national policies and program aimed at achieving rapid agriculture growth. This year the ministry has allocated 27K crores for agriculture apart from that 1K crores proposed to continue support to the new green revolution in Eastern States and plan to spend 500 crores to promote technological innovation and motivate farmers to choose crop alternatives in the original green revolution states. This budget clearly shows India majorly supporting the Inorganic agriculture system which was initially promoted by Swaminathan. The same Swaminathan agrees that India can achieve sustainable agriculture growth only in Organic agriculture method not in Inorganic method

Agriculture in Tamilnadu

It is the most predominant sector of the Tamilnadu economy. 70 per cent of the population are engaged in agriculture and allied activities. In recent years, In India more number of farmers is winding up from their occupation and that to its very high in Tamilnadu. There are few poems which says about the agriculture system in Tamilnadu.

This line revealed that during the period of "Karikala Chozhan" the farmers used to yield 4,900 kg of paddy per acre but now in India the average yielding of paddy per acre is 1000 kg and in Tamilnadu it is 1400 kg of per acre. In spite of not using any modern pesticides like Urea, Potash, A.T.P (adenosine tri phosphate), Endosulfan, etc. they yield three to four times more than the current yield. So it clearly shows after investing lot of efforts and money in terms of fertilizer and pesticides the productivity is coming down and this makes the farmers to wind up from their occupation.

When the situation is like this the Tamilnadu government is very keen in implement the Act called Tamilnadu state agricultural council Act, 2009. The Tamilnadu government says that the objective of this act is "At present there is no law to regulate the agricultural practice in Tamilnadu. Therefore it is essential to consider necessary action to regulate the agricultural practice and for the registration of agricultural practitioners in the state and establish a council called Tamilnadu State Agricultural Council"

This act clearly stated that the agriculture knowledge should be shared only to the people who have completed their degree in agriculture in any one of the following universities. The University of Chennai, Tamilnadu agriculture University of Coimbatore, the Annamalai University. This act also says that the person who completes their degree in the above mentioned universities should be registered in "Tamilnadu State Agricultural Practitioners Register" are eligible to discover new things in agriculture, if others do that they will be punished by law. So our organic farmer and traditional farming practitioners like Dr. Nammalvar, Selvam, Sundarraman and many other are not holding this degree not eligible to discover new things in agriculture, if they do so they will be punished by law. The punishment is fine of Rs. 5000 for the first time and it will Rs. 10000 or six months imprisonment or both for the second time. The organic farmers saying that this act is try to wind up the organic agriculture from our country there by, they will introduce all their pesticides, fertilizer and hybrid seeds in the name of development. After a successful struggle from the Tamilnadu farmers the law has been withdrawn from the Tamilnadu government.

The Consequences of Inorganic and Organic Agriculture System

Even though it is believed that the inorganic agriculture system increase the productivity it's mandatory to see the quality of the product and how it affects the environment. There are many environmentalist talks about the consequences of Inorganic Agriculture system and Ms. Rachel Carson is one among the famous environmentalist. Her thoughts about the Inorganic Agriculture system is mentioned below

Rachel Carson

The Marine biologist Rachel Carson clearly explains how the synthetic fertilizer and pesticides causes the environmental damage in the book called "Silent Spring". This book was translated in Thamizh as "Mauna Vasantham". This led to launching of many environmental movements. In her book she revealed the reason for wash out of a bird species called "robin". It is described on next page.

She also adds the pesticides not only kill the pest but also the human beings. The substances accumulate in the tissues of plants and animals, penetrate the germ cells and alter the very material of hereditary upon which the shape of the future depends. So these substances should not be called as pesticides or insecticides, they should be called as "biocides". For the first time in the history of world every human being is now subjected to contact with dangerous chemicals, from the moment of conception until death. The chemical are now stored in the bodies of the vast majority of human beings regardless of age. They occur in the mother's milk and probably in the tissue of unborn child.

The trees affected with diseases

↓

DDT (Dichloro diphenyl tri chloro ethane) a synthetic Pesticides was sprayed on the tree

↓

The pesticide dew and rain water and adulterated into the soil

↓

The leaves which fell on the earth contain the pesticides and pollute the soil

↓

The earthworm who lives in the soil takes the contaminated leaves and gets contaminated with the pesticides

↓

The bird which takes the contaminated earthworm leads to death.

Conclusion

The inorganic farming may increase the yield of agriculture products but it compromises in the quality and that leads to many biological problems for all the species in this earth. Even the polar bears that live in the polar region get affected because of pesticides. The earth lost many species because of the pesticides which was clearly explained by many environmentalists like Rachel Carson. The increase in the usage of inorganic farming is also one reason for increasing in farmer suicide in India. Most of the European countries banned the hybrid seeds because it is not good for health. The MNC companies who involves in the manufacture of hybrid seed and pesticides and other requirement of agriculture's tries to control the agriculture system of all the countries. Some of the examples are in Iraq the Article 21 says that the farmers should not use the indigenous seeds if they do so they will punished by the law. So this insists them to use the products of Multinational companies. So it's right time for us to think our agriculture system in our country

REFERENCES

Vivasayam – Oru Arimugam by Veerakumar in 2008.

Tamilnadu Velanmandra Sattam by Dr. Nammalvar in 2011.

One Straw Revolution by Mosanobu Fukuoko in 2008.

The Silent Spring by Rachel Carson

Changing Scenario of Agriculture in India Since 1947

Miss Anusree Krishna Mandal

ABSTRACT

The changing scenario has recorded that the agriculture becomes more as a business proposition than merely tradition at least in the agriculturally progressive states. The traditional agriculture, which was a way of life of the majority of Indian farmers, has gradually shrunken to fewer pockets. India adopted significant policy reforms focused on the goal of foodgrain self-sufficiency. This ushered in India's Green Revolution. It began with the decision to adopt superior yielding, disease resistant wheat varieties in combination with better farming knowledge to improve productivity. Even though, India has shown remarkable progress in recent years and has attained self-sufficiency in food staples, the productivity of Indian farms for the same crop is very low compared to farms in Brazil, the United States, France and other nations.

Introduction

The changing scenario has recorded that the agriculture becomes more as a business proposition than merely tradition at least in the agriculturally progressive states. The traditional agriculture, which was a way of life of the majority of Indian farmers, has gradually shrunken to fewer pockets. It is rightly believed that the traditional farming was consistent for cropping patterns, mixed crop composition, cultivation practices, etc., and it was based on the hereditary and the community level experiences. In terms of subsistence, the traditional agriculture ensured the farming families more or less self-sufficiency because of an array of harvests even though individual commodities harvested were little in quantities. The farmer did not have to pay for these commodities in the local market. Rather they sometimes earned a little profit by selling their marginal surplus in the weekly haats (Singh, 2004).

Indian Agriculture Since 1947

Over 50 years since its independence, India has made immense progress towards food security. Indian population has tripled, but food-grain production more than quadrupled: there has thus been substantial increase in available food-grain per capita.

Prior to the mid-1960s India relied on imports and food aid to meet domestic requirements. However, two years of severe drought in 1965 and 1966 convinced India to reform its agricultural policy, and that India could not rely on foreign aid and foreign imports for food security. India adopted significant policy reforms focused on the goal of foodgrain self-sufficiency. This ushered in India's Green Revolution. It began with the decision to adopt superior yielding, disease resistant wheat varieties in combination with better farming knowledge to improve productivity. The Indian state of Punjab led India's green revolution and earned itself the distinction of being the country's bread basket.

The initial increase in production was centred on the irrigated areas of the Indian states of Punjab, Haryana and western Uttar Pradesh. With both the farmers and the government officials focusing on farm productivity and knowledge transfer, India's total foodgrain production soared. A hectare of Indian wheat farms that produced an average of 0.8 tonnes in 1948, produced 4.7 tonnes of wheat in 1975 from the same land. Such rapid growths in farm productivity enabled India to become self-sufficient by the 1970s. It also empowered the smallholder farmers to seek further means to increase food staples produced per hectare. By 2000, Indian farms were adopting wheat varieties capable of yielding 6 tonnes of wheat per hectare.

India and China are competing to establish the world record on rice yields. Yuan Longping of China National Hybrid Rice Research and Development Centre, China, set a world record for rice yield in 2010 at 19 tonnes per hectare in a demonstration plot. In 2011, this record was surpassed by an Indian farmer, Sumant Kumar, with 22.4 tonnes per hectare in Bihar, also in a demonstration plot. Both these farmers claim to have employed newly developed rice breeds and System of Rice Intensification (SRI), a recent innovation in rice farming. The claimed Chinese and Indian yields have yet to be demonstrated on 7 hectare farm lots and that these are reproducible over two consecutive years on the same farm (Yuan, 2010 and World Bank: "India Country Overview 2008").

Draw Backs of Agriculture

India lacks cold storage, food packaging as well as safe and efficient rural transport system. This causes one of the world's highest food spoilage rates, particularly during Indian monsoons and other adverse weather conditions. Food travels to the Indian consumer through a slow and inefficient chain of traders. Indian consumers buy agricultural produce in suburban markets known as 'sabzi mandi' such as one shown or from roadside vendors.

Indian agriculture includes a mix of traditional to modern farming techniques. In some parts of India, traditional use of cattle to plough farms remains in use. Traditional farms have some of the lowest per capita productivities and farmer incomes.

"Slow agricultural growth is a concern for policymakers as some two-thirds of India's people depend on rural employment for a living. Current agricultural practices are neither economically nor environmentally sustainable and India's yields for many agricultural commodities are low. Poorly maintained irrigation systems and almost universal lack of good extension services are among the factors responsible. Farmers' access to markets is hampered by poor roads, rudimentary market infrastructure, and excessive regulation."—World Bank: "India Country Overview 2008".

A 2003 analysis of India's agricultural growth from 1970 to 2001, by Food and Agriculture Organisation of the United Nations, identified systemic problems in Indian agriculture. For food staples, the annual growth rate in production during the six-year segments 1970-76, 1976-82, 1982-88, 1988-1994, 1994-2000 were found to be respectively 2.5, 2.5, 3.0, 2.6, and 1.8 per cent per annum. Corresponding analyses for the index of total agricultural production show a similar pattern, with the growth rate for 1994-2000 attaining only 1.5 per cent per annum. The low growth rates may constitute in part a response to inadequate returns to Indian farmers. India has very poor rural roads affecting timely supply of inputs and timely transfer of outputs from Indian farms, inadequate irrigation systems, crop failures in some parts of the country because of lack of water while in other parts because of regional floods, poor seed quality and inefficient farming practices in certain parts of India, lack of cold storage and harvest spoilage causing over 30 per cent of farmer's produce going to waste, lack of organised retail and competing buyers thereby limiting Indian farmer's ability to sell the surplus and commercial crops. The Indian farmer receives just 10 to 23 per cent of the price the Indian consumer pays for exactly the same produce, the difference going to losses, inefficiencies and middlemen traders. Farmers in developed economies of Europe and the United States, in contrast, receive 64 to 81 per cent of the price the local consumer pays for exactly the same produce in their supermarkets.

Even though, India has shown remarkable progress in recent years and has attained self-sufficiency in food staples, the productivity of Indian farms for the same crop is very low compared to farms in Brazil, the United States, France and other nations. Indian wheat farms, for example, produce about a third of wheat per hectare per year in contrast with wheat farms in France. Similarly, at 44 million hectares, India had the largest farm area under rice production in 2009; yet, the rice farm productivity in India was less than half the rice farm productivity in China. Other food staples productivity in India is similarly low, suggesting a major opportunity for growth and future agricultural prosperity potential in India. Indian total factor productivity growth remains below 2 per cent per annum; in contrast, China has shown total factor productivity growths of about 6 per cent per annum, even though China too has smallholding farmers. If India could adopt technologies and improve its infrastructure, several studies suggest India could eradicate hunger and malnutrition within India, and be a major source of food for the world.

Indian farms are not poor performing for every crop. For some, Indian farms post the best yields. For example, some of India's regions consistently post some of the highest yields for sugarcane, cassava and tea crops every year (Wikipedia, the free encyclopedia).

One study suggests Indian agricultural policy should best focus on improving rural infrastructure primarily in form of irrigation and flood control infrastructure, knowledge transfer in forms of better yielding and more disease resistant seeds with the goal of sustainably producing as many kilograms of food staples per hectare as already produced sustainably in other nations. Additionally, cold storage, hygienic food packaging and efficient modern retail to reduce waste can also dramatically improve India's agricultural output availability and rural incomes (Renuka, 2003).

Reason for Low Productivity: The low productivity in India is a result of the following factors:

- The average size of land holdings is very small (less than 2 hectares) and is subject to fragmentation due to land ceiling acts, and in some cases, family disputes. Such small holdings are often over-manned, resulting in disguised unemployment and low productivity of labour. Some reports claim that small holder farming may not cause poor productivity, since the productivity is higher in China and many developing economies even though China smallholder farmers constitute over 97 per cent of its farming population. Chinese smallholder farmer is able to rent his land to larger farmers, China's organised retail and extensive Chinese highways are able to provide the incentive and infrastructure necessary to its farmers for sharp increases in farm productivity.

- Adoption of modern agricultural practices and use of technology is inadequate, hampered by ignorance of such practices, high costs and impracticality in the case of small land holdings.
- According to the World Bank, Indian Branch: Priorities for Agriculture and Rural Development", India's large agricultural subsidies are hampering productivity-enhancing investment. Overregulation of agriculture has increased costs, price risks and uncertainty. Government intervenes in labour, land, and credit markets. India has inadequate infrastructure and services. World Bank also says that the allocation of water is inefficient, unsustainable and inequitable. The irrigation infrastructure is deteriorating. The overuse of water is currently being covered by over pumping aquifers, but as these are falling by foot of groundwater each year, this is a limited resource.
- Illiteracy, general socio-economic backwardness, slow progress in implementing land reforms and inadequate or inefficient finance and marketing services for farm produce.
- Inconsistent government policy. Agricultural subsidies and taxes often changed without notice for short term political ends.
- Farmers' access to markets is hampered by poor roads, rudimentary market infrastructure, excessive regulation

and middlemen intervention in selling the products is very big problem in marketing the products. Hence the Indian farmers need easily accessible and highly structured markets with out middleman interventions.

Irrigation facilities are inadequate, as revealed by the fact that only 52.6 per cent of the land was irrigated in 2003-04, which result in farmers still being dependent on rainfall, specifically the Monsoon season. A good monsoon results in a robust growth for the economy as a whole, while a poor monsoon leads to a sluggish growth. Farm credit is regulated by NABARD, which is the statutory apex agent for rural development in the subcontinent. At the same time overpumping made possible by subsidised electric power is leading to an alarming drop in aquifer levels.

- A third of all food that is produced rots due to inefficient supply chains and the use of the "Walmart model" to improve efficiency is blocked by laws against foreign investment in the retail sector.
- The Indian Agricultural Research Institute (IARI), established in 1905, was responsible for the search leading to the "Indian Green Revolution" of the 1970s. The Indian Council of Agricultural Research (ICAR) is the apex body in agriculture and related allied fields, including research and education. The Union Minister of Agriculture is the President of the ICAR. The Indian Agricultural Statistics Research Institute develops new techniques for the design of agricultural experiments, analyses data in agriculture, and specialises in statistical techniques for animal and plant breeding.
- Recently Government of India has set up Farmers Commission to completely evaluate the agriculture programme. However the recommendations have had a mixed reception.
- In November 2011, India announced major reforms in organised retail. These reforms would include logistics and retail of agricultural produce. The reform

announcement led to major political controversy. The reforms were placed on hold by the Indian government in December 2011.

Similarly, in tribal areas, the combinations generally seen are trees, cereallegume mixed cropping, cows and/or goats and poultry. These farming systems have developed on the perceptions of men and women farmers, tribals and agropastoralists over the generations. It has been observed that in the semi-arid to arid areas or when the rains fail, income from livestock is the main farm income. In tribal areas, small ruminants replace the livestock, which is semidomesticated rather than being stall-fed. Further, in the better rainfall areas, there is shift towards buffalo. The majority of tribal families, and the underprivileged community in general, rear poultry in the traditional backyard system. The main developmental concern in these systems, however, is the verification of improved local technology and its delivery system.

Water is another important vital resource for economic development. At the global level, three-fourth of the earth's surface is covered with water and the total water resources amount to 1385.5 million km^3, comprising 97.3 per cent as salt water and 2.7 per cent as fresh water. Of the latter, 75.2 per cent occurs as polar ice and glaciers, 22.6 per cent as ground water, 1.9 per cent as soil moisture and atmospheric vapour, and 0.3 per cent in lakes and rivers. This indicates that very limited water is available for domestic, industrial and agricultural use. Fresh water is finite but renewable through continued hydrologic cycling. India is one of the well-endowed countries in terms of annual rainfall and has about 4 per cent of the world's fresh water resources. It is projected that the present per capita per annum water availability of 2001 m) will reduce to stress level of 1700 m) in the next 2 to 3 decades. Further the projected reduction in water availability to the agricultural sector from the present share of 89 to about 75 per cent by 2020 would adversely affect our capacity to produce more food. Future gains in agricultural productivity depend upon integrated development and utilization of surface and ground water resources. The indiscriminate use of canal water is leading to waterlogging and salinization in the major irrigated commands. The increased ground water extraction has declined water table at an alarming rate, putting an additional burden on farmers in terms of investments, equipments and energy. Further, it is estimated that even after achieving the full irrigation potential, nearly 50 per cent of the total cultivated area will remain rainfed in the country (Singh, 2004).

Globalization, as a consequence of WTO, linked with the international trade liberalization, opening up of economies, and a free flow of capital, labour, information and technology is a major paradigm shift making significant changes in the world economy. It has a considerable potential to significantly influence both the food/nutritional security and poverty for better or worse, but its implications and consequences are not yet fully understood (Singh, 2004).

Challenges of Agriculture

The challenges in the agricultural sector at present are quite different from those met in the previous decades. The enormous pressure to produce more food from less land with shrinking natural resources is a tough task for the farmers. This calls for spe-cial efforts to manage the key inputs without eroding the ecological assets and sound knowledge base to sustain agricultural productivity and profitability.

The recent trends in globalization and increased interest in factory and corporate farming should not be al-lowed to jeopardize the role of millions of small and marginal farmers and land-less agriculturists who form the back-bone of the agricultural economy in India. Their interests should be protected. This could only be made possible by empowering the farmers with the new techniques and skills that foster sustainable agriculture.

The "information revolution" that has brought about remarkable changes in the industrial sector will prove to be an ideal tool for achieving the goal of knowledge and skill development among farmers. Simplified versions of information technology backed by easy-to-follow text and illustrations highlighting environmentally benign agricultural technologies would prove to be a low cost and powerful tool in im-parting training to the farmers.

Such well designed information tech-nology package can help serve as a market information network, weather, pest and disease monitoring system and can be a storehouse of various farming technologies and practices in vogue. Setting up of "information kiosks" with computer network in dif-ferent clusters of villages will form the foundations of a meaningful extension.

Vision for 2020: The President of India, A.P.J. Abdul Kalam, outlined his vision for making India an economically empowered nation by the year 2020 and gave out specific solutions to tackle long-standing problems of the poor. (The Hindu 6th August, 2004). The President drew up a seven-point plan of action for promot-ing the interests of farmers which included the creation of cooperatives in major centers involving Government, NGOs, Consultancy services, R & D Organizations and people as partners for the dissemination of the vital informa-tion such as soil nature, water availability, crops that can be raised, fertilizer to be used, arrival of monsoon, combating natural calamities, availability of finance, critical inputs, value addition, marketing, crop insurance etc.

Agri-portal kiosk: Agri-portal kiosk is an internet cafe that provides infor-mation on agriculture and its allied activities. It is designed to address the specific needs of the rural farming com-munity and catalyze e-commerce in agricultural and non-farm products by offering a network of partnerships in the areas of Content, Connectivity and Commerce.

Weather information: local weather forecasts to help farmers decide agricultural operations.

Best agricultural practices: Infor-mation for farmers to increase their productivity - area specific crops and its varieties, fertilizers, pesticides etc.

Market information: Options to ex-plore world demand, crop prices, world production, 'mandi' trading volume, and 'mandi' price list.

Q & A forum (FAQs): The website provides an interactive feature, which allows the farmer to ask a question and have it answered by the appropriate panel of experts.

News page: The website holds ex-cerpts of relevant news items, including Government decisions on subsidies or minimum support prices (MSPs) and in-novation in other countries. Local news pertaining to farmers' successes is also posted. The Government, NGOs, Public or Private Agribusiness Corporations may own these kiosks. Some of the suc-cessful agri-portal kiosks are listed below:

1. It should be multi-dimensional in nature, addressing problems of rural communities in holistic manner cover-ing all aspects of rural life including agriculture, human/animal health, education, banking, governance, enter-tainment etc.
2. The existing agencies of knowledge dissemination in the country such as Indian Council of Agricultural Research Institute (ICAR), State Agricultural Universities (SAUs), Krishi Vigyan Kendras (KVKs), National Information Centres and other non-government and private sector institu-tions need to be networked rather than creating a new institution. This would result in sharing the available information/knowledge and transmitting it freely to the end users.
3. Suitable mechanisms need to be developed for the creation of location specific knowledge capsules in the form of CD-ROMs, Portals, Kiosks, etc. through in-volvement of specialized institutions.
4. Complexities in the second- generation agriculture would require greater role of emerging ICT tools and methods in complementing the existing extension system. This would require capacity building of extension functionaries for the transfer of knowledge without dissemination losses to the end users.
5. Enthusiastic young entrepreneurs may be encouraged to run Rural Information Clinics or Rural Internet Chaupals.

This would offer employment opportunities to the rural youth. They may be (*a*) trained as ICT agents by the State Agricultural Univer-sities (SAU) and ICAR institutions and (*b*) supported financially by NABARD, SBI and other financial institutions) (Rani, 2007).

Farmer Suicides

Following the liberalising economic reforms of 1991 the government withdrew support from the agricultural sector (Balakrishnan P et. al., 2008). These reforms, along with other factors, led to a rise in farmer suicides. Various studies identify the important factors as the withdrawal of government support, insufficient or risky credit systems, the difficulty of farming semi-arid regions, poor agricultural income, absence of alternative income opportunities, a downturn in the urban economy which forced non-farmers into farming, and the absence of suitable counseling services (Mishra, 2007).

The required level of investment for the development of marketing, storage and cold storage infrastructure is estimated to be huge. The government has not been able to implement various schemes to raise investment in marketing infrastructure. Among these schemes are *Construction of Rural Godowns, Market Research and Information Network,* and *Development/Strengthening of Agricultural Marketing Infrastructure, Grading and Standardisation.*

The Indian Agricultural Research Institute (IARI), established in 1905, was responsible for the search leading to the "Indian Green Revolution" of the 1970s. The Indian Council of Agricultural Research (ICAR) is the apex body in agriculture and related allied fields, including research and education. The Union Minister of Agriculture is the President of the ICAR. The Indian Agricultural Statistics Research Institute develops new techniques for the design of agricultural experiments, analyses data in agriculture, and specialises in statistical techniques for animal and plant breeding.

Recently Government of India has set up Farmers Commission to completely evaluate the agriculture programme. However the recommendations have had a mixed reception.

In November 2011, India announced major reforms in organised retail. These reforms would include logistics and retail of agricultural produce. The reform announcement led to major political controversy. The reforms were placed on hold by the Indian government in December 2011.

In the summer of 2012, the subsidised electricity for pumping, which has caused an alarming drop in aquifer levels, put additional strain on the country's electrical grid due to a 19 per cent drop in monsoon rains, and may have helped contribute to a blackout across much of the country. In response the state of Bihar offered farmers over $100 million in subsidised diesel to operate their pumps.

REFERENCES

Balakrishnan P *et. al.* (2008): Agricultural Growth in India Since 1991, Reserve Bank of India, Mumbai

Directorate of Wheat Research (2011): "Brief History of Wheat Improvement in India", ICAR India.

Guillaume P. Gruère, Purvi Mehta-Bhatt and Debdatta Sengupta (2008): "Bt Cotton and Farmer Suicides in India: Reviewing the Evidence", International Food Policy Research Institute.

Mahadevan, Renuka (2003): "Productivity Growth in Indian Agriculture: The Role of Globalisation and Economic Reform", Asia-Pacific Development Journal, December, 10 (2): 57-72.

Mishra, Srijit (2007): "Risks, Farmers' Suicides and Agrarian Crisis in India: Is There A Way Out?". Indira Gandhi Institute of Development Research (IGIDR).

Panjab Singh (2004): "Indian Agricultural Development in Changing Scenario Past, Present and Future", Journal of The Indian Society of Agricultural Statistics.

Rani, Pushpa (2007): "Agri-Portal Kiosk: A Tool to 'Information Hungry "Farmers", Southern Conomist, Vol. 46, No. 6, Bangalore, p. 7-8.

Yuan, L.P. (2010). "A Scientist's Perspective on Experience with SRI in CHINA for Raising the Yields of Super Hybrid Rice".

Web Sites

Scientificamerican.com. Retrieved 2011-09-17.

Books.google.com. 2004-11-01. ISBN 9781597268936. Retrieved 2011-09-17.

"India Country Overview 2008". World Bank. 2008.

(http://www.preservearticles.com/201106168058/irrigation-importance.html and Directorate of Wheat Research, 2011).

Nature and Performance of Self-help Groups (SHGs) Promoted Under Agricultural Technology Management Agency (ATMA) Programme in Nagaland

Sanjoy Das
N.K. Patra

ABSTRACT

The group provides women, a base for self-employment and empowerment through group dynamics. In India the mutual help based groups are known as self help group. This approach aims at inculcating the habits of saving even in small amounts, supplemented by borrowing from outside sources and rotation of saved and borrowed funds by lending within the group. The results from SHGs are promising and it helps significantly in reducing poverty in present days. Out of different organisations supporting for SHG formation, ATMA programme is one of the important ones in supporting and sponsoring of SHGs for rural livelihood improvement.

Introduction

Self Help Group (SHG) plays a very vital and critical role especially towards empowering women in almost all the fields. In recent years the group approach to various poverty alleviation programmes is getting recognition in India. Mostly, women are mobilized into groups for undertaking mutually beneficial social and economic activities. The group provides women, a base for self-employment and empowerment through group dynamics. In India the mutual help based groups are known as self help group. It is being realized in India that SHGs can establish relationship between the formal institutions and the poor for providing information, credit and other facilities. It has been very well established that providing finance to the poor after organizing them into homogenous group commonly known as SHGs have given statutory results in India and other developing countries, especially among the rural poor women. Group approach to poverty alleviation is gaining momentum in India and other developing countries. This approach aims at inculcating the habits of saving even in small amounts, supplemented by borrowing from outside sources and rotation of saved and borrowed funds by lending within the group. The SHGs generally have members 8-20 and each group selects among its members a leader called animator.

A new extension reform programme "Support to State Extension Programmes for Extension Reforms" in the name of ATMA (Agricultural Technology Management Agency) was launched in the country during 2005-06 by the Department of Agriculture and Cooperation (DAC), Ministry of Agriculture, Govt. of India to make extension system more farmer driven and farmer accountable. Among the different cafeteria of activities under the programme, one most important thrust area was mobilisation of farmers groups in the name of SHGs, FIGs, CIGs etc. Every year under the ATMA programme, a considerable amount was spent for constitution of SHGs for economic upliftment of their members through skill up-gradation and capacity building programmes. In Nagaland also ATMA programme has been operational since 2005-06 with variety of cafeteria of activities. Keeping in view the faulty system of agricultural extension programme in the past, new extension reform programme in the name of ATMA was introduced to disseminate agriculture and allied technologies in the hands of farmers.

Research Methodology

This manuscript was prepared based on master's level research work carried out at Nagaland University, Nagaland, India. Study was carried out at Dimapur District, an important district of North Eastern States Nagaland, India where ATMA programme was in operational since 2005-06. It was tried to study the nature and performance SHGs promoted under ATMA programme in Dimapur district of Nagaland State. Two blocks viz. Niuland and Medziphema were selected purposively for this study out of total four blocks in the district, as these are the most representing blocks to carried out the present study. From each block 10 SHGs were selected randomly that are sponsored or supported by ATMA and from 1 SHG, 4 member beneficiaries were selected as respondent. Altogether 80 respondents were selected from 20 SHGs for the study and due consideration was given on selection of SHGs, so that SHGs with less than 3 years of existence could not be taken into consideration. Primary data were collected pertaining to year 2010-11 from sample respondents.Year 2005-06 was considered as base year and 2010-11 as current year.

Results and Discussion

One important activity of ATMA programme is the formation of Self Help Groups (SHGs) for the economic upliftment of its members. Since the beginning of the ATMA programme in 2005 -06, ATMA Nagaland had started to form SHGs including persons from various social groups.

Nature of SHGs According to Gender Category, Member Strength and Saving Pattern

Table 12.1 indicates the gender category, member strength and saving pattern of the selected 20 SHGs (10 from each block) under study. The significant development was that 90 per cent SHGs belonged to female only against 'nil' for male. The rest 10 per cent SHGs belonged to category of mixed members.

Table 12.1: Nature of SHGs According to Gender Category, Member Strength and Saving Pattern

Sl. No.	Name of the Block	No. of SHGs	Gender Category			Member Strength		Saving rate per member		
			Male	Female	Mixed	Upto 10	10-15	Less than Rs. 50/- month	Rs. 50/- month	Rs. 100/- month
1.	Medziphema	10	0	9 (90.0)	1 (10.0)	8 (80.0)	2 (20.0)	3 (30.0)	4 (40.0)	3 (30.0)
2.	Niuland	10	0	9 (90.0)	1 (10.0)	3 (30.0)	7 (70.0)	1 (10.0)	4 (40.0)	5 (50.0)
	Total	20	0 (00.0)	18 (90.0)	2 (10.0)	11 (55.0)	9 (45.0)	4 (20.0)	8 (40.0)	8 (40.0)

Figures in parentheses indicate per cent to total

Table 12.1 also indicates that 55.0 per cent SHGs had member upto 10 members and rest 45.0 per cent had member strength between 10-15 members. However, block level information indicates some differences among the two selected blocks. In Medziphema block, 80 per cent SHGs had member upto 10 numbers and rest 20 per cent had between 10-15 members. On the other hand, in Niuland, 30 per cent SHGs had upto10 members and rest 70 per cent had between 10-15 members. As for the saving pattern followed, 40 per cent SHGs followed contribution pattern of Rs. 50 per month followed by 40 per cent SHGs with contribution pattern of Rs. 100 per month and the rest 20 per cent with contribution pattern of less than Rs. 50 per month.

Nature of SHGs Based on Linked Bank

Table 12.2 indicates the nature of SHGs based on linked bank by these SHGs. It was observed that all the SHGs were linked to some banking institutions. Most common linked bank was SBI (50%), followed by UBI (30%). Some other banks involved as linked bank to SHGs are Vijaya bank, Syndicate bank, Bank of Baroda and Cooperative bank (5% each). Although banking infrastructure in Nagaland is not good, the two blocks under study were seen little developed in banking infrastructure. On the other hand, the role of cooperative bank as well as rural bank was found less significant in this respect.

Nature of SHGs Based on Disbursement of Revolving Fund

Revolving fund or seed money is one of the important inputs provided to SHGs as one time assistance to take up some productive activities. Table 12.3 indicates the status of SHGs based on disbursement of revolving fund. Eighty per cent SHGs under study had got revolving fund to starts some productive activities. Among the two blocks, in Medziphema 90 per cent SHGs had got revolving fund against 70 per cent for Niuland block.

Table 12.2: Nature of SHGs According to Linked Bank

Sl. No.	Name of the Block	No. of SHGs	Number of SHGs with Linked Bank					
			SBI	Vijaya Bank	UBI	Syndicate Bank	Bank of Baroda	Co-operative Bank
1.	Medziphema	10	4	0	5	0	1	0
2.	Niuland	10	6	1	1	1	0	1
	Total	20	10	1	6	1	1	1
			(50.0)	(5.0)	(30.0)	(5.0)	(5.0)	(5.0)

Figures in parentheses indicate per cent to total.

Table 12.3: Nature of SHGs Based on Disbursement of Revolving Fund

Sl. No.	Name of the Block	No. of SHGs	Number of SHGs Received Revolving Fund	
			Frequency	Per cent
1.	Medziphema	10	9	90.0
2.	Niuland	10	7	70.0
	Total	20	16	80.0

Nature of SHGs Based on Major Activities Undertaken

Table 12.4 shows the classification of SHGs according to major activities undertaken. In Medziphema block, the study showed that 30.0 per cent of the SHGs were involved in activities such as horticulture + sericulture and sericulture + livestock, whereas in Niuland block majority of the groups were involved in agriculture + horticulture activities followed by agriculture + livestock, horticulture + sericulture, and agriculture + horticulture + fishery.

Nature of SHGs According to Training Exposure Under ATMA

Table 12.5 indicates status of SHGs based on training exposure. Mostly SHGs were exposed to various activities on agriculture, horticulture, sericulture, livestock, fishery etc. by the ATMA programme. In case of Medziphema block, highest number of SHGs (90%) attended sericulture related training, followed by agriculture (80%), livestock (80%) and horticulture (60%). Table 12.5 also indicates that altogether 145 numbers of participants had participated in the above cited training. On the basis of number of participants, agriculture had represented the highest (25.52%), followed by sericulture (22.76%), livestock (20.69%), horticulture (19.31%) and fishery (11.72%). In case of Niuland block also, almost similar picture was visible in relation to training area. In Niuland block, altogether 143 participants participated in the various training programmes, out of which highest was on agriculture (26.57%), followed by livestock (24.48%), sericulture (18.18%) etc.

Table 12.4: Nature of SHGs According to Activities Undertaken

Sl. No.	Name of the Block	No. of SHGs	Major Activities Undertaken	No. of SHGs Involved
1.	Medziphema	10	Agriculture + Horticulture	2 (20.0)
			Agriculture + Livestock	1 (10.0)
			Horticulture + Sericulture	3 (30.0)
			Sericulture+ Livestock	3 (30.0)
			Agri. + Horti. + Fishery	1 (10.0)
2.	Niuland	10	Agriculture + Horticulture	3 (30.0)
			Agriculture + Livestock	2 (20.0)
			Horticulture + Sericulture	2 (20.0)
			Sericulture+ Livestock	1 (10.0)
			Agri. + Horti. + Fishery	2 (20.0)
3.	Total	20	Agriculture + Horticulture	5 (25.0)
			Agriculture + Livestock	3 (15.0)
			Horticulture + Sericulture	5 (25.0)
			Sericulture+ Livestock	4 (20.0)
			Agri. + Horti. + Fishery	3 (15.0)

Figures in parentheses indicate per cent to total.

In the district, as a whole the major activities undertaken were identified as agriculture + horticulture (25%) and horticulture + sericulture (25%), followed by sericulture + livestock (20%).

Income and Employment Status of SHGs Beneficiaries

After introduction of ATMA programme in the district, SHG members were exposed to various activities and accordingly they adopted some of the techniques/ technologies in their field. Table 12.6 indicates the changes in monthly average income of the beneficiaries after they have joined in the programme. Income and employment status of the beneficiaries' farmers was studies with the help of categories of farmers based on land holding. Average monthly income recorded an increase for all categories of farmers after

ATMA programme in both the blocks, however average monthly income found to be less in case of marginal and small farmers. Among the two blocks, respondents of Medziphema block recorded a bit higher average monthly income for all the categories of respondents except for marginal as compared to Niuland block.

Table 12.5: Nature of SHGs According to Training Exposure

Sl. No.	Name of the Block	No. of SHGs	Training Area Under ATMA	No. of SHGs Participated	No. of Participants
1.	Medziphema	10	Agriculture	8 (80.0)	37 (25.52)
			Horticulture	6 (60.0)	28 (19.31)
			Livestock	8 (80.0)	30 (20.69)
			Fishery	6 (60.0)	17 (11.72)
			Sericulture	9 (90.0)	33 (22.76)
			Total		145 (100.0)
2.	Niuland	10	Agriculture	7 (70.0)	38 (26.57)
			Horticulture	7 (70.0)	23 (16.08)
			Livestock	8 (80.0)	35 (24.48)
			Fishery	7 (70.0)	21 (14.69)
			Sericulture	9 (90.0)	26 (18.18)
			Total		143 (100.0)

In terms of percentage increase in income after ATMA, for all categories, Medziphema block recorded better position compared to Niuland block.

The impact of ATMA on income level of the sample respondents was studied by calculating t-statistic and a significant t-statistic value of 23.2 at 1 per cent probability level indicated a significant increase of income after ATMA programme. The mean of average scores were found as 3613 and 3995 respectively for before ATMA and after ATMA.Changes in Employment Status of SHG Members

Table 12.7 indicates the change in employment level (in man days) of sample respondents after the implementation of ATMA programme in various activities. On an average 504.3 man days were created before ATMA started in the district, it remained same even after the implementation of the programme.

Table 12.6: Average Monthly Income of Sample SHGs Beneficiaries at Block Level

Sl. No.	Name of the Block	Category of Respondents (according to land holding)	No. of Respondents	Average Monthly Income (Rs.)		Per cent Increase
				Before ATMA	After ATMA	
1.	Medziphema	Landless	0	0	0	0
		Marginal (< 1 ha)	13	1535	1940	26.4
		Small (1-2 ha)	14	2942	3387	15.1
		Medium (2-10 ha)	12	5084	5627	10.7
		Large (> 10 ha)	1	7100	7540	6.2
2.	Niuland	Landless	0	0	0	0
		Marginal (< 1 ha)	3	1717	1947	13.4
		Small (1-2 ha)	15	2827	3182	12.6
		Medium (2-10 ha)	17	4516	4791	6.1
		Large (> 10 ha)	5	7090	7372	4.0

Table 12.7: Changes on Employment Status of SHG Members (in man days)

Sl. No.	Enterprise	Before ATMA		After ATMA		Increase/decrease in employment
		Employment	%	Employment	%	Employment
1.	Agriculture	134.5	26.7	130.7	25.92	-3.8
2.	Horticulture	67.25	13.3	68.25	13.53	1
3.	Livestock	100.8	20	101.4	20.11	0.6
4.	Fishery	67.25	13.3	67.65	13.41	0.4
5.	Others	134.5	26.7	136.3	27.03	1.8
	Total	504.3	100	504.3	100	

It indicates that over all there was no change on employment after the implementation of the programme in the district. However, there was a change on creation of man days at activity level. In case of agriculture aspect, number of man days reduced to 130.7 from 134.5 after ATMA started in the district. However, there was an increase of man days in horticulture, livestock, fishery and other activities in the district after the implementation of the programme.

Conclusion

SHG concept originated from Grameen Bank of Bangladesh is performing as one of best form of micro finance programme in India. The results from SHGs are promising and it helps significantly in reducing poverty in present days. Out of different organisations supporting for SHG formation, ATMA programme is one of the important ones in supporting and sponsoring of SHGs for rural livelihood improvement. In Nagaland, specially in Dimapur district SHGs are women based and most of them were linked to financial institutions. Because of ATMA programme, members were benefited in terms of different activities; prominent in income and employment generation.

REFERENCES

Self-help Groups: A Keystone of Microfinance in India – Women Empowerment & Social Security; CS Reddy, APMAS CEO, Sandeep Manak, APMAS Intern.

NABARD 1998 SHG Bank Linkage Programme, Status As on March 31, 1998, NABARD, Mumbai.

NABARD 1999 SHG Bank Linkage Programme, Status As on March 31, 1999, NABARD, Mumbai.

Bora, Pallabi and Talukdar, R.K. 2012 Functioning and Sustainability of Women Self-Help Groups of Assam: An Analysis Based On Credit System and Income Generation, *Indian Res. J.Ext.Edu.*12(2): 107-112.

Environment and Changing Agricultural Scenario in North East India

Mrs. Archana Mandal

ABSTRACT

In spite of the population explosion, it is possible to substantially augment the carrying capacity of the land, doubled or even tripled the food grain production and achieved rapid industrialization to provide economic security and improve the quality of life of the people of North East India. Since the planning period starts, stress has always been laid on the production of food grains to meet the requirements of the increased population. In this respect of North Eastern India it can not be compared with all other states of Indian Federation as growth of population is most alarming in this region due to immigration from neighbouring border countries and the flow of population to this region from other states of Indian Union. This problem of food insecurity can be linked with the backwardness in agricultural development.

Keynotes: Population explosion, food grain production, rapid industrialization, food insecurity and agricultural development.

Introduction

The North Eastern India (NEI) comprises seven states of Indian Territory forming 7.8 per cent of the total land area and about 4 per cent of the total population of the country. More than 70 per cent of total geographical area of NEI is covered by hills and about 3 million hectares are estimated to be under soil erosion hazard as a result of practice of jhum cultivation. In Assam alone, 83.2 per cent of area are suffered from erosion of slight (35.3 p.c.), moderate (37.7 p.c.), severe (10.0 p.c.) and very severe (0.3 p.c.) intensity. Improvement of soil conservation and soil fertility is a critical component of low income people. Traditionally, agriculture has been the mainstay of people of this region but the agro-based economy fails to flourish as it should have due to lack of proper involvement and utilization of technological aids. As a result, the stamp of 'backwardness' has been attached to this region suffering from food scarcity, while the country moves ahead from its target of production to food surplus in different phases of the Post-Independence era. Increasing the yield of crop in a complex system and in an environmentally positive manner is a challenge that will not be easy to meet in the region.

NEI is dominated by the tribal population and the development of agriculture and production of food grains in the region is highly depending upon the custom, culture and the food habit of the tribal people. At the same time, due care should be taken for the protection of the environment of the region and hence sustainable development in agriculture is highly welcome in the north east region. According to 2001 census about 80 per cent of the State's populations are living in rural areas and all are directly and indirectly involved in jhum cultivation (Shifting Cultivation). It is also claimed that slash and burn agriculture (Shifting Cultivation) leads to deterioration of the vegetative cover on the hills and forest lands degenerate into infertile grassland and barren land space. The shorter the jhum cycle preserves the lower level of soil fertility. Five year jhum cycle generates very low level of soil fertility. Therefore, it is contended that this system of agriculture is unsustainable, unscientific and economically unprofitable labour intensive method. It should be stopped for sake of environment and thereby to save the human being. This necessitates switching over to settled cultivation.

The area under shifting cultivation and number of families are engaged are shown in Table 13.1 in context of North-East States. This was a report of the Task Force Report on Shifting Cultivation, Ministry of Agriculture, 1983 which was so old report. The number, at present, is so high because of heavy pressure of population on land. Per capita availability of cultivable land is going to be low and low as time goes.

Table 13.1: Shifting Cultivation in the North-East Region

State	Annual Area Under Shifting Cultivation (Sq.Kms)	Fallow Period (in years)	Minimum Area Under Shifting Cultivation one time or other (Sq.Kms)	No. of Families Practicing Shifting Cultivation
Arunachal Pradesh	700	3-10	2,100	54,000
Assam	696	2-10	1,392	58,000
Manipur	900	4-7	3,600	70,000
Meghalaya	530	5-7	2,650	52,290
Mizoram	630	3-4	1,890	50,000
Nagaland	190	5-8	1,913	1,16,046
Tripura	223	5-9	1,115	43,000
Total	3869		14,660	4,43,336

Table taken from " Globalisation, Growth and Inequality in North East India" by P.C. Dutta and R.K.Mandal.

It is well established fact now that Jhum cultivation is not an eco-friendly practice. It is a curse to the existence of mankind. Therefore, it needs to be reduced and jhum practitioners should be won over to adopt alternative way for livelihood. The environmental problems caused by increased sedimentation has extensively affected the capacity of the reservoirs as well as the aquatic eco-system in the inland waters just as soil erosion, in addition to loss of fertility, has drastically reduced the recharging capacity, resulting in severe depletion of under ground water. Extensive deforestation has resulted in increased carbon-di-oxide concentration in the atmosphere. The changes in climate and rain pattern gradually setting in because of deforestation. Water and soil erosion have affected the maximum lands used for agricultural purpose. The climatic fluctuation and changes in the rain pattern have further compounded the problem of providing adequate food security to our increased population. The gross neglect of environment also resulted in polluting not only river water but also surface water, making them fertile breeding grounds of many communicable diseases due to indiscriminate discharge sewage, dumping of solid wastes etc. Further, the tragedy of the commons due to common ownership of the property right also adversely affects not only the loss of fuel and food but also fodder to a large extent.

Objectives of the Study

This paper is an attempt to search the problems arisen by the Jhum Cultivation and to focus how the problems of agricultural development can be linked with the social system and the governmental policies of the region.

The primary objective of agricultural development is to satisfy the essential materials needs of the society, but the same can not be achieved at the cost of local environment and the culture of the people. To analyze the agricultural backwardness of the region, some of the social indicators have been chosen. As it is very much customary in this region to blame the rise of insurgency as the major factor which impedes the development of the region in general and the agricultural development in particular, the study rejects the notion as some of the states of the region made rapid progress in agriculture during the period of insurgency and rise of terrorism.

Methodology and Data Source

Percentage, per capita and coefficient of variation are calculated. The study is based on the statistical data of secondary sources collected from the offices, Agricultural census, Government Reports, Newspapers and basic statistics of north east states. It is concluded with some remedial measures and suggestions for the future planners of the country as well as people of this region to cope with the current new millennium so as to achieve hunger free North-East India.

Jhum cultivation is creating so many problems which are discussed below:

1. *Environmental and Socio-Cultural Problems:* The recent debates and developments with regard to the draft National Environment Policy (NEP), 2004 and the Scheduled Tribes (Recognition of Forest Rights) Bill (STB), 2005 are illustrative in different ways of the manner in which social concerns are dealt with in environmental policy and legislation in India. Yet, while the pros and cons of specific policies and legislations have been central to the academic debates on the environment, very little attempt has been made to trace the changes in environmental policy making. The ecological balance favouring the complete hydrological cycle has been seriously upset over vast areas due to ignorance or lack of appreciation of methods of conserving and managing natural vegetation (whether a forest, grass land or mixed type) and of clearing the vegetation for cultivation. This misuse and destruction of plants cover combined with great increase in human and livestock population has created intense competition for natural resources, in many cases residual, as between forestry, grazing and crop production. In the continued absence of conservation and correctly integrated land use system, overall habitat deterioration has become very widespread.

   The 1988 National Forest Policy (NFP) was the first "environmental" policy document in India that explicitly recognized the linkages between environmental and social concerns in terms of community rights to natural resources. Unlike the previous forest acts that privileged revenue and commercial interests, the NFP was strikingly different section different. Section 4.6 of the policy highlighted the symbiotic relationship between tribals and forests and the need to involve tribal communities in the management of forests. It also emphasized that domestic requirements of firewood, fodder and minor forest produce should be the first priority of forest management, not commercial or industrial needs.

2. *Soil Erosion:* High rainfall and undulated topography is always associated with problem of severe soil erosion, which affects the environment adversely. The excessive deforestation caused by excessive cutting down of trees for commercial purpose as well as shifting cultivation are resulting in alarming and frightening signals for human survival. Estimates reveal that nearly 181 M.T. of soil is lost annually as a result of shifting cultivation from north eastern hill region (Task Force Report on shifting cultivation, 1983). Developments in the hills and its fall out on the ecology have caused soil erosion, landslides, floods and droughts in the plains.

3. *Soil Fertility:* Burning of vegetation in the process of shifting cultivation chemically alters the plant nutrient supply from organic form to a mineral form in ash, major portion of which is often lost in course of run off. The effect of burning affects the soil properties.

4. *Loss of flora and fauna:* The extent of deforestation of tropical forest has caused world wide alarm as tropical forests provide more than 50 per cent of modern medicine. Tropical forests are living museums and laboratories that have yielded only a tiny fraction of their treasures to scientific study. The NEI is, as if, a natural garden of more than 20,000 identified species of medicinal plants and so many still remain unidentified. In course of shifting cultivation remarkable varieties of flora and fauna are disappearing, which need immediate attention for extensive and intensive studies. The type of vegetations destroyed depends upon the length of jhum cycle. A dense forest of long cycle has more tree species than grasses, whereas a forest of short cycle has more number of grasses. About 300 plant species out of native flora in North-Eastern India are used for edible purpose.

Of these, over 25 provide tubers/rhizomes etc., which are eaten raw or boiled. Over 50 are consumed as green with their leaves/tender shoots cooked as vegetable; about 170 ripe fruits, which are pulpy and sweet/sub-sweet are eaten raw and many of these are used for pickles/vegetables, when unripe; about 15 have edible seeds are eaten raw or roasted.

Wildlife in the natural situation constitutes the most important component of the ecosystem, which participates affectively in the energy flow and bio-geo-chemical cycling. Animal-plant, plant—plant and animal-animal interactions are the basic milestone of the success of an ecosystem and its productivity. As such, the richness of the ecosystem means the capacity of hold high species diversity but deforestation has threatened the very fabric of the survival of wildlife and the ecosystem in the region. This area is the habitat of as many as 55 major mammalian species of which 17 are rare or extremely rare. 21 rare species of extremely rare birds are found in this region and there are innumerable species of insects. As such, there are different species of wild lives found in this region. Almost all of them are dared as protected species under the protection Act of 1972. Like flora, other forest resources are also disappearing and become rare.

5. *Water Resources:* There is ample of water resources in North-Eastern Hill Region. Almost 10 per cent of the total rainfall of the country is received in this region. Soil erosion and deforestation favour in less retention of water under ground and more run off water causing flood in the plains. This causes great loss to human and animal lives as well as crops. Now -a-days, supply of drinking water has become serious problem in every town in the hill region.

Agricultural Development and Allied Problems

Indian economy is pre-eminently agrarian and North-East India is no exception to it. Agriculture occupies a key position in the economy of NEI because of its contribution to:

(a) Overall economic growth through supplies of food, raw materials and export,
(b) Source of livelihood for over 70 p.c. of population and
(c) Providing a large market for non-agricultural goods and services.

Agriculture in NEI has considerable social and political influence. Agriculture has a vital role to play in the economic development of NEI, which is a key factor in the economic growth in absence of mushrooming growth of industries as seen in other parts of India especially in western and southern states. NEI produces a wide array of crops although the food crops preponderate over other crops accounting for maximum total cultivated area of the entire region. Among food crops, rice is the major crop followed by maize and pulses. But the slow growth in agricultural sector results the slow growth of north east economy. Again, the policy makers are keener on accelerating industrialization than the development of agriculture. However, the agricultural backwardness of the region is clearly visible in the context of present day India. While other states of India like Punjab, Haryana, West Bengal are marked by food surplus in the production of rice, wheat, fish etc. and they blamed the government of India for not having purchasing capacity and an adequate market facility to supply the surplus food grains, the people of NEI are importing two million tones of food grains from other regions of the country at a higher prices.

It is very customary in this region to blame the rise of terrorism as one of the major factors which impedes development of the region in general and the agricultural development in particular. However, during the period of insurgency, the studies show that states of Nagaland, Manipur, Mizoram made rapid progress in the production of food grains. Hence, we can not generalize the problem of terrorism as the greatest hindrance in the development of agriculture and in the production of food grains of the region for which the security of life is always threatened.

Food originates from efficient, effective and environmentally benign production technique and conserve and enhance the natural resource base of crops and animal husbandry, forestry and fishery. In Assam rice production in this year is surplus to the tune of 41 thousand tones. The problem lies in the fact that there is high level of poverty and lack of purchasing power of the poor which reduce the ability to access to food and adequate nutrition. However, economic and ecological access will remain as the main challenge at present.

The impending food crisis over the world is due to increasing population, increasing purchasing power of effluents leading to the consumption of more animal products, increasing damage to the ecological foundation of agriculture, depleting per capita availability of land and water and the absence of technologies that can further enhance the yield of potential of major food crops.

The most important problem which creates hindrance on the way of agricultural development is the problem of population explosion in the region. The total population of the region is about 38.5 million representing about 3.75 per cent of India's total population in 2001. The region's growth rate of population is much higher than the national average. It is striking to note that India's total population increased by 51.80 p.c. in the period 1951-71, 54.39 p.c. in 1971-91 and 21.35 p.c. in the period 1991-2001 whereas for the NEI the respective growth rates are 90.86 p.c., 62.11 and 22. 02 p.c. At the same time the share of population of NEI , in comparison to India , increased from 2.84 p.c. in 1951 to 3.75 p.c. in 2001 (Table 13.2).

Increased population at an alarming rate in the region is due to immigration from outside the country as well as from within the country. The population explosion caused by immigration poses serious threat on the natural resources of the region and the availability of cultivable lands for the people of NEI. As a result, the agricultural production could not cope with the growing population and socio economic changes of the region for which the food grain production is short by 2 million tones of demand in this region.

Table 13.2: Population Trend in North East India (in'000)

Year / State	1951	1961	1971	1981	1991	2001
Arunachal Pradesh	–	337	468	632	865	1091
Assam	8029	10837	14625	18041	22414	26638
Manipur	578	780	1073	1421	1837	2389
Meghalaya	606	769	1012	1336	1775	2306
Mizoram	196	266	332	494	690	891
Nagaland	213	369	516	775	1210	1989
Tripura	639	1142	1556	2053	2757	3191
N E R	10260	14501	19582	24752	31547	38495
India	**361088**	**439235**	**548160**	**683329**	**846303**	**1027015**
Decadal growth Rate of NER	–	**41.34**	**35.04**	**26.40**	**27.45**	**22.02**
p.c. of NER with respect to India	**2.84**	**3.30**	**3.57**	**3.62**	**3.70**	**3.75**

Table taken from " Globalisation, Growth and Inequality in North East India" by P.C. Dutta and R.K.Mandal

The absolute number of the migrants was more than 91 thousand in 1901. Since then it has been steadily increasing and reached at nearly 745 thousand in the census year 1991. The share of migrants from Bangladesh was between slightly more than 87 per cent in pre-independence era. In post independence era it reached at 94 per cent in 1951- the highest among the periods 1901-1991. From 1961 onwards the share started to decline and became around 89 per cent in the census year of 1991.It is also clear from the statistical information that Bangladesh was followed by Nepal in sending migrants to the NEI of India. Again, the number of migrants who came from other states of India varied between 0.5 million to around 0.8 million during the pre independence era. But it declined to around 0.4 million in 1951 and reaching slightly more than 0.5 million in 1991. In recent years the flow of immigration again shows an increasing trend.

Since north eastern society is dominated by the tribal population, the reference may be made to the tribal method of cultivation. Out of 23.78 lakh hectare of land in the country as a whole 19.91 lakh hectare (83.73 p.c.) of land in the northeast is under shifting cultivation or jhuming adopted in the ancient farming system, which was once considered as a farmer friendly practice has now become an ecological menace. Rapid deforestation over the years 1987-1997 due to the shifting cultivation in the region have reduced the total forest cover amounting to 1312 sq. km (Table 13.3). An inevitable consequence of deforestation is increased run off rain water, precipitation and extensive soil erosion resulting in unacceptable deterioration of top soil, degradation of land and sedimentation of water bases resulting in desertification and frequent flooding. The high rate of soil erosion in deforested areas in our country ranges from 10 tones per hectare in the plains to about 30 tones per hectare in the north eastern hilly region 10 to 50 times larger than in the forest areas.

The Union Government has sanctioned Rs. 68 crore to the eight North Eastern States including Sikkim during the past three years for modernizing the forest protection force, forest protection system and strengthening the forest management. Tripura and Assam got the maximum amount of Rs. 16 crore each while the other states of the region received 5-9 crore for this purpose. Among the eight NE States, including Sikim, the forest cover had increased in Arunachal Pradesh and Tripura (N E News Letter, Vol. 5., No. 4, April, 2003).

Table 13.3: Forest Cover in NEI of India (Sq. Km.) during the period 1987-1997

State	1987	1989	1991	1993	1995	1997	Total Change Over Decade	Total Geographical Area of Land (in sq. km.)
Arunachal Pradesh	60500	68783*	68757	68661	68621	68621*	- 162	83578
Assam	26386*	26058	24751	24508	24061	23824*	- 2562	78523
Manipur	17679	17885*	17685	17621	17558	17318*	- 567	22356
Meghalaya	16511*	15690	15875	15769	15714	15657*	- 854	22489
Mizoram	19092*	18178	18858	18697	18576	18775*	- 317	21087
Nagaland	14351	14356*	14321	14348	14291	14221*	- 135	16527
Tripura	5743*	5325	5535	5538	5538	5346*	- 397	10477
NER	**160262**	**166255***	**165777**	**165142**	**164359**	**164943***	**- 1312**	**255039**
India								**3280483**

Table taken from " Globalisation, Growth and Inequality in North East India" by P.C. Dutta and R.K. Mandal.

The Ministry had allocated an amount of Rs. 47.00 crores (10% of Gross Budgetary Support) under various non conventional energy programmes during 2002-2003 including Rs. 1.50 crore for setting up of State nodal agencies in all the NE States for exclusive implementation of various conventional energy programmes. During March, 2003 an expenditure of Rs. 34.23 crore has been incurred, making a cumulative expenditure of Rs. 46.69 crores during April2002-March, 2003.A total of 323 Family Type biogas plants were installed in Arunachal Pradesh, Manipur, Meghalaya, Mizoram, Nagaland, Tripura and Sikkim ,making a total 3841 plants up to February, 2003 during 2002-2003. Under Village

Electrification Programme 178 villages were sanctioned for electrification in NE region during 2002-2003.

In the entire north east, the valley districts of Manipur are among the most productive zones in the production of paddy. However, the same can not be said to be true about the districts of Assam. Moreover, the average yield of paddy in Assam is also lower than the regional yield. Lack of assured irrigation seems to be the major factor behind it. The productivity of paddy in Manipur–Tripura Valley and Mizoram is higher than the regional average and also above Assam which alone accounts for more than 70 per cent of area and output in the region. Mizoram has achieved remarkable growth in the yield rate of paddy since around the middle of 1980. It is due to increase in fertilizer consumption and the new land use policy in Mizoram. Also it is observed from the table 13.8 that while the Government of Assam fixed the amount for expenditure in agricultural sector (Rs. 1557.82 lakhs) as on 01.04.1998 but disbursed only 23.60 per cent while only 15.95 per cent of the disbursed amount actually utilized. The same is true in the states of Arunachal Pradesh and Meghalaya. On the other hand, the government of Tripura and Manipur are not only disbursed more but also actually utilized 70.25 p.c. and 47.09 p.c. respectively on agricultural sector. Perhaps corruption at the governmental level and bad intention of the bureaucrats are responsible for this problem in the states of NEI. Although the paddy productivity is the lowest in the state of Arunachal Pradesh, the yield of oil seeds and pulses is the highest in the state along with Meghalaya, Mizoram and the hill districts of Manipur. As the region is classified into hill areas and plain areas, the cropping pattern in hill districts is more varied and not similar to the plain areas. The development of infrastructure facilities like roads, banking, health and communications are perhaps responsible for the above gaps.

The low productivity of food grains explains the shortage of food in the NEI and is responsible for poverty of agricultural masses. Agricultural productivity is in inverse proportion in NEI to the number of people engaged in it.

There is excessive pressure on land resulting in small uneconomic and fragmented holdings. Such small and scattered holdings coupled with defective land tenure system are bound to keep the agricultural productivity very low.

A sizable area in the region is in plantation of tea. Its share to the total production of tea in the country in the year 1980 was 53.44 per cent. Many parts of the region are showing good potential for the cultivation of rubber, coffee and a variety of horticultural crops. The region has a total cultivable area of 6.13 million hectare out of which net area sown is only 0.80 million hectare. However, the above production has not reached the target due to various socio-economic problems of the region.

Nutrition and Food Security

It is now a well-known fact that the nutrition plays an important role in physical efficiency of the people and act as a device to determine the food security in a country and in different parts of the country. India is a vast and varied country. There are large differences in per capita income, availability of the food stuffs, purchasing power, dietary habits, habitual consumption of food stuffs, health and nutritional status between different states in the country and even in different areas of a state. In almost all the states, there are substantial urban-rural and inter district variations along with the marked variation between tribal and non-tribal population within the district, for which it is always a difficult task to measure the nutritional standard of the population living in a particular region and the case of NEI is highly apparent. It is always a fashion in India to relate food problem with income or private household consumption expenditure. The nutritional value of food items is implicitly or explicitly assumed to be constant. The income elasticity of poor households is supposed to be always less than unity. The income elasticity is sometimes calculated for the sake of deriving relationship with food expenditures. The nutrient intake, household income and working capability of individuals in the household are interrelated. The expenditure incurred on food items is an indication of nutrition intake. Each food item has some calorie value and therefore total calories purchased and consumed as indicated through private consumption expenditure of a household. At the same time it should also possible to say that lower is the consumption expenditure of a household, lower is the calorie intake and that is why intake of calories determines the food poverty. Further, poverty on account of lower intake of calories that are needed to maintain health as the particular household was unable to earn adequate wages or income to purchase the nutrient required. Food provides energy and body spent energy. Once the food intake activity is stopped, the death is certain. Food items are comprised of carbohydrates, proteins, fats, vitamins and minerals. Besides, water is essential for digesting the intake of food ingredients. Although the climatic conditions, food habits, money in hand, age, height, weight and other factors influence the diet and calorie needed, still we can derive the consumption norm based on food items like rice, wheat, pulses, fish, egg, meat, milk and vegetables etc. Hence, the above description may serve as the indicators to determine the nutrition deficit in the population of the NER. The dietary standards differ from one country to another. The recommended intakes of nutrients of a nation differ from those of international norms set up by FAO and WHO. The term used to describe dietary standard is "Recommended Dietary Allowance (RDA)".

Education is the main instrument of social change. It is the index of social progress and economic development of a region. Normally it has been considered an agency helping economic production through the development of skills and efficiency highly necessary for the said production. Education is an organic entity, changes, grows with the time, responds to the needs of the society adapts to the environment. It was mostly an ornament in the agricultural civilizations, a tool in economic development in the industrial era and has become today all pervasive resources, a resource that can find substitutes for other resources, but has no substitute for it. A look into the table 13.4, it is observed that the female literacy rate is highest in Mizoram (95 p.c.) followed by Nagaland (77 p.c.) and lowest in Arunachal Pradesh (48 p.c.) which is the only state in NER below the national level in this respect. There is a big gender gap in literacy which is one of the major obstacles in attaining total literacy. Enrolment in various stages of education is growing at a fast rate, but the proportion of girls is low and declines sharply at higher stages of education. The highest gender gap has been found in the states of Manipur (24.03 p.c.), Arunachal Pradesh (21.76), Tripura (20.93) and lowest in Mizoram (7.01) followed by Meghalaya (8.27). However, all the states of NEI are below all-India level (24.84 p.c. points).

The development of an area is best reflected in the distribution of basic needs. Table 13.5 confirms the fact of region's backwardness as it is observed that the per capita consumption of electricity is much lower in the states of NEI as compared to the country's consumption (338.5 kwh). Among the states of NEI, the highest per capita consumption is observed in the state of Meghalaya (134.5kwh) and lowest in Tripura (80.4 kwh).

The North Eastern Council (NEC) has contributed to the North Eastern Region power supply through its power projects. The county's third hydel power project and the first in the North East, which is located in the heart of Shillong at Mawprem is all st to be revived after a gap of 81 years since its inception. The Ministry of Non-Conventional Energy Sources (MNCES) will finance the restoration of the Sonapani Hydel Power Plant, which is expected to light Mawprem and part of Mawlai area. The power plant, which will be "totally unmanned and remote control based" is expected to generate its full capacity of 1.5 Mega Watt for six to seven months especially during the Monsoon and 50 per cent to 62 per cent during other seasons. The unique feature of remote controlling is the first of its kind in the North East and will be managed by the Mawlai 132 KV sub-station.

Table 13.4: Female Literacy Rate, Female Work Participation, Gender Gap in literacy and Density of Population (per sq. km.)

State	Female Literacy Rate (in p.c.)		Female Work Participation (in p.c.)	Density of Population (population per sq. km.)			Gender Gap in Literacy	
	1991	2001	1991	1951	1991	2001	1991	2001
Arunachal Pradesh	29.69	44.24	37.5	–	10	13	21.76	19.83
Assam	43.03	56.03	21.6	102	184	340	18.84	15.90
Manipur	47.60	59.70	39.0	26	82	107	24.03	18.17
Meghalaya	44.85	60.41	34.9	27	79	103	8.27	5.73
Mizoram	78.60	86.13	43.5	9	33	42	7.01	–
Nagaland	54.75	61.92	38.0	13	73	120	12.87	9.85
Tripura	49.65	65.41	13.8	61	263	304	20.93	16.06
NER				**40**	**124**	**151**		
India	**39.29**	**54.16**	**22.3**	**117**	**273**	**324**	**24.84**	**21.69**

Table taken from " Globalisation, Growth and Inequality in North East India" by P.C. Dutta and R.K.Mandal.

Table 13.5: Per Capita Food Grain Production, Consumption of Electricity and Percentage of Households having Electricity , Safe drinking water in N.E.States

	1*	2*	Per capita Food Grain Production (in kg.)				3*
	1996-97	1991	1972-73	1980-81	1990-91	1997-98	
Arunachal Pradesh	80.8	40.85	104	207	253	186	70.02
Assam	107.6	18.74	158	150	154	139	45.85
Manipur	127.9	50.92	159	205	155	152	38.72
Meghalaya	134.5	29.16	120	116	87	83	36.16
Mizoram	127.8	59.20	244	70	118	123	16.21
Nagaland	88.0	53.42	107	136	160	150	53.37
Tripura	80.4	36.93	116	196	187	152	37.18
India	338.5	42.37	172	190	208	198	62.30

1. *per capita consumption of electricity (in kwh)
2. *percentage of households having electricity
3. *percentage of households having safe drinking water, Table taken from "Globalisation, Growth and Inequality in North East India" by P.C. Dutta and R.K. Mandal.

Drinking water is the most precious commodity in our daily life. Supply of safe drinking water is essential to sustain life. It is remarkable to note that in the state of Mizoram, only 16.21 per cent of households can enjoy the facility of safe drinking water while water is the life blood of the environment (Table 13.5). With a view to ensure community participation in creation and maintenance of source and in the interest of long term sustainability of the sources, Government has introduced reforms in the rural water supply schemes which is called SECTOR REFORMS. West Tripura is one of the 63 districts in the country which have been chosen for implementation of the reforms programme. District Water & Sanitation Mission (DWSM) has been constituted for overall supervision of the project, while District Water & Sanitation Committee (DWSC) and Village Water & Sanitation Committee (VWSC) have been formed for implementation of the programme.

The Centre has constituted a separate cell for the North East in the Ministry of Rural Development to bring the region at par with the rest of the country. The cell, headed by Union Rural Development Ministry Joint Secretary would look after the development of infrastructure in the region besides, generation of employment. The cell has made it mandatory for all the Ministries of the Central Government to allocate 105 of their budget to the region. The Union Rural Development Ministry had also allocated 10 per cent of its budget for the North East since 2000-2001.

Despite of several governmental measures, the purchasing capacity of the people of NEI has not increased up to that level what our planners and policy makers desired. The statistics of per capita income of the people of NEI may be stated as, in 1992-93 the per capita income of Nagaland and Mizoram was just slightly above the national average (Rs. 5781 at current Prices) whereas in case of Arunachal Pradesh it was marginally below Rs. 5551 (Table 13.9). In case of Manipur, it was Rs. 1429, Meghalaya Rs. 1361, and Tripura Rs. 1323. The per capita income in 1980-81 was not only so significantly below the national average over the periods (1980-81 to 1992-93).

Per Capita Net State Domestic Product (PCNSDP) gives a rough idea about the economic condition of NEI with respect to all-India level. It is observed that all the states of NER except Arunachal Pradesh (Rs. 2119 - Rs. 3265) and Mizoram (Rs. 2119 - Rs. 7743) are below the all India level (Rs. 1857 - Rs. 2553) for the years 1985-86 to 1994-95. In this respect Assam's position is the lowest for ever during the period 1990-91 (Rs. 1544) to 1996-97 (Rs. 1628) and also in the period 1980-81 (Rs. 1254). The picture shows the economic backwardness of the region in general and Assam in particular (Table 13.6).

Table 13.6: Per Capita Net State Domestic Product (At Current Prices 1980 - 81)

State	1980-81	1985-86	1990-91	1994-95	1995-96	1996-97
Arunachal Pradesh	1571	2119	2710	3265	3304	3059
Assam	1284	1510	1544	1585	1606	1628
Manipur	1419	1598	1739	1986	1993	–
Meghalaya	1361	1412	1733	1673	1808	1837
Mizoram	1289	2658	4474	7743	–	–
Nagaland	1448	1653	1916	2270	–	–
Tripura	1307	1240	1646	1898	2113	2197
India	**1625**	**1857**	**2267**	**2533**	**2664**	**2814**

Table taken from " Globalisation, Growth and Inequality in North East India" by P.C. Dutta and R.K.Mandal.

Monthly Per Capita Expenditure (MPCE) may be accepted as an indicator of standard of living for people, on the basis of minimum calorie intake, suggested by Indian Council of Medical Research (ICMR) which should be 2400 calorie for an Indian working person in rural India and 2100 calorie in urban India. This exercise yielded the official or Planning Commission's poverty line (per capita expenditure for 30 days) of rural and urban India at 1973-74 prices as Rs. 49.02 and Rs. 56.64 respectively. Thus an estimated people of 46.02 p.c. in urban India and 56 p.c. in rural India were below the poverty line in the year 1998. Considering the economic condition of

NEI, it is estimated that the percentage of population below the poverty line is higher in respect of all-India level in 1998 and which come out as 56.83 p.c. and 42.33 p.c. for the rural and urban people of NEI respectively. However, as per NSSO's round survey, the poverty ratio has declined in the north east. It has declined to 40.01 per cent in 2000 as round survey, 2000 as compared to 45.01 per cent in 1993-94.

It should be noted that, as for example, the state of Nagaland could not spend the Ninth Plan outlay fully. The Tenth Plan outlay had been projected for Rs. 2227.65 crore which was 11 per cent higher than the Ninth Plan outlay. State Government was advised to have regular monitoring so that tenth plan outlay could be utilized fully. Concern was expressed on the large size bureaucracy eating into resources meant for developmental activities, high rate of population growth, lower literacy in two districts, lower sex ratio, tardy implementation of developmental programmes and absence of banking facilities affecting credit supply in rural areas.

In the north eastern hill areas food production is subject to wide fluctuations due to shifting cultivation. Hence estimate of production may not give the true picture. However, during the last two decades per capita production has declining in the states of Assam, Manipur, Meghalaya and Mizoram and are lower than the national average except in the state of Arunachal Pradesh. While the population is rapidly increasing in the states of the region, it is observed that in case of Assam, the per capita food production decreased from 158 kg. In 1972-73 to 154 kg. in 1990-91 which further decreased to 139 kg. in 1997-98. The respective figures for Meghalaya are 120 kg., 87 kg. and 83 kg. only (Table 13.5).

It is interesting to note that on a global basis, only 8 p.c. increase in food grain production in the last 50 years, has been through expansion of cultivable area, the rest 92 p.c. coming from improved irrigation techniques and use of high yielding cultivates. About 46 p.c. of the global food grain production comes from irrigated area, which has increased from 80 million hectares in 1950 to 240 million hectares in

1993. It will not be possible to increase the total annual food grain productivity in the country beyond 250 million tones, with the present agricultural practices, which totally falls short of the requirement to produce a minimum of 400 million tones by the year 2050 to provide adequate food security to the projected 1.8 billion populations.

A look at the table 13.7, it is observed that the performance of the northern states in comparison to all-India level, regarding availability of cereals, all the states of NEI excluding Arunachal Pradesh and Tripura, are below the national average (522.7 gm. per capita per day). In case of per capita per day availability of pulses, it is observed that all the states of NEI are below the all-India average over the period 1983-1999.

Table 13.7 gives a picture of per capita per day availability of food grains production where same picture is observed as in case of pulses. It is observed that Arunachal Pradesh, the only state in NEI tried to maintain its superiority till 1994 but declined thereafter.

Table 13.7: Per Capita Availability of Cereals and Pulses (in Gms.) Per Day in NEI

State \ Year	Cereals				Pulses			
	1983	1988	1994	1999	1983	1988	1994	1999
Arunachal Pradesh	569.8	675.4	653.9	446.6	–	–	15.3	16.8
Assam	365.8	359.5	410.2	373.9	7.10	7.71	6.72	7.69
Manipur	418.5	461.0	492.4	476.4	2.93	–	–	–
Meghalaya	293.8	235.1	208.2	225.9	3.88	4.03	3.54	3.07
Mizoram	179.1	233.2	398.6	395.8	0.52	4.39	35.2	28.6
Nagaland	392.6	247.2	432.1	423.6	3.88	9.58	19.82	22.1
Tripura	535.6	475.8	457.1	391.9	3.02	4.13	5.91	3.9
India	**448.4**	**443.6**	**520.5**	**522.7**	**45.2**	**37.6**	**40.5**	**41.1**

Table taken from " Globalisation, Growth and Inequality in North East India" by P.C. Dutta and R.K.Mandal.

Table 13.8: Agricultural Development In NEI (Rupees in Lakhs)

State	Unutilised Amount of Money	Amount Fixed for Expenditure as on 1.4.98	Amount Disbursed	Expenditure
Arunachal Pradesh	421.96	980.32	327.05	94.11
Assam	1440.65	1557.82	365.65	58.67
Manipur	919.52	1538.84	474.90	223.64
Meghalaya	334.20	878.91	523.06	74.01
Mizoram	204.72	1434.17	941.18	283.48
Nagaland	415.22	1799.22	1333.18	574.92
Tripura	537.38	1015.77	438.90	308.34

Table taken from " Globalisation, Growth and Inequality in North East India" by P.C. Dutta and R.K.Mandal

Table 13.9: Per Capita Output (At Current Prices, in Rs.)

State	1980-81	1986-87	1992-93
Arunachal Pradesh	1561	3274	5551
Assam	1200	2313	
Manipur	1429	2362	4230
Meghalaya	1361	2250	4180
Mizoram	1289	2658	4458
Nagaland	1448	2591	5910
Tripura	1323	2108	5910
India	1625	2703	3569
Coefficient Variation:			
India	**31.04%**	**27.84%**	**30.39%**
NER	**7.69%**	**14.31%**	**18.21%**

Tables are taken from " Globalisation, Growth and Inequality in North East India" by P.C. Dutta and R.K.Mandal.

Thus food insecurity is a matter of great concern not only to the people of NEI but also to the policy makers and planners of NEI. It is further observed that no proper care has been taken for the development of agriculture to increase production by which the living condition of the society of NEI may be a better one.. Modern technologies, irrigation facilities, scientific and modern equipments are not being properly used for the real development of agriculture in the age of globalisation and liberalization and for which the region stepping back day by day.

Conclusion and Suggestion

The continuous neglect of soil health and fertility exhaustive methods of cultivation must be rectified through appropriate soil conservations methods and efficient use of organic and inorganic plant nutrients through improved soil management practices. Though reduced use of fertilizers is advocated for environmental effects, the use of inorganic fertilizers is a must in the present moment where soil fertility is low and loss of soil and nutrients are more and large section of population are poor and insecure in food supply.

Distribution of improved varieties of crops, arrangement for fertilizer and proper irrigation facilities, availability of these inputs of farmer's level, demonstration and training for effective and efficient use of organic and inorganic fertilizers in various farming system through Integrated Nutrient Management System and plant protection through Integrated Pest Management by bio-pesticides etc can be effectively managed in these areas. Besides long term property rights to land, access to credit, marketing facilities of produce and investment in roads and rural transportation system are to be efficiently managed.

Educated youths of the villages must be attracted in farming through spreading science-based precision farming techniques which are both intellectually stimulating and economically rewarding. Increased investment in effective Agricultural research through private sector, NGO's and other agencies is most important NER in particular to achieve household food security and nutritional security.

In the Indian Council of Agricultural Research (ICAR) vision 2020 strategic plan to achieve food and nutrition security it propose to address the issues of bio diversity, natural resource management, farming system approach, rain-fed agriculture, post harvest management, farm mechanization, information networking and effective partnership with other public and private institutions.

It is necessary to improve all the factors employed in agricultural viz. land, labour, capital and enterprise. Poor quality of seeds, non-adoption of modern technologies, non-use of plant protection measures, out-of-date implements, lack of adequate or biased finance (agricultural credit), absence of productive investment in land due to defective land tenure system, poor communication between research and extension or development agencies and lack of irrigation facilities are the low agricultural productivity in the region.

REFERENCES & NOTES

Bhalla, G.S. and P. Hazell (1997): *Food Grains Demand in India to 2020,* Economic and Poliical Weekly, December 27.

Dutta, P.C. (2003): *"Regional Disparity and its Consequences in North Eastern Region of India"*, in Mahapatra, A.C. and Pathak, C.R.(eds.), Economic Liberalization and Regional Disparities in India: Special Focus on the North Eastern Region, Star Publishing House, Shillong.

Dutta, P.C. and H. Choudhury (1995): *"Per Capita Household Consumption Inequalities in North Eastern Region (NER)"*, Indian Journal of Regional Science, No. 27(1 & 2).

Dyson, T and A. Hanchate (2000): *India's Demographic and Food Prospects-State Level Analysis,* Economic and Political Weekly, November 11.

Mandal, R.K. (2009): "Forest in Arunachal Pradesh: What is its Future? Arunachal Review", Vol.-I, No.5, November, IPR, Govt. of Arunachal Pradesh.

Mandal, R.K. (2008): "Herbs and Their Sustainability in Arunachal Pradesh", Kurukshetra: A Journal on Rural Development, Vol. 56 No. 5, March, Ministry of Rural Development, New Delhi.

Mandal, R.K. (2006): "Constraints of Economic Development in Arunachal Pradesh with Special Reference to Globalization and Inner Line System" Artha Beekshan,Vol. 15, No. 3, December, IIDS, 221A, APC Road, Kolkata.

Mandal, R.K. (2006): "Control of Jhum Cultivation in Arunachal Pradesh: Retrospect and Prospect", Kurukshetra: A Journal on Rural Development, Vol. 55 No. 02, Ministry of Rural Development, New Delhi.

Misra, V.V. and M. Govinda Rao (2003): "Trade Policy, Agricultural Growth and Rural Poor – Indian Experience, 1978-79 to 1999-2000", Economic and Political Weekly, 38(43), 4588-4603.

Agricultural Practice Under Jhum Cultivation in the North East India With Special Reference to Arunachal Pradesh and Its Impact on Environment

Mr. Toku Chokio

ABSTRACT

The North Eastern Region of India (NER) consists of eight states, namely, Assam, Arunachal Pradesh, Meghalaya, Mizoram, Manipur, Tripura, Nagaland and Sikkim. The hills constitute about 70 per cent of its total land area, where shifting agriculture, locally called "jhum" is the chief land use. The region covers 7.76 per cent of the geographical area of the country. Traditionally, agriculture has been the mainstay of people of this region but the agro-based economy fails to flourish as it should have due to lack of proper involvement and utilization of technological aids. As a result, the stamp of 'backwardness' has been attached to this region suffering from food scarcity, while the country moves ahead from its target of production to food surplus in different phases of the post-Independence era. Increasing the yield of crop in a complex system and in an environmentally positive manner is a challenge that will not be easy to meet in a place like NER. NER is dominated by the tribal population and the development of agriculture and production of food grains in the region which is highly depending upon the custom, culture and the food habit of the tribal people. At the same time, due care should be taken for the protection of the environment of the region and hence sustainable development in agriculture is highly welcomed in the north east. The ethnical, linguistics and cultural diversities of the region make it a mini-modal for representing the country as a whole. There are hundreds of different tribes in the region differing linguistically and culturally.

Introduction

The North Eastern Region of India (NER) consists of eight states, namely, Assam, Arunachal Pradesh, Meghalaya, Mizoram, Manipur, Tripura, Nagaland and Sikkim. Large sections of the people in the region are Tibeto-Mangoloid origin speaking variety of languages. The hills constitute about 70 per cent of its total land area, where shifting agriculture, locally called "jhum" is the chief land use (Ramakrishnan, 1996). The Brahmaputra and the Barak Valley in Assam is the largest valley land where settled agriculture is confined. The region covers 7.76 per cent of the geographical area of the country. About 3 million hectare are estimated to be under soil erosion hazard as a result of practice of jhum cultivation. In Assam alone, 83.2 per cent of area are suffered from erosion of slight (35.3 p.c.), moderate (37.7 p.c.), severe (10.0 p.c.) and very severe (0.3 p.c.) intensity. Improvement of soil conservation and soil fertility is a critical component of low income people. Traditionally, agriculture has been the mainstay of people of this region but the agro-based economy fails to flourish as it should have due to lack of proper involvement and utilization of technological aids. As a result, the stamp of 'backwardness' has been attached to this region suffering from food scarcity, while the country moves ahead from its target of production to food surplus in different phases of the post-Independence era. Increasing the yield of crop in a complex system and in an environmentally positive manner is a challenge that will not be easy to meet in a place like NER.

NER is dominated by the tribal population and the development of agriculture and production of food grains in the region is highly depending upon the custom, culture and the food habit of the tribal people. At the same time, due care should be taken for the protection of the environment of the region and hence sustainable development in agriculture is highly welcomed in the north east. The ethnical, linguistic and cultural diversities of the region make it a mini-modal for representing the country as a whole. There are hundreds of different tribes in the region differing linguistically and culturally.

Geographical Features: The entire region is more or less geographically isolated from the rest of the country. The only gateway to rest of India for all the seven states is Guwahati, the capital city of Assam. The whole of the region is almost surrounded by international borders with Bangladesh, China and Myanmar. The long stretch of border areas not only creates occasional sense of insecurity but also disrupts the inter-regional communication link. The road communication along the border areas through hilly terrain has become difficult and many places are still inaccessible to vehicular traffic. This has heavily affected the economy of the border areas of every states of the north eastern region (Barua 1990).

Demographical Features: The growth rate of population is much larger in all the states of NER as compared to the all India average. While some states like Assam, Tripura and to some extent Meghalaya and Mizoram have experienced a large scale influx of people from neighbouring countries like Bangladesh and Nepal, the other states are characterised by much higher birth rate than death rate (Lekhi and Choudhury, 1994). As a result the decadal variation in the states of NER seems to be very high as compared to all India average.

The high rate of decennial variations is in the NER as compared to the country as whole. The all India trend shows decline in the variation from 1971-81 to 1981-91, the north eastern states individually or the region as a whole showed an increasing trend during the period. While the average annual exponential growth rate shows that in both the decades 1971-81 and 1981-91 in almost all the states of N.E. region the growth rate becomes higher than all India average. This trend will surely have an impact on the socio-economic condition of the region (Dutta and Mandal, 2011).

Agricultural Development and Allied Problems: Indian economy is pre-eminently agrarian and North-East India is no exception to it. Agriculture occupies a key position in the economy of NER because of its contribution to:

(a) Overall economic growth through supplies of food, raw materials and export;
(b) Source of livelihood for over 70 p.c. of population; and
(c) Providing a large market for non-agricultural goods and services.

Also, it is a source of revenue for the state governments of NER. Agriculture in NER has considerable social and political influence. Agriculture has a vital role to play in the economic development of NER, which is a key factor in the economic growth in absence of mushrooming growth of industries as seen in other parts of India especially in western and southern states. NER produces a wide array of crops although the food crops preponderate over other crops accounting for maximum total cultivated area of the entire region. Among food crops, rice is the major crop followed by maize and pulses. But the slow growth in agricultural sector results the slow growth of north east economy. Again, the policy makers are keener on accelerating industrialization than the development of agriculture.

However, the agricultural backwardness of the region is clearly visible in the context of present day India. While other states of India like Punjab, Haryana, West Bengal are marked by food surplus in the production of rice, wheat, fish etc and they blamed the government of India for not having purchasing capacity and an adequate market facility to supply the surplus food grains, the people of NER are importing two million tones of food grains from other regions of the country at a higher prices.

It is very customary in this region to blame the rise of terrorism as one of the major factors which impedes development of the region in general and the agricultural development in particular. However, during the period of insurgency, the studies show that states of Nagaland, Manipur, Mizoram made rapid progress in the production of food grains (Dutta, 1994)

Hence, we cannot generalize the problem of terrorism as the greatest hindrance in the development of agriculture and in the production of food grains of the region for which the security of life is always threatened.

Food originates from efficient, effective and environmentally benign production technique and conserve and enhance the natural resource base of crops and animal husbandry, forestry and fishery. In Assam rice production in this year is surplus to the tune of 41 thousand tones. The problem lies in the fact that there is high level of poverty and lack of purchasing power of the poor which reduce the ability to access to food and adequate nutrition. However, economic and ecological access will remain as the main challenge at present.

The impending food crisis over the world is due to increasing population, increasing purchasing power of effluents leading to the consumption of more animal products, increasing damage to the ecological foundation of agriculture, depleting per capita availability of land and water and the absence of technologies that can further enhance the yield of potential of major food crops.

The Union Government has sanctioned Rs. 68 crore to the eight North Eastern States during the past three years for modernizing the forest protection force, forest protection system and strengthening the forest management. Tripura and Assam got the maximum amount of Rs. 16 crore each while the other states of the region received 5-9 crore for this purpose. Among the eight NE States, including Sikim, the forest cover had increased in Arunachal Pradesh and Tripura (N E News Letter, Vol. 5. No.4, April, 2003).

The environmental problems caused by increased sedimentation has extensively affected the capacity of the reservoirs as well as the aquatic eco-system in the inland waters just as soil erosion, in addition to loss of fertility, has drastically reduced the recharging capacity, resulting in severe depletion of underground water. Extensive deforestation has resulted in increased carbon-di-oxide concentration in the atmosphere. The changes in climate and rain pattern gradually setting in because of deforestation. Water and soil erosion have affected the maximum lands used for agricultural purpose (Dutta and Mandal, 2011).

The Ministry had allocated an amount of Rs. 47.00 crores (10% of Gross Budgetary Support) under various non conventional energy programmes during 2002-2003 including Rs. 1.50 crore for setting up of State nodal agencies in all the NE States for exclusive implementation of various conventional energy programmes. During March, 2003 an expenditure of Rs. 34.23 crore has been incurred, making a cumulative expenditure of Rs. 46.69 crores during April 2002-March, 2003.A total of 323 Family Type biogas plants were installed in Arunachal Pradesh, Manipur, Meghalaya, Mizoram, Nagaland, Tripura and Sikkim ,making a total 3841 plants up to February, 2003 during 2002-2003. Under Village Electrification Programme 178 villages were sanctioned for electrification in NE region during 2002-2003.

The climatic fluctuation and changes in the rain pattern have further compounded the problem of providing adequate food security to our increased population. The gross neglect of environment also resulted in polluting not only river water but also surface water, making them fertile breeding grounds of many communicable diseases due to indiscriminate discharge sewage, dumping of solid wastes etc. Further, the tragedy of the commons due to common ownership of the property right also adversely affects not only the loss of fuel and food but also fodder to a large extent.

The low productivity of food grains explains the shortage of food in the NER and is responsible for poverty of agricultural masses. Agricultural productivity is in inverse proportion in NER to the number of people engaged in it. There is excessive pressure on land resulting in small uneconomic and fragmented holdings. Such small and scattered holdings coupled with defective land tenure system are bound to keep the agricultural productivity very low (Sarma and Pal, 2000).

Arunachal Pradesh is a hilly state lying geographically between 26°42′ to 29°30′ N.L and 90°36′ to 97°30′ E.L. The state has an area of 83,743 sq. km. with 10,97,968 persons and density 13 person per sq. km. according to 2001 census. It is the home of more than 20 major tribes and 110 sub-tribes. This state has vast area of forest covering 51,540 sq. km which forms about 62 per cent of her total geographical area the proportion of arable plain land is very low.

As on 31st march 2003 the state has an estimated gross cropped area of 2.53 lakh Hect. of which net area sown is about 2.01 lakh Hect. accounting for about 2.39 per cent of the total geographical area of 83,743 sq. km. (Eco. Review of Arunachal Pradesh 2003, p. 13). There are distinctly two types of agricultural practices: (*i*) settled cultivation; and (*ii*) jhum i.e., shifting cultivation. Shifting cultivation is our main concerned here. Almost all the tribes except Apatanis and Khamptis in Arunachal Pradesh are practicing shifting cultivation. The Apatanis and Khamptis are engaged in settled cultivation. The jhumias produce all the crops, which they need. These types of cultivation are widespread among the hill dwellers of Assam, Meghalaya, Nagaland, Mizoram and Arunachal Pradesh. It is known in different areas by a variety of local names. In North-East India, it is called Jhum. In these wide-spread areas, there is a remarkable uniformity of the method of cultivation. It is the most primitive form of agriculture which is still in vogue in most parts of N.E. Hill Region of the country. According to 2001 census about 80 per cent of the states populations are living in rural areas and all are directly and indirectly involved in jhum cultivation. It is known through archaeological discoveries that in the Neolithic period around 1000 B.C., man's attitude to his environment underwent fundamental changes. It might be an accident when he took hoe from bow i.e., from hunter he became food producer. Man began to plant, cultivate and improve species of edible plants by selection. This is regarded as the first step in the transition from food gathering/hunting to food production. Among the food plants cultivated by the Neolithic people, rice, wheat, barley, millet, maize, yam, sweet potatoes provided staple food.

The shifting cultivation is also called as slush and burn method of cultivation. It is labour-intensive process of farming with extensive use of land. The technology being primitive, the level of production and income is very low. It occupies a distinct place in the socio-economic fabric of tribal economy of this state. The man who practices jhum cultivation i.e., shifting cultivation is called the jhumia. The jhumia selects the same field on the slope of the hill on rotation basis. Due to deterioration in fertility of soil the jhumia is compelled to shift his cultivation on another plot. He keeps the land fallow for a number of years for regeneration of forests. Again he uses the same land. That is why, this process is also called shifting cultivation. Its chief characteristics are (*i*) slash and burn operation of vegetal species; (*ii*) Use of human labour as chief input; (*iii*) Non- employment of animal; and (*iv*) use of simple implements such as dibble stick, scrapper, etc.

The cycle of agricultural operation in all these areas of North-East Region is marked by the following stages:

1. Selecting the forested hilly track.
2. Cleansing the forest tract by cutting down the jungle during December/-January.
3. Drying and burning of felled shrubs/trees into ashes during February-/March.
4. Fencing cleared plots.
5. Worship and sacrifice.
6. Dibbling and sowing of seeds for mixed cropping.
7. Weeding operation.
8. Watching and protecting the crops against depredation by wild animals, pests, etc.
9. Harvesting.
10. Threshing and storing.

The area under shifting cultivation and number of families are engaged are shown in the following table 14.1.

Table 14.1: Shifting Cultivation in the N.E. Region

State	Annual Area Under Shifting Cultivation (Sq. KMs)	Fallow Period (in years).	Minimum Area Under Shifting Cultivation One Time or Other (Sq. KM)	No.of Families Practicing Shifting Cultivation
Arunachal Pradesh	700	3-10	2,100	54,000
Assam	696	2 -10	1392	58,000
Manipur	900	4-7	3600	70,000
Meghalaya	530	5-7	2650	52,290
Mizoram	630	3-4	1890	50,000
Nagaland	190	5-8-	1913	1,16,046
Tripura	223	5-9	1115	43,000
Total	3869 (1.5%)		14660 (5.7%)	443336

Sources: Report of the Task Force on Shifting Cultivation, Ministry of Agriculture (1983).

The following table 14.2 shows the position of different states of North East India in respect of only shifting, shifting combined with permanent, permanent and not doing any cultivation.

Table 14.2: Shifting, Permanent and Combined Cultivation in the Tribal Society

State	Percentage of Tribal Households in Respect of Cultivation			
	Shifting Cultivation	Shifting Combined With Permanent Cultivation	Permanent Cultivation	Not doing any Cultivation
Arunachal Pradesh	33.50	24.20	29.60	12.70
Assam	18.60	24.00	29.50	07.70
Manipur	46.10	24.50	15.40	04.10
Meghalaya	15.40	38.20	21.60	14.80
Tripura	12.10	11.60	53.20	23.10

Source: Patnaik, 1984. [Majumdar, D.N. (1990), "Shifting Cultivation in North East India," Omsons publications, Guwahati, New Delhi, p-29]

Problems

1. **Environmental and socio-cultural problems:** The ecological balance favouring the complete hydrological cycle has been seriously upset over vast areas due to ignorance or lack of appreciation of methods of conserving and managing natural vegetation (whether a forest, grass land or mixed type) and of clearing the vegetation for cultivation. This misuse and destruction of plants cover combined with great increase in human and livestock population has created intense competition for natural resources, in many cases residual, as between forestry, grazing and crop production. In the continued absence of conservation and correctly integrated land use system, overall habitat deterioration has become very widespread. It has been undisputedly accepted that shifting cultivation creates environment and socio-cultural problems. The growth in the number of members per jhumia family and in the number of jhumia families cannot be absorbed in settled and jhum cultivation, as a result a consumption gap develops in the hills. The greater food requirements cannot be met out of dwindling yields from smaller plots of land devoted to jhuming with smaller and smaller fallowing periods. The over exploitation of forests of jhuming and for commercial purposes also leads to a deterioration of the condition of the forests. The misuse and destruction of plants cover combined with great increase in human and livestock population has aggravated the problem of eco-system. Ecological damage in the hills, widespread poverty among hill-dwelling tribal, social discontent and the growth of extension has been the fall-out of the development of the hill economy. Development in the hills has obviously not led to development of the hills. It has also produced external diseconomies. A climate of uncertainly has been generated among the jobless tribal.
2. **Soil Erosion:** High rainfall and undulated topography is always associated with problem of severe soil erosion, which affects the environment adversely. The excessive

deforestation caused by excessive cutting down of trees for commercial purpose as well as shifting cultivation are resulting in alarming and frightening signals for human survival. Estimates reveal that nearly 181 mt of soil is lost annually as a result of shifting cultivation from north eastern hill region. Development in the hills and its fall out on the ecology and economy of the hills has caused soil erosion, landslides, floods and droughts in the plains.

According to the forestry experts' soil conservationists, "The ecological balance favouring the complete hydrological cycle has been seriously upset over vast areas due to ignorance or lack of appreciation of methods of conserving and managing natural vegetation".

Shifting cultivation is regarded as one of the most destructive method of land operation causing ecological imbalance, which raises temperature of the environment.

3. **Soil Fertility:** Burning of vegetation in the process of shifting cultivation chemically alters the plant nutrient supply from organic form to a mineral form in ash, major portion of which is often lost in course of run off. The effect of burning on some soil properties studied at laboratories is shown in the following table.

Effect of Burning on Soil Properties

Soil Properties	Before Burning	After Burning
PH	5.10	5.50
Organic Carbon (%)	1.32	1.05
P20s (Kg.ha-1)	3.30	3.31
K20 (Kg ha-1)	210.00	570.00
Exch.Ca (Meg%)	7.15	9.46

Sources: 1. Borthakur, et al. 1983. [Majumdar, D.N. (1990)(Ed.), "Shifting Cultivation in North East India," Omsons publications, Guwahati, New Delhi, p-147].

2. Task force report on shifting cultivation in India, Ministry of Agriculture, 1983.

The shorter the jhum cycle preserves the lower level of soil fertility. Five year jhum *cycle* generates very low level of soil fertility. Thus, jhum cultivation becomes uneconomic progressively. This necessitates switching over to settled cultivation.

4. **Loss of flora and fauna:** The extent of deforestation of tropical forest has caused world wide alarm as tropical forests provide more than 50 per cent of modern medicine. Tropical forests are living museums and laboratories that have yielded only a tiny fraction of their treasures to scientific study.

   Arunachal Pradesh is as if a natural garden of more than 20,000 identified species of medicinal plants and so many still remain unidentified. In course of shifting cultivation remarkable varieties of flora and fauna are disappearing, which need immediate attention for extensive and intensive studies.

   The type of vegetations destroyed depends upon the length of jhum cycle. A dense forest of long cycle has more trees species than grasses, whereas a forest of short cycle has more number of grasses. About 300 plant species out of native flora in North-Eastern India are used for edible purpose. Of these, over 25 provide tubers/ rhizomes etc., which are eaten raw or boiled. Over 50 are consumed as green with their leaves/tender shoots cooked as vegetable; about 170 ripe fruits, which are pulpy and sweet/sub-sweet are eaten raw and many of these are used for pickles/vegetables, when unripe; about 15 have edible seeds are eaten raw or roasted.

   Wildlife in the natural situation constitutes the most important component of the ecosystem, which participates affectively in the energy flow and bio-geo-chemical cycling. Animal-plant, plant—plant and animal-animal interactions are the basic milestone of the success of an ecosystem and its productivity. As such, the richness of the ecosystem means the capacity of hold high species diversity but deforestation has threatened the very fabric of the survival of wildlife and the ecosystem in the region. This area is the habitat of as many as 55 major mammalian species of which 17 are rare or extremely rare. 21 rare species of extremely rare birds are found in this region and there are innumerable species of insects. As such, there are different species of wild lives found in this region. Almost all of them are dared as protected species under the protection Act of 1972. Like flora and other forest resources are also disappearing and become rare.

5. **Water Resources**: There is ample of water resources in North-Eastern Hill Region. Almost 10 per cent of the total rainfall of the country is received in this region. Soil erosion and deforestation favour in less retention of water under ground and more run off water causing flood in the plains. This causes great loss to human and animal life as well as crops. Now -a-days, supply of drinking water has become serious problem in every town in the hill region.

Solutions

Jhum cultivation today is regarded as an alternative farming to permanent or settled cultivation on mountain slopes. But the government has to try his level best to abolish it completely. The following issues may be considered for positive approach towards shifting cultivation.

Diversification of the hill Economy: For the development of the hill economy of the state in an effective manner, ecologically harmful method of jhuming should be discouraged on the steep slopes. All round development can diversify the -hill economy and offer the tribal new avenues of employment but this cannot create job opportunities for uneducated, untrained and unskilled tribal. At best they can find employment as wage labourers. Till the jhumias are rehabilitated in higher income occupying for their upliftment, the public distribution system in the hills will have to be revamped and reinforced and new employment opportunities and guaranteed employment schemes will have to be created for the jhumias.

A. **Land Reforms:** Any plan for improved farm practices cannot be materialized without settling the question of land reforms and land distribution. In Arunachal Pradesh, the following three broad categories of land ownership system are found:

1. Land owned by the Community.
2. Land owned by the Chiefs who distribute land among the individual households for jhum cultivation.
3. Land owned by individual families.

It is well accepted that the transition from shifting to settled agriculture cannot be successfully achieved without abolishing the system of ownership of lands by the Chiefs. It is impossible to radically solve the problem of transition from nomadism to a settle life without fundamentally changing the pattern of social relationship in this state. This is most vital issue. S ate government has taken several achemes to reform the land. But it is not so much effective to its function. As there is no systematic land record, land reform policy maker should consider the following suggestions to get factual results in this respect.

1. The customary land laws of all communities should be documented and studied and then a uniform land policy should be formulated.
2. As plain land in Arunachal Pradesh is scare, ceiling on cultivable land should be fixed. Ceiling should be varying depending on the quality of land.
3. Landless poor people should be given some cultivable land.
4. Poor people having small amount of land should be prevented from selling their land.
5. Sharecropping should be discouraged.
6. All land sales should be compulsory registered.
7. Restriction should be placed on the sale of cultivable land to non-cultivators.
8. Progressive land tax should be introduced.

B **Land Management:** The soil and land use survey should be conducted to examine the eligibility for what type of forest or what type of horticulture or for what type of crop for settled cultivation can be cultivated! Adequate protection measures including soil conservation should be adopted where settled land management should be supported by effective supply of inputs including seeds, manures, fertilizers, tools and implements, etc. It is necessary to undertake studies to improve the farming practices of the jhumias so as to cause minimum soil erosion and loss of soil fertility.

1. **Soil Survey:** The terracing of land for settled cultivation may be suggested as remedy for the evils effect of shifting cultivation. But terracing is costly and cannot be immediately undertaken in many steep hills of this state. The essential pre-requisite for terracing is survey.' A soil survey can assess the soil potentiality for agriculture identifying erosion, salinity, acidity and alkalinity, water-logging, etc. Soil survey is, also essential for pasture development, horticulture and forestry. A complete soil survey is not undertaken till now in this state. A detailed survey work should be undertaken keeping in view the nature of slope, soil depth and prevalent practices to reclassify the land for proper use in the form of terraces.
2. **Conversion of jhum land into settled Cultivation:** In Arunachal Pradesh the main plan on which the jhum control scheme rests is the introduction of terrace cultivation. According to a recent report, of about 70,000 hectares of jhum area, 2300 hectares have been reclaimed for wet rice cultivation4. The govt. should accelerate the process of conversion as much as possible and try to convince the jhumias about good effect of settled cultivation. Agricultural practice by slash and burn method must be avoided. Their practice has to be improved upon so that productivity per hectare rises without causing soil erosion.

3. **Surrender of land:** The jhumias should be persuaded to surrender at least 50 per cent of their jhum cultivable land to the government on the basis of sale, pension, lease, and donation. Government should use this land only for forest purpose.

C **Agricultural Knowledge:** Agricultural school should be opened in every district head quarter so as to give a practical training to the jhumias for different types of cultivation. Again the school authority will also organize sometimes seminar, symposia in almost all villages to convey the jhumia about the ill effect of jhum cultivation.

Subsidiaries to Agriculture

(a) Tribal should be encouraged to take up horticulture, floriculture, silviculture, agro-forestry, growing of medicinal and aromatic, plants on hill slop and fodder crops with special emphasis on crops which will not damage the fragile hill ecology. Arunachal Pradesh with its undulating topography and rich diversity of agro-climatic condition has scope for growing wide variety of tropical, sub-tropical and temperate fruits. The government has been trying to enhance the scope of horticulture since 1987-88 with set up of Directorate of horticulture at Itanagar. But this is much lagging behind the expectation due to lack of proper marketing, transportation etc. The area under fruits has gone up from 12,175 hectares in 1987-88 to 49,102 hectares in 2002-03 and production rose form 29,025 M.T. in 1987-88 to 96,438 M.T. [Directorate of Economics and statistics, Govt. of Arunachal Pradesh, Itanagar].

(b) **Cultivation of Tea, Coffee, Rubber and Black pepper:** Tea, Coffee, Rubber and black pepper can occupy an important place in the hill economy of Arunachal Pradesh. Proper development of these industries will not only contribute to generation of revenue but also create employment opportunity for growing population of the state. Tea cultivation is the state was started in 1978-79 by the Arunachal Pradesh Forest Corporation Limited at

Kanubari in Tirap District. Being encouraged by success of the forest corporation many big and small private tea garden have come up in recent past. Besides tea, the Arunachal Pradesh Forest Corporation is also growing Coffee, Rubber and Black pepper in Tirap, Lohit and Changlang District. Therefore, horticulture, cultivation of tea, coffee, rubber and black pepper as alternative and subsidiary occupations may be desirable and feasible to bring the jhumias from their attachment with the traditional practice of jhum cultivation.

(c) **Fisheries, Piggeries, dairies and duckeries:** Whenever possible water bodies should be created for starting fisheries, piggeries, dairies and duckeries. These should be encouraged among the hill people to diversity the hill economy.

Livestock rearing is an integral component of the rural economy. It plays an important role in improving the economy of the rural population. For livestock development Govt. has paid his attention on (*i*) Animal and disease control (*ii*) cattle development (*iii*) poultry development (*iv*) piggery development (*v*) dairy development and (*v*) Education and Training.

The total livestock and poultry population as per 1997-98 livestock census was 11.87 lakhs whereas in 1992-93 livestock census it was 9.59 lakhs. But it is very little supply as per demand. There are bright scopes to develop the livestock in the state. Government should pay more attention in this respect.

D. **Forest based industries:** Industries based on forest products should be set up on a priority basis throughout the hill region so as to engage the jhumias in the industrial work. The tendency to preserve forests will grow if the forest products will have a ready market. In fact the setting up of such industries will revolutionize the economy in the tribal areas and will have a negative impact upon the jhuming practice. The forest-based industries such as paper pulp, plywood, vineer, matches, saw mills, wooden railway slippers, etc. If once Arunachal Pradesh gets herself industrialized at least 50 per cent, it would greatly help to achieve economic rehabilitation of the jhumias. When they will realize the potential value of bamboos, timber species, etc., which they will sell to the industrial authorities, they will automatically try to conserve these resources which will be a permanent source of income for them. The industrialization programme is a necessary and unavoidable part of overall planning for development of the region. Without an industrialization programme agricultural improvement programme cannot succeed. Industrialization programme would provide employment to surplus farm hands. This will reduce the excessive pressure of growing population on land. Thus, industrialization programme would indirectly help soil conservation programme.

E. **Tourism, Power and Trade:** Arunachal Pradesh is gifted with many basic resources necessary for tourism development such as unique natural beauty, different species of wild life, religious places, historical sites, diverse attractive tribal culture and friendly and hospitable people. A proper development of tourism sector can provide alternative employment to the growing population in tourism activities.

Although, Arunachal Pradesh possessing immense potential of power in the form of hydro, oil, natural gas and coal resources) the progress in this sector in the state has not taken place on scale proportionate to resources availability. As a result, there is a big gap between availability and requirement for power in the state. As per 2001 census out of 2,12,615 households only 116,275 households (54.7%) are having electricity facility.

The National Hydro power corporation (NHPC) has undertaken survey and investigation works of Siang and Subansiri basin mega hydro power project with an estimated installed capacity of 20700 MW. If once power is available, it will bring revolution of, infrastructural development with set up of different industries. It will open a new era for employment in the state. The unexploited Hydro-Power potential of the state is estimated to be 49,000 M.W. Even if a part of the available hydro potential is harnessed, the state will not only be self-sufficient in meeting its own demand for power but at the same time it can earn revenue by supplying power to the other neighbouring states.

Border trade with neighboring countries is a priority of central govt. for which infrastructure would be developed in Arunachal Pradesh, said Secretary of External Affairs Ministry, Shyam Saran while addressing a high level official meeting at Itanagar dated 26.12.2004. The Chief Minister, Gegong Apang said that due to cross-border trade, priority development of border areas through infrastructure development in terms of road, health, education, etc., could boost states economy. Free flow of goods and trade with China and South East Asian countries as part of "Look East Policy" would neutralize the disadvantage of North-East Region, particularly Arunachal Pradesh (The Arunachal Times, 27.11.2004). Arunachal Pradesh has a long international border with Bhutan to the West (160 Km), China to the North and North-East (1,030 Km) and Myanmar to the east (1440 Km).

Transport and communication play a vital role on the over all development of an area in general and industrial development in particular. Arunachal Pradesh being hilly State no any other suitable and viable mode of communication like railways and waterways. Road is the principal mode of communication for movement of goods as well as movements of passengers. At present, total length of road is 14,450 Km. Now all the Districts' Head Quarters are not interlinked with each other by road. The Government has to take attention on priority basis to develop transport and communication so as to bring the jhumias in the main stream of the people.

1. An appropriate mechanism should be devised to help extension of bank credit to the jhumias even though the property relation prevailing among them prevents it. It is not necessary that the banks should give loans only when land is held as security.

2. Planned development with simultaneous steps for forestation, conservation of germ plasm through establishment of national parks, of arboreta of biosphere reserves should be a satisfactory solution.
3. Jhumming, wherever it is a necessity, should be promoted and not eliminated. For the upgradation of jhuming two ways are advocated. First, jhum land may be converted to economically more viable horticultural gardens. Horticultural gardens can pave the way for a roaring business and income for the people.

   Second, the idea of implementing scientific jhumming can equally be entertained. Scientific jhumming has something to do with minimizing the bad effects of jhumming and capitalizing on its benefits.
4. Question arises if a change is brought looking at the entire terrain conditions of the region, will it be acceptable to the local population and fit into their pattern of life. In this regard it may be suggested that some scientific measures should be taken to put an end to the erosion of top soil and studies should be carried out to explore the possibility of introducing modern innovations on jhum land so as to obtain higher yield per unit area. Besides, replacement of crop cultivation by other types of alternative livelihood like plantations, economic and conservational forestry, horticulture, development of animal husbandry i.e., livestock rearing like poultry farming, sericulture, bee keeping and so on may also be encouraged. The problems arising out of jhumming in Arunachal Pradesh can be solved keeping in view the many facts of shifting cultivation, the socio-cultural life of the people, the feasibility of change over the expenditure involved, and the maintenance of a changed pattern.

Conclusion

As an economic proposition, till the shifting cultivation is replaced by an improved form of land management, it is essential to make the above alternative techniques more productive so that it can sustain the growing pressure of population and improve the quality of life of the people concerned without creating imbalance in the fragile eco-system of the reason.

It can be argued that if it is as pointed out above why did shifting cultivation not show the evil effects during so many millennia of human existence? The devastating effects of shifting cultivation came into operation when population increases beyond the optimum limits of shifting cultivation.

While bringing the change from shifting cultivation to settled cultivation, there will necessarily come about some changes in the social and land reforms. Special care should be taken so that there is no undesirable social consequence.

We think, question may arisen if such a change is brought looking at the entire terrain conditions of the region, will it be acceptable to the local people and to fit in their pattern of life? The population arising out of jhuming can be solved keeping in view the many facets of shifting cultivation such as the socio cultural life of the people, the feasibility of change over the expenditure involved and the maintenance of a changed pattern

Last of all, I feel that it is necessary to make an integrated research on the basic problems arise with the shifting cultivation by scientists of all the disciplines including social scientists.

The solution of the problem arisen by the shifting cultivation is greatly depended on integrated and coordinated affords of all concerned - Government, District Council, Village Organization, Village Leaders and farmers. But assistance of the agricultural scientists, economists, sociologist, political leaders and social workers in formulation and implementation of the action plan to solve these problems is also equally important.

REFERENCES

Arunachal Times (Daily News Paper) November 27, 2004 and December 3, 2004.

Barua, P.C., (1990): Development Planning of North East India, Mittal Publications, New. Delhi.

Dutta, B.B. (1994): Insurgency and Economic Development in India's North East in India's North East – The Process of Chance and Development (Ed.) R.K. Samanta, B.R. Publishing Corporation, pp. 1-38, New Delhi.

Dutta, P.C. and Mandal, R.K. (2011): Globalisation, Growth and Inequality in North East India, Kalpaz Publications, Delhi.

Das Gupta, M. (1999), 'Planning for the Hill Economy of Trupura' Edited by Amlash Banerjee and Biman Kar under the title 'Economic planning and Development of North-Eastern States': Kanishka Publishers; New Delhi, pp. 78-91.

Economic Review of Arunachal Pradesh, Govt. of Arunachal Pradesh 2000, 2001, 2002 and 2003.

Lekhi, R.K. and Choudhuiy, R.K, (1994): Economy of India Including Assam and North East, Kalyani Publishers, Kolata.

Majumdar, D.N. (1990), "Shifting Cultivation in North East India," Omsons Publications, Guwahati, New Delhi.

Mandal, R.K. (2006), "Control of Jhum Cultivation in Arunachal Pradesh: Retrospect and Prospect", Journal of North-East India Council for Social Science Research, April, Vol. 30, No. 1 pp. 21-27.

Mandal, R.K.(2005), "Arunachal Economic: Socio-Economic Transformation, Champion Publishers, Itanagar, pp. 116-26.

Mitra, A. (2002), " Internal Migration and Economic Development in the Hills" Omsons publication, New Delhi, p. 5.

Osik, N.N. (1996), "A Brief History of Arunachal Pradesh", Omsons Publication, New Delhi, pp. 1-3.

Rarnakrishnan, P.S. (1996): Shifting Agriculture and Sustainable Development, UNESCO and the Parthenon Publishing Group.

Roy, N.C and Kuri, P.K., "Land Reform in Arunachal Pradesh", Classical Publishing Com., New Delhi.

Gopalkrishnan, R, (1991), "The North-East India: Land, Economic and People" Vikas Pub., New Delhi.

Sarma, B.K. and Pal, P.P. (2000): Food Production, Food Problem and Public Distribution System in North East India , Paper Presented in the National Seminar on Food, Nutrition, Food Security, Public Distribution System, NEICSSR, Shillong, 27-28 November.

Index

D

E

F

❑❑❑❑❑❑